Soul Snatchers

A Quest for True Human Beings

Robert W. Morgan

Pine Winds Press

Pine Winds Press

An imprint of Idyll Arbor, Inc.
39129 264th Ave SE, Enumclaw, WA 98022
360-825-7797, www.pinewindspress.com

Front Cover and Title Page Photographs: Robert W. Morgan
Back Cover Photograph: N. Erika Morgan
Pine Winds Press Editor: Thomas M. Blaschko

Pictures on pages 11 and 143: N. Erika Morgan
Picture on title page: Robert W. Morgan
Pictures of masks on page 278-279 Courtesy of the Lelooska Foundation
Other picture credits are included with the pictures.

Library of Congress Cataloging-in-Publication Data

Morgan, Robert W., 1935-
  Soul snatchers : a quest for true human beings / Robert W. Morgan.
    p. cm.
  ISBN-13: 978-0-937663-14-1 (alk. paper)
  1. Indians of North America--Folklore. 2. Ghost stories. 3. Tales--United
States. 4. United States--Folklore. I. Title.
  E98.F6M84 2008
  398.25--dc22

                                                                          2008017291

ISBN 9780-937663-14-1

This work is dedicated to all those True Human Beings around the world regardless of their race, religion, faith, creed, or nationality who sincerely wish to discover who they are, why they are, what they are, where they came from, and where they may choose to go.

Contents

Acknowledgments

Above all, I am both grateful and humbled by the patience and understanding of my life's missions by my beloved daughter Natalie Erika Morgan and Alicia Dorey, my forever soul mate and my heart's true companion. Words cannot express my abiding love for them. Indeed, Alicia endured the countless hours I spent composing this work while my "Riki-Doo" lost years of my presence to allow me to search the world while seeking the whys of life itself. Was it selfish and unfair of me to do so? Perhaps so, for I was not there when she first learned to ride a bicycle or play her softball games, nor was I there when Alicia needed me the most. Even as I write this confession, my heart aches over my selfishness that lost us such precious moments. Yet, somehow, neither lost faith in me nor did their love dim. My greatest hope is that they will consent to share their future lives with me, too. I shall do better.

I must also express my sincerest thanks to those who helped me peel away uncounted layers of fiction from those few kernels of truth that remain. These include W. Ted Ernst; Eliza Moorman; Eva Phillips; Michael and Sonja Polesnek; Norman Jones, DEA-retired; Frederick Coward, FBI-retired; Count Pino Turolla; Carleton S. Coon; George Shaller; Jim Butler; John Shelley; Peter and Julie Reid; Len Aiken; Jim and Colleen Helbert; Steve & Michelle Jones; Robert Purser; Richard Van Dyke; Bill Lee; Colleen and Judah Parry; Serge, Sunny, and Dominique Georgeon; Scott Kleinhans; Robert and Toni Hipp; Chris Kimball; Joe Decker; Robert Gimlin; Christopher Murphy; Ron Morehead; Ralph Burris; Catt LeBaigue; Ann Swain Perry; Mary Jo Florey; Scott Church; Neil Spring; Mike Wilson; Mike Hupp; Tenaya Torres; Don Smith (Lelooska); Fearon Smith (Tsungani); Patty Fawn; Shono-hah of the Lelooska Foundation.

I also thank the spirit of Nino Cochise, my true father of a thousand years.

This work may never have seen the light of day without my uncompromising proofreader, Roger Schmitt, my literary agent Stephanne Dennis, or the introduction by Autumn Williams and her mother, Sali Sheppard-Wolford, to my understanding publisher and editor, Tom Blaschko and Dawn Craft.

Prologue:
The Perfect Encounter

Mehaffey Ridge, When you are ready

This day, this hour, and with each quickening step you can feel the Fear gaining on you as you hurry along that narrow and winding forest path. You want to turn, to see its face, to stare it down, to ask it why, why? You don't because there is no time, no time — the Fear prods you up and over Mehaffey Ridge and down through the valley of shadows and ferns and past the beaver pond and around that shallow lake. All along that path, furtive little rustling sounds remind you of the Fear's hiding places, dark and mean. Now, for the first time ever, it is hounding you through the brooding marsh — it wants you to know that something is out there, something that you cannot see. It wants you to *feeeel* its presence.

Until last week, hiking this particular route was such a soul-satisfying pleasure — what went wrong? What in the hell is happening? Everything in the forest seems on edge, from the bugs to the birds and the animals — and most of all, you.

It's only your imagination, you have told yourself over and over again, but you can no longer deny it. You know now that certain parts of this forest are forbidden to you and that something is out there watching your every move.

This very afternoon the Fear ambushed you less than a mile from your secret camp; it dogged you all the way up to the ridge, down into the valley, past the lake, and now it is clinging to you like mud in a marsh. You feel like a scared little kid rushing to get home before dark — you sneak another look behind you while you fake tying a shoelace —

listen, listen, there they are again. All this week those same owls hooted all along the trail as if you had somehow invaded their territory — do owls normally hoot in daylight? Gotta check that out in your Audubon manual, by golly.

Even as you quicken your pace out of the marsh, an acrid stench of something fleshy and warm crinkles your nose. You pause to sniff the air — you listen harder. Nothing stirs, damn it, but the hair curls on your arms and up the nape of your neck anyway.

Be smart, be safe, you tell yourself, and you deliberately rush past the mouth of the game trail that leads up to your hidden encampment. Instead, you stamp your feet hard so that anything evil listening in the forest behind you will know that you are traveling on to where the creek rounds the bend between two giant boulders. Once there, you slip off the trail to stand still as a stone's shadow. Ten throbbing minutes go by — then twenty. You strain your eyes while dusk closes its shutters to the paling light. Not even a leaf dares to fall.

The owls have stopped hooting as if they too are waiting for the darkness to hide them.

While you listen for telltale footsteps, you allow your mind to slip back to when it all began one short week ago. You set out quite cheerfully from your campsite and took your usual hike up along Mehaffey Ridge. Reaching its crest, you followed a narrow and twisting deer path down through the tall ferns until you dropped into your favorite valley. You had intended to stick to your routine the same as every previous afternoon since you chose this part of the wilderness as your research area. You always went halfway down to the valley floor before skirting its quiet beaver pond and then struggling up and over the steep saddleback on the far side. After regaining your breath, you plunged down again to loop around a lake where wild ducks and geese raised their messy broods. From there you cut through the marsh before making that last climb back up to the tiny meadow where your secret observation camp awaited you so cozy and safe among maples and oaks.

It was such a pleasant routine — until last week, that is. You had barely set foot on the floor of the valley when the Fear bit into the back of your neck like a starving cougar. You spun around at least a dozen times as you hurried on toward the ridge, your eyes darting this way and that. Oddly, you saw not a single bird, none of the usually plentiful deer, and that old beaver that lives alone in the pond failed to smack his tail to greet you. Instead, a feeling of some unknown power stalked you until you left that valley floor. Only then had that noxious feeling faded away to leave you sweating and trembling and cussing your way back to camp.

Nevertheless, that day ended well. By the time you were ready to crawl into your sleeping bag you were laughing aloud at your antics. After all, there was no one in that valley but you, right? Right? C'mon, right?

However, the Fear slammed into you again the following day as you topped Mehaffey Ridge. Made stubborn by the absence of anything tangible, you jogged down through the ferns anyway and crossed the valley that was still devoid of wildlife. This time that silent fury escorted you all the way up the saddleback. Had it wanted to make certain that you did not tarry?

The third day was worse. This time the Fear lay in wait below the ridge. This time it kept a steady pace with you until you were quick-trotting over the ridge, through the valley, and over the saddleback — but then it also dogged your heels past the lake, even to the edge of the marsh. It was as if each day the Fear came closer to your safe and secret hideaway. It was as if — something moving up along the creek snapped you back into the present. You don't move. Wisely, you do not hold your breath, either. You let it flow out slowly, slowly, so that you can be sure to hear any clicking stone, a scrabbling of pebbles, or a splash made by an incautious step — damn! You cannot help but sigh relief when a fat old boar raccoon comes bustling past you, whirring and chirring up a storm as if something has made it angry… or scared.

The stillness of the forest folds in again as the insulted creature fusses off into the distance. After another hour of calming silence, you melt again into the trackless woods. After all, whatever or whoever is back there might be human, and they are the most dangerous stalkers of all.

You allow yourself to return to your camp, the tips of your boots nudging under the leaves and brittle twigs one careful step at a time. Staying silent, you put your full weight down only after you feel solid ground. You glide silently in between twin knots of browsing whitetail deer without a rustle. You are proud of your acquired prowess. Only last week a fox hunted mice beneath the dry brown grass only yards from where you sat motionless. Practice has been making you more skillful with each passing day. It is pitch dark before you finally slip into your little clearing and are greeted by Hoo, hoo-hoo, hoo-hoo-woo-oo-ohm.

Interesting creatures, owls. Sometimes they start out like a great horned owl, but these seem to end up moaning like a common barn owl. Oh, and remember that time early last spring when you were pitching your first camp here and they hooted and moaned for three days and nights running? They had not sounded all that pleased about your arrival. Then one fine day everything became quiet and serene as if they had moved on for the summer.

It's nearing autumn again, the air is chilling, and everything in nature is steeling itself against the trials of winter. Perhaps, when those owls returned last week, they were surprised to find you still here.

Your hands quiver as you scratch a match to your propane lantern — at its first flare a coyote yaps somewhere off to your left — was that a fox barking to your right? How odd! Since when do foxes and coyotes exchange information — no, no, your inner voice murmurs a caution. Something could be imitating them. Remember, your Observer's manual warns that the Forest Giants are among the world's greatest imitators…

and intimidators. What is happening at this moment was predicted; you've been expecting it; it's what you've worked for, so stay strong — listen, listen…! A cadenced thumping rolls in from a faraway ridge. It sounds like Babe Ruth smack-smacking his bat against a tree, bam, bam, bam-bam!

You spin the knob of your lantern back until its propane is choked down to a trickle before you edge out to its rim of light. Perhaps the darkness will make you hear better — kee-eeeeerack! The sharp sound of wood striking wood somewhere in the forest behind you is immediately answered by a measured Kee-rack-rack-rack just to the left, closer still, and you scramble back to choke that lantern to blackness. It's wise and it's prudent, you say; after all, you can't afford to have any late-night hikers stumbling in to destroy the privacy your research demands, not after all this time alone — but maybe, maybe, maybe that was only one confused hiker signaling another?

Or, maybe not.

The city kid in you wants to curl into a ball and pull a sleeping bag over your head, but you manage to stand tall even though your heart is slamming around inside your chest looking for a new way out. Again comes the silence. Again, too, your heart puts its escape on hold and your ever-forgiving mind begins to rationalize it all. Maybe a woodpecker had hammered into a hollow tree for one last snack before he tucked in — maybe those snappings and cracklings were just some young buck deer getting an early start on the rutting season.

Aw, you've been coming out here most weekends for over a year with nothing like this happening, right? You've put your entire vacation into this last ditch effort before the cold winds come and you could no longer greet the longest rays of the morning sun in the nude like the Indians of old. You're just disappointed, that's all. Remembering too that manual's instructions, when in doubt, check it out, you creep back down to the main path.

It's easy to walk by starlight now; you've become accustomed to it and soon you are doing your own lurking so near the main trail that you could reach out and touch anyone or anything passing by. Another half hour of silence grinds by — wait, wait! That silence is exactly what has been setting you on edge! Where are the usual peeper tree frogs, the mournful cries of lonely loons, the whirring cicadas, the flapping bats, and everything else that sings in the woods at night? Why is everything so eerily silent?

Bat-crap! Enough, already! You stomp back to your camp to noisily strike up that lantern until it hisses cheerfully before you set about your nightly routine of preparing more slides for your microscope. Making slides is engrossing; the nights slip by so quickly, and today granted you a boon for your wildlife hair collection when you discovered that bobcat den in the hollow below the old bat caves.

You begin by methodically setting everything up just as explained in the biology 101 manual that you got from the library. You place on your folding table the cutting blades for whole mounts and sectioning, the alcohol swabs, the empty glass slides and cover slips, the various fixatives and stains, some Canadian balsam for mounting, and your precious hair samples. However, when you reach for your scissors, you discover that they are not in their assigned spot. Where are they? A quick search locates them lying in the grass beneath the rain fly to your tent. Impossible! All summer long, you have been so careful, so attentive to detail. A closer look around jump-starts your heart yet again. Not a single tool is toeing the outlines you marked out for them in silhouette. Look, look! Even your soap, toothbrush, toothpaste, deodorant, have been moved. You do an item-by-item check-off against your prepared diagram to realize that this disturbance is not the result of nosy blue jays, crows, or those ravens that have an attraction to shiny things, because nothing is missing and yet everything has been touched...

This night seems darker than most. Worse, the moon won't rise until it's nearly dawn. You've lost your concentration; making slides is impossible. All you can do now is to sit back, to listen, and to wait — what was that? Did you really hear someone laughing from behind those thick brambles? Where, where? Right over there! That's ridiculous, the right side of your brain argues while the left side shouts back, "Pay attention, fool!"

Ka-thump! You whirl around as dead wood smacks against live wood on your left — crack! An answering wallop sounds somewhere off to your right.

You don't dare to blink even as something huge, dry, and strong begins to creak louder and louder until it snaps with a great pop. Whoosh, at the far end of your little meadow an old hollow tree keels over and slams onto the earth with a sad shudder.

"Hey, no sweat, dude. It's a coincidence," some lazy brain cells from your idiot side offer with a shrug. "Yeah, the wind did it, so chill out, man."

Nevertheless, that same idiot side is proven wrong as heavy footfalls begin to circle your camp. As if drawn by a magnet to those crunching sounds, you turn with each step like the second hand of a giant clock, tick-tick.

What to do, what to do?

Your memory recalls the instructions in the manual. You must not stare into the shadows… but your eyes do it anyway.

Circle completed, the pacing halts, but then the air is compressed close beside your left ear as something round and hard ziiiiiiips past at sonic speed — you cannot move, you cannot breathe, you cannot cry out for mercy. You can only listen as that hard rock bounds off to lose itself somewhere in the woods behind you — you want to run, you want to scream, shout, yell, cry, plead, and beg; you want to do anything except what you have trained to do. However, before you can unglue your feet from the ground, the woods around your camp are filled with the distinct and unmistakable sound of… a baby crying?

I've snapped, you mutter to yourself. I'm mad, insane, nuts, flipped out, gone, I'm over the edge for sure — should I go to that baby's rescue? Maybe there really are some lost hikers; maybe they saw my light; maybe someone collapsed out there and threw that rock just to get my attention; maybe, maybe — get a grip! You know exactly who and what is out there. Remember the rules, remember what you've studied, and remember why you are here. You press your fingers together, just as the manual said. You automatically begin to count 10, 9, 8, 7… another deep breath, in and out. 6, 5, 4, 3, 2, 1. Your breathing and your heart rate slow, your blood pressure drops, and you return to comparative calmness.

Now you lift your arms up and out from your sides and you open your empty hands as you pivot slowwwly for one complete revolution. As you turn, you say aloud, "I hope you don't mind my waiting here all summer, but I am determined to meet you. I want to know who you are, what you are, and why you are here…"

At that moment, the most incredible shrieking that has ever chilled a human's bones fills the forest around you with a cacophony of outrageous sounds. It is terrifyingly loud, yes, but it includes — dare you think it — it includes words in English strung together in between the cries of a crow and an eagle and the hoots of a dozen different owls mixed in with bird whistles and rabbit shrieks, coyote howls, and even fox barks — and yet words — words — are being articulated in a language foreign to your ear, but words nonetheless.

Somehow, you manage to shout back, "And perhaps then I will know who, what, and why I am! Come in where I can see you! I can't see in the dark the way you can. Please, come in and share with me. Look, I have no weapons; I have nothing in my hands at all. I really would like you to be my friend…"

No hard wood is bashed, no tree is shoved over, no one stomps about, no one laughs, and no baby cries. After a while, was it five minutes or fifty, you allow yourself to sink down to wait and to let your fear seep into the ground.

It is in the wee hours before moonrise when you are startled from a quick doze not by any sound, but by a presence. Before you can focus your eyes, you know something close to you has changed. You rub your weary eyes to peer into the blackness of the forest directly ahead of you. There a great and tangible mass is taking form. You don't utter a word when that mass takes a small step into the rim light of your lantern. The first thing you notice is this powerful being is opening its hands and is holding them out as if to show you those hands are empty of stones or clubs or anything bad. The second thing you notice is the glittering eyes that peer back at you from behind tufts of unruly hair. Those eyes are wary, to be sure. However, they are also intelligent, gentle... and curious. This perfectly adapted being is wildly beautiful... and at this moment you know that both of your lives have forever changed.

You, my friend, are face-to-face not with a legend but with a reality.

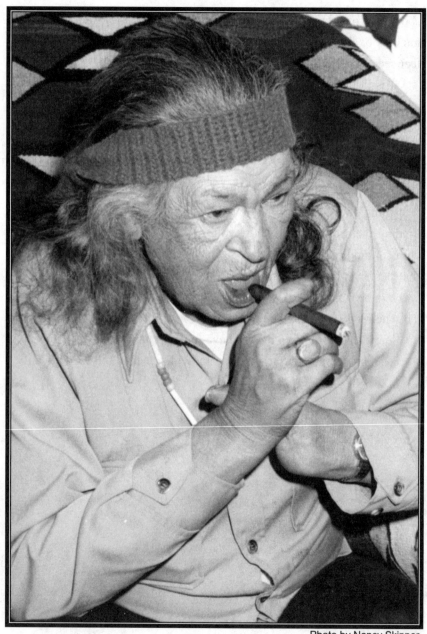

Ciyé Nino Cochise

1. Conversations with Cochise

The leathery old Apache eyed me through the thick haze of his cigar smoke. Over his shoulder and through windows sealed shut with cheap plastic and masking tape I could see the Dragoon Mountains fading into the desert twilight. Amid that mass of jumbled rocks was the legendary Chiricahua Apache stronghold where less than 100 years ago the U.S. Cavalry had not dared to plant a single horse's hoof.

"Yeah, I've seen what our people called the Yamprico," the man known as Ciyé Nino[1] Cochise said in a gravely growl. "Does that make me just another superstitious old Indian, or one privileged fella?"

Hunched across from me sat a man who was described in legends as swapping campfire tales with Teddy Roosevelt on the Arizona border ranch of John Slaughter,[2] riding with the Mexican rebel Pancho Villa,[3] and playing stud poker with Wyatt Earp.[4] Nearing the age of 99, Nino

---

[1] Although Niño (with a tilde) is the correct spelling for 'male child' in Spanish, Nino Cochise did not use that spelling or pronunciation. He pronounced his name 'Nee-noe'.
[2] Verified by 101-year-old Tombstone cowboy Sid Wilson who had worked on the Slaughter ranch at age 15. He also claimed he had met Nino there when both were youths.
[3] Substantiated via a brief telephone conversation with Mrs. Villa shortly before her death.
[4] Substantiated by Hobart (Hobie) Earp, of Grass Valley, CA, who recalled hearing that his cousin Wyatt had become friends with a relative of Cochise.

11

was reputed to be the last living Chiricahua Apache who had been born wild and free. He also claimed to be a grandson of the fierce Cochise, the only son of Tahza,[5] and a nephew to Gothlaka,[6] the warrior known to history as Geronimo. Was it true? I had no clue. For the time being, I accepted it all at face value if only to learn where it might lead.

I also noticed the sweat-polished handle of an antique Colt .45 Peacemaker sticking out from under his seedy couch, so I chose my words carefully. My earlier use of the term "Bigfoot" had turned him stiff as starch.

"As I was saying, Mister Cochise, the bits and pieces I've scraped together about early Native American legends dealing with these... er... creatures, only makes me want to know a lot more."

"If you think the Yampricos are creatures, you got 'em dead wrong. They're people just like us, only bigger."

"Whatever it is, was it near here where you had your encounter, or—"

"Waugh! Aren't you cuttin' me a tad short? Either give it to me straight and full, or not at all."

Cleo, Nino's nasty Chihuahua mutt, bared her needle teeth as if she, too, demanded it "straight and full."

"Cutting you short? I don't follow you, sir."

That tough old cob took his sweet time lighting another cigar while eyeing me from stem to stern. When his match flared, I could see that his fierceness had not faded over time. Some who knew him best whispered that, as a young war chief, Nino had ordered the dynamiting of a gunpowder factory down in Old Mexico. The blast had obliterated most of the town.

Equally intriguing, recent historians have yet to confirm the exact fate of the murderous Apache Kid, although descriptions of his escapades

---

[5] White man's history records no male heirs for Tahza. Nino claims that he and his mother had been part of the No-Name clan that had chosen to escape into Mexico rather than submit to being moved to a new and more barren reservation.

[6] Sometimes spelled Goyathlay.

still fascinate us. Some believe he became a successful melon farmer and died a peaceful death as a converted Mormon;[7] others are certain he had fallen under the guns of Mexican Rurales, while more will swear he had slipped back onto the reservation to die in obscurity. Nearly a century had passed, yet his name still spawned tall tales and wild speculation. However, my whisperers expressed full confidence that Nino Cochise held the key to that mystery. After all, they said, he was barely 16 years old when he had been sliced armpit to elbow during a knife brawl near the Sonoran village of Bacochic with an Apache warrior his frightened mother had called Apachlakit.[8] That fight had ended abruptly when young Nino's bowie knife slammed up and under his opponents jaw — I watched carefully when he reached for his ashtray. Clearly, an old scar seamed the length of his inner arm.

The old man's grumble interrupted my musings.

"You say you don't follow me? I think you do. Ya'see, after you left last night, I gave a call to our mutual pal down there in Key West. Ted Ernst[9] told me you'd caught sight of a few Yampricos yourself, but they always left you in the dust."

"True enough," I said. "I've seen much I can't explain, but that's not the proof science demands. I only want to know if you…"

"You want to know my stuff without sharing your side, eh? Well, maybe I want some answers first, tu comprende, amigo?" he said as his

---

[7] Many Indians professed Mormonism as a convenient dodge to Christianity, which they found cruel and preposterous, especially when they learned the Holy Roman Catholic See debated if they even had souls into the 1940s.

[8] I later discovered much of the skepticism surrounding Nino's authenticity came from his purported biography where several items did not add up. However, when he gifted me a copy of his original manuscript, I found glaring discrepancies between it and the published version. It became clear that his white co-author had arbitrarily changed several things to make a better read. Nino's credibility suffered because he had made the mistake common to many Native Americans — he had trusted a white man. Minnie claimed Nino had not received a dime of the royalties paid to his writing collaborator.

[9] Ted was my attorney and a close friend who, like myself, wanted to know all and everything. He was first to meet Nino and had immediately called me to follow suit ASAP. Good call!

right hand dropped to dangle scant inches above that exposed gun butt. I wondered if he might forget what century he was in; I wondered too if he might consider gunning me down just because I had cut him "a tad short." I decided not to blink an eye when an evening dust devil, a twister in miniature, rattled the windows. While I was facing a man said to have been born in 1874, there were modern cars and trucks whizzing along a highway less than 100 yards away.

"Ted said some of your college-educated pals give you the raspberries about this stuff," Nino sniffed.

"Not so much anymore. When he and I formed Vanguard Research in Florida, we were able to recruit a volunteer science advisory board that now lists seventeen scientists, most of whom have doctorates in a variety of complementary disciplines."

"Like who?"

"We have Carleton S. Coon, professor emeritus at Penn State; George Agogino, curator to the Paleo-Indian Institute in New Mexico; S. Dillon Ripley, the secretary of the Smithsonian; E. E. Hedblom, the senior physician in the U.S. Navy; and Grover Krantz of Washington State University at Pullman. We also consult with Pino Turolla and J. Manson Valentine of Miami, Tracy Blair, Jim Butler, George Shallar, Mary Jo Florey, and..."

"No Indians, huh?"

"Not yet, but I've interviewed quite a few; in fact, now that the snows chased me out of my base camp in Cougar, Washington, I'm heading back to the Florida Everglades to link up with some Miccosukees —"

"So what do your great white experts think?"

"Drs. Coon and Krantz express no doubts something is out there; Pino Turolla had a sighting of his own in Venezuela[10] and was actually chased from a cave in Ecuador in an up-close encounter."

---

[10] See his book, *Beyond the Andes*, for details.

"What about all these reports that make the news?"

"We generally agree some are simple errors made by folks who heard something going bump in the night, but far too many are outright hoaxes that leech time, money, and damage the credibility of the project. Unfortunately, those are the ones the media prefer to report."

"Yeah, well, I saw what I saw but nobody's gonna believe some superstitious old Indian, so why bother with me?"

"To be frank, sir, I am intrigued to know the long-term effects your encounter had on you as an individual. There's more to consider than simple physical attributes they might share with the family Hominidae; are there also intellectual and spiritual similarities?"

"Ol' Ted warned me you were a smart bird," he snorted. "So just what have you seen that humans share with our giant hairy friends?"

His folksy way of speaking was not fooling me. He was the smartest person in that room, so I gave him my best "university" response.

"Like humans and unlike apes, these creatures habitually walk erect; they also have buttocks like ours, opposing thumbs, the hallux, and an articulated speech pattern. None of these attributes exists in any of the lower primates and that could place them in the genus Homo that is dominated by a single species — Man.

"Here's the conundrum: when — not if — their existence is proven, it will shake the foundations of most faith-based religions whose core doctrines beat the drum about how special we are."

I paused to allow comment, but he waved me on like an Indian pope giving his blessing.

"As I see it, what elected politician would dare help us at this early stage? That is probably why no study grants are available that involve public money. With the exception of a single grant by the duPont family, Ted and I and our volunteers do everything on our own hook."

Once again, Nino's sole response was a hand-flick, so I ploughed ahead.

"The bias I've faced in the media and among some religious groups reminds me, sir, of the Dark Ages when the common citizenry was ruled by fear, fire, and flowery promises of heavenly rewards. If anyone questioned the divine authority of kings, popes, or priests, they were burned alive, and it was a great sin to learn to read and write unless you were a priest."

Nino chuckled, "Maybe that's why they don't teach much history today and, when they do, they make it as boring as dried spit. How can kids know where they're going if they don't know where they've been?"

Finding common ground at last, I said, "I remember being shocked to learn they had considered killing Galileo only because he had discovered that the sun and the universe did not revolve around our precious little earth after all. It was also hard to believe that in those times the microscope I was using in biology class — and even the printing press — were condemned by Rome as instruments of Satan.

"Nowadays when I lecture, Mister Cochise, I stress that whatever is, is, no matter what we wish things could be. For me, true learning is the literal process of discovering more and more things that I know nothing about.

"Anyway, nothing more can be said through science about your Yampricos until we gain access to their genetic codes. If they prove to be humanoid to any degree —"

"Boy, oh, boy, won't that be some hullabaloo!"

Nino's laugh sent a ball of cigar smoke rolling at me like a misty cannonball; it also launched Cleo into another fit of snapping and snarling.

"Are you flicking ashes on Cleo again, Nino?" a voice called out from the rear of their mobile home. "One of these days you're gonna set that dog on fire!"

Photo by N. Erika Morgan

Figure 1: Nino Cochise, Minnie, and Robert Morgan.

"Aw, she's all right, Minnie," he bellowed back. To me, he said, "When they figure out we've got Yampricos for kissing cousins, it'll bring back the Inquisition with Hell's fire, brimstone, and damnation!

"Doggone it, Robert, before the white people got a strangle hold on us, every Indian knew who they were as true human beings, where they came from, why they're here, and where they were going. I hear some Buddhists are on to it, but most whites ain't got a clue.

"So why not kill just one, so some money can pour your way? You'd be famous, too," Nino cooed.

"It's getting late," I sighed. "Maybe I'd better push on."

"Relax, son," he chuckled. "Ted told me you wouldn't hurt 'em. He said you don't even carry a gun and you like to go out alone so no one knows your best spots."

"Yeah, just me and my monsters, mano-a-mano."

"So where do you get your grubstakes for all this running around?"

"I've sold a few feature film and TV concepts, a couple scripts, and sometimes a commercial. Every time I scrape enough together for a break, I head back into the bush. It's become an expensive obsession."

"What's your angle? You gonna sell all this stuff as a monster movie?"

I flipped my notepad into my briefcase.

"I am what you see, sir. Help us if you wish, but I don't want to waste either your time or my own."

"Yep, there's that short fuse Ted warned me about," he cackled. "What about flying saucers? You believe in them, too?"

"I believe in what I know are facts, not what I think I know. Look, Mister Cochise, a few years back I occupied a responsible position with the Federal Aviation Administration in Washington, DC. I saw for myself some of those blips zipping all over radar screens, and they definitely weren't airplanes; I also listened to airline pilot's chatter about lots of shiny disks following them up and down the eastern seaboard."

"Sounds like a good job. Why'd you leave?"

"I couldn't take all the hypocrisy I saw inside the Beltway; life's too short. Now, when I see respected scientists like Grover Krantz being criticized for telling a truth that might upset the status quo — just like Galileo — it only makes me more determined."

"If nobody believes him, why come to this old Indian?"

"To tell the truth, I'm not all that sure, but Ted kept insisting that I stop by," I said and shrugged. "He thought you might help somehow."

"You really don't know why you're here, do you, son?"

Confusion washed over me like an icy wave. From the first moment we had met, I had been curiously willing to share my innermost thoughts, fears, and wonderings with a person who should be a stranger. Perhaps I was at a personal crossroad; perhaps I must make a choice about something... but what?

"Maybe it's time to learn who you really are," he said with a smile. But, before he could continue, Minnie Cochise emerged from her evening bath. She was a short, round, Anglo woman who habitually wore beaded moccasins that slap-slap-slapped with each step.

"Nino, you stop being so mean," she puffed while tossing fresh coffee grounds into a dented percolator. "Mister Morgan brings us steaks and all the trimmings and then you start talking all that nuts-stuff. Shame on you."

"She thinks she's the boss," Nino chuckled while deftly adjusting the red wool headband with his left thumb, the only digit remaining on a hand that had been mutilated in a biplane crash sometime in the 1930s. When I had pressed for details, he had tapped one empty trouser leg.

"Lost this stick at the same time because I was dumb enough to fly into a cloud," he had said as if it still surprised him. "Darned thing had a mountain in it."

I glanced at my wristwatch. My Miccosukee friend, Victor Osceola, had promised to take me out to his ancestral hummock if I got back before the waters feeding the Florida Everglades slowed for the winter. He felt we had an excellent chance to see a legendary Sha-wan-nook-chobee, their version of the Sasquatch, Bigfoot, or Yamprico — Nino's voice snapped me back to Arizona.

"Okay, so you've seen a Yamprico a time or two on your own. Like I said, is that all I get?"

Minnie scratched a match under the coffee pot and turned the gas up full blast.

"Robert Morgan, you'd better bark back at that dog or he'll keep you up a tree 'til the cows come home."

"Aw, you just hurry up with that coffee, Minnie. How do you expect us menfolk to talk turkey without some good java in us?" To me he said, "Now, let's put some meat into this powwow; where were you when you first saw what you think you saw?"

"I was up in Mason County, Washington. That's out on the Olympic Peninsula, not far from Bremerton."

"What were you doing up there?"

"I was in the Navy and my ship, the aircraft carrier *Princeton*, was in dry-dock so I —"

"That rain forest up there is a good place for Yampricos — they call them Skookums, I think. They're all over the Quinault Reservation, too. Good loggers, those Quinaults. Salish talkers, you know. Were you hunting or just walking out kinks?"

"We'd just got back from a nine-month Far East cruise so I needed some time alone. I had hiked part way up this one mountain to make a hide among some rocks above a small canyon, and —"

"What were you packing?"

"Half a sandwich. I was only there for the day."

"I mean did you have a rifle, a pistol, a bow and arrow — two rocks and a baseball bat — what?"

"Ohhh... I had a Marlin .30-.30 Texas carbine."

"That's okay unless you get a big bear looking down your barrel. Then it would get downright puny. So how did the Yamprico get mixed up in all this — and don't give me any cute answer, either!"

"It was about nine or ten o'clock in the morning and I guess I'd dozed off..."

"Good way to miss bear."

"Keep it up, Nino, and you ain't getting supper," Minnie groaned.

"Something fooling around in the brush behind me woke me up. When I couldn't make it out, I stood up and yelled."

"Why'd you do that?"

"If it was a hunter, I didn't want to get shot. But that's when I started feeling weird." I paused to take a deep breath and my heart began thumping all over again despite all those intervening years.

"The minute I called out, everything went dead silent and eerie — and it wasn't just because I was there. There was something more to it. No birds were doing their morning chirping, no bugs were rustling around among the leaves, and not one little critter was scampering around like you'd expect when the sun starts warming things up."

"Did the hairs on your neck prickle up and your mouth pucker dry?" Nino asked.

"Yeah, and my arms looked like bottle brushes."

"You got some pictures in your brain, too, didn't ya?"

How could he know that? He went on before I could ask.

"Sometimes you can see those Yampricos inside your brain even before your eyes take hold. Once you get to know those fellers real well, they might even talk to you inside your head."

"Hush, Nino! What happened next, Mister Morgan?" Minnie said breathlessly.

"When I called out that second time, something big — and I mean big-big — went plowing up through the brush toward the nearest ridge. I tracked its wake through my rifle sights after I saw patches of reddish-blackish hair. Then, just as it got to a break in the bushes, it stopped and…"

"Milk and sugar?" Minnie chirped as she presented mugs of steaming coffee and plopped a tall stack of gingersnaps beside me. "Here's some of them good cookies you brought. They're Nino's favorites, too."

"Just milk, thanks. Anyway, it was some 40 yards out when it pushed up through some hip-high bushes."

"You sure are slow on the hammer," Nino bellowed. "Quit calling them an it; they're a *them* just like us! Yampricos are wild people, and you'd better get it straight from the get-go. Now stop waltzing around with that safe-science lingo and tell me what in the blue blazes happened next!"

"That's when it... er... he swiveled around to look straight at me."

"Young or old one?"

"Fairly young, I would guess. I don't know why I say that, but he—"

"He was young."

"How do you know?"

"An old one would've known you were there and you wouldn't have seen hide nor hair of him. How did this fella hold his hands? Was his palms toward you or away from you?"

I squeezed my eyes shut to study the picture etched inside my eyelids.

"I'd have to guess his palms were toward me."

"You didn't shoot," Nino said matter-of-factly.

"Never crossed my mind."

Other odd things about that day still puzzled me. I had seen animals with wild and angry eyes, frightened eyes, sleepy eyes, and just plain dumb eyes. Not this character. His eyes were bright, intelligent, and, instead of being either frightened or menacing, he appeared equally amazed and perplexed by my sudden appearance. Above all, not for an instant did he appear threatening. Nevertheless...

"I got out of there as fast as I could. When I reached that first gas station, I called the Highway Patrol."

"Did they come out with sirens and all?" Minnie asked.

"Not after I told them I thought some passing circus had lost their gorilla — what are you laughing about? Look, I came from the backstreets of a steel town in Ohio; I was ten before I found out milk came from more cows than Elsie Borden. It was years later and only after I'd read about Jerry Crew's encounter near Eureka, California, that I realized what it — he — had been."

"Where's my cookies, Minnie?" Nino asked.

"You said you didn't want any."

"You never asked! Sometimes you treat me like an unwanted stepchild!"

"Lookee here, Nino, I can't keep fooling with you if I'm to get supper on the table before midnight," she said as she stomped in to plop a saucer of two cookies on the coffee table between us. "I got potatoes to pare, steaks to broil, and a pie to bake, so I can't be serving you every time you think you need something!"

Nino compared his two against my stack.

"Maybe she's saving 'em for Christmas..."

The evening before, these two had generously shared with me their leftover stew and stale oyster crackers. Minnie's eyes had lit up like blue fireflies when I had pushed in today with four grocery bags bulging with goodies; even Cleo had stopped yapping and snapping to sniff and snuffle at everything. That rat in dog's clothing came up short on doggie treats. My heels were still raw from her sneak attacks the previous night, so I had no charitable feelings toward that bug-eyed bandito. I was ready for her this time. I had smeared my bare heels with gooey Vaseline made blood red by gobs of fiery cayenne pepper.

I had to hand it to Cleo, though. She was a crafty bitch. She deftly swiped Nino's biggest cookie the moment he was distracted by relighting his cigar.

"Let me tell you about the first Yamprico I ever saw," he mumbled in between sucks on that stogie. "I was in the Mexican Sierras not far from the Cañon del Cobre at the time..."

"No sir! You saw it right near the Arizona border," Minnie sighed amid flying potato peels.

"... with what was left of our tribe. Right after my grandfather died, the government went to canceling every promise that lying General

Howard[11] had made about letting us live in peace on the land of our ancestors. That's when Tom Jeffords, our first Indian agent,[12] quit the government to go mining up in the Tortolito Mountains. Ol' Tom hated liars worse than he hated thieves, and he'd shoot a thief quicker than bees will sting a bare butt.

"Anyway, when the Army brought in John Clum to take Tom's place, my father's whole clan decided it was time to vamoose."

"We all hate that John Clum," Minnie said with a solemn nod.

Nino continued.

"I was a just a toddler when Clum and his army decided to herd my tribe up onto that hellhole San Carlos Rez with those Sierra Blancos and Tonto Apaches and such. That was a bad idea. Us Chiricahuas always scuffled with those fellers even if they were our kissing cousins. Different spins on the same ball, don't you know?

"Anyway, when we saw which way the wind was blowing, about 38-40 men, women, and kids of our clan vamoosed down to our secret hideout in Mexico. Ol' Clum didn't want to admit that any of us had slipped away, so when we started popping up here and there, he called us No-Name Apaches and claimed we must be broncos out of Mexico."

While Nino appeared to be veering away from my main topic of interest, I had to ask, "Why No-Name?"

"Aw, that Clum couldn't get his stiff Yankee tongue around our language so he took to calling us by numbers. How would you like to be called Mister 8-9-2? Plumb arrogant! As it was, we scooted out before he got his dog tags around our necks. Not having a number made us the No-Names, get it?"

---

[11] General Oliver Otis Howard, a Civil War veteran whose impatience with the Nez Perce Indians triggered the infamous war with Chief Joseph. In 1871, he negotiated the boundaries to the Chiricahua Apache's first reservation in Arizona. That treaty was broken when Cochise died and the Apache Wars broke out.

[12] The close personal relationship between Thomas Jeffords and Cochise is described in the book, *Blood Brother*.

"Then you've never lived on a reservation?"

"Not this hoss. See that jumble of rocks this side of the Dragoons? That's where I was born. It's a doggoned park now. Campers throw trash where proud people used to live." He wagged his head. "A way of life that'd been there for a couple thousand years got snuffed out. Ain't that a shame?

"Anyway, my mama tossed me on her cayuse and we rode all night and the next day until we got over the border into Mexico. We ended up way high in the Sierra Madres on a mesa we called Pahgotzinkay; that means 'our little piece of heaven.' Pretty soon lots more Chiricahua, Mescalero, and Mimbreno runaways started showing up. Chatto and young Mangus and their gangs all came around until the Army got 'em down.

"I remember my mama crying when some Yaqui renegade plugged Beduiat — that's the feller the Pinda-Lick-O-Ye — the white-eyes — called Victorio.

"There was always a big show when my other uncle showed up, too. He was Gothlaka to us but the Mexicans tagged him with that handle Geronimo."

"I thought that was his Indian name."

"Naw, some Nakai-ye Mexican Rurales had an officer from Spain whose favorite stage play was about some sheriff named Jeronimo. That sheriff's whole family was murdered and he went crazy. Since Spaniards are Catholics and Catholics can't do suicide, he commenced taking revenge against those murderers in the hopes somebody would put him out of his misery. No matter how hard he tried to get himself killed off, he had to live with it.

"See, that's what set off my uncle, you know. When Gothlaka was away doing some honest trading in one village, some Nakai-ye from another place went out and killed and scalped his mama, his wife Alope, and even his little kids. Just like Catholics, Apaches won't do suicide, so he started taking crazy chances in the hopes somebody might shoot straight for once.

"I remember one time he showed up after he and his gang had rode over 1,200 miles in a month — he kept busting out from San Carlos, see. Oh, what a shindig we had! All us kids were a-laughin', singin', and dancin' right along with 'em."

"What kind of an uncle was he?"

"I'll tell you this: he had a sense of humor no whites ever saw. Once I tripped him with a stick just funning around so he threw me up a tree. He laughed like the dickens when I got stuck. All us kids liked him. He gave me a pocket watch one time. He said the white man who owned it didn't need it anymore, hee-hee!

"You ever hear of Nana? He was another one to be proud of, especially when I hear people nowadays wailing about getting old and rickety even before they hit the 50-year mark. By jeepers, Nana was over seventy when he busted loose from the Rez; he and his fighters were chased high and low by General Crook's best troopers — or maybe that Miles was on the job by then. I was too little to know the difference. That Nana fought a dozen battles and never lost a single man.

"Want to know the rotten truth? No whites could ever catch my people, but things were so miserable at that San Carlos hellhole that some of our young bucks signed up as scouts. It took Apaches to catch Apaches, and that's the solemn truth."

"This Pahgotzinkay must have been a pretty special place," I said.

"There were a few spells when we couldn't find a rotten acorn to eat; still, we'd rather starve than live on the dole. Want to see an Apache's lights go out? Pen him up!" Nino's gaze shifted over my shoulder to somewhere outside and in the fading light. "When I was born we had about a thousand or so true human beings living right here where all our ancestors were buried. We called ourselves the Chockonen Teneh, the People of the Mountains. Before I had reached thirty, we were down to three hundred or so, and about all of those were ganged up at Fort Sill, Oklahoma. None of those poor souls ever came home again. There was just a few of us that held out and even we had to change our ways to fit in with this new world."

"Awful mean thing to do to people," Minnie said, adding her sighs to his.

"About your encounter with the Yamprico..."

"When food got too scarce, our old folks would go out and sit on a rock until they died just so our young could keep the tribe going," he said wistfully. "That's the way it was back then. People cared more about the tribe than they did about themselves."

"Excuse me, but didn't you just say Apaches never committed suicide?"

"Suicide is what you do for yourself. Sacrifice is what you do for others," Nino said while scanning the abundance of food Minnie had scattered around in their kitchen. "Our spread could've fed an awful lot of hungry folks back then."

"What about the first time you saw a Yamprico?" I asked again.

"First tell about Dee-O-Det. Mister Morgan will like that story," Minnie said.

"Could we make that just plain old Robert so I don't feel like another unwanted stepchild?"

"Well, sir, that old man is the smartest feller I ever met, bar none," Nino said with a chuckle. "Ya'see, he'd been the shaman to my grandfather until my father took over and then he was his shaman, too. I even inherited the old goat when I got old enough. See, a good shaman will live a long time because their only job is to keep things going.

"Back when Clum was inviting my father back East to palaver with President Grant, Dee-O-Det warned him not to go because his dreams told what would happen. Dreams like that don't lie, if you know how to read them."

"Like Freud's interpretations?"

"Hell, no! For us, it's more about the mission of the soul, not just the wishings of the crotch."

"They murdered Nino's father to death," Minnie sniffed. "He's buried in the Congressional Cemetery. I saw his grave. Nino wouldn't go. He said he didn't want to see his father surrounded by the same white people that killed him. Indians are funny about dead people, you know."

"Huh! That Clum claimed my father got mad and sat up all night in a park across from the White House where he caught pneumonia because it was wintertime. That never happened. Dee-O-Det dream-watched him being strapped to a bed where they poured water on him and then propped the windows open until he died. Yep, just the other night, Dee-O-Det said —"

"Hold it, wait, wait, wait! Dee-O-Det still talks with you?"

"Yeah, and when he heard you were coming, he told me to warn you about those people who only look like regular people, but they ain't. They're the ones who are always trying to snatch your soul so you can't go home, don't ya see?"

"Whoa, whoa! No, I don't see! Let's start again; Dee-O-Det is still alive? He must be 150!"

"Ain't you never heard of dream-talking?"

"Now, that's enough, Nino," Minnie exploded. "If you start talking that nutsy stuff, I'm going to cart you off to the loony bin!"

"Aw, Guynatay[13] here knows more than he thinks he knows," he said with a wink in my direction. "Ain't that right, Guy?"

"Well, sir, I've always likened waking dreams in a human brain to a computer clearing its memory when it's first switched on. For instance, if you and I each dream of the Eiffel Tower, mine might be triggered by a

---

[13] I was confused by his use of this term until later when he deigned to mention that he had named me Guynatay. How I found out the meaning of the name is described in Chapter 12.

movie I've seen, while you may have been there playing kissy-face with Minnie. I don't believe blanket interpretations work for everyone or in all cases. That's sort of a blanket cop-out."

"Aw, that ain't dream-talking. Dream-talking is when your dream-self talks with your awake-self, or sometimes it's when other souls of your clan are talking to you even if they're far away or maybe even with the dead."

"But-but-but, Mister Cochise —"

"My name is Nino," he yawned.

"Please, Nino, I know everyone wants to believe there is something beyond this life, but what does it have to do with the Yampricos — hello?"

Damn. Too late. His chin had dropped onto his chest and his long hair was sweeping over his face like twin gray curtains. Rats! The previous night, smack in the middle of a similar conversation about Native American beliefs in past and future lives, he had lowered his head this way and had fallen fast asleep.

Cleo took the cue and scored Nino's last cookie.

I was getting antsy. No matter if this man was a delusional liar or a wise survivor, his account of Dee-O-Det's purported warning stirred powerful emotions within me. Was it mere restlessness or some abiding fear that I felt each time I found myself wondering how any human being with a soul could torture or murder a child, steal from the aged, or start a war. It had baffled me since childhood. Was it possible that a human body could walk, talk, and function... if it was soulless? If it was a sort of fear that I felt, was it an unreasonable and paranoiac fear or something more, something so sinister that the id within my psyche could only utter muted screams to beware, beware.

"Nino! You wake up and tell Robert all about that Yamprico or you're going to bed hungry!" To me, Minnie said, "It's a darned good story — gives me the goose pimples!"

Nino's bony shoulders twitched as if shaking off some somber reverie. Perhaps that magical light of Arizona eventide blurred my vision for the moment; perhaps I was exhausted or confused. Whatever it was, when Nino's head lifted and his hair folded away, his cheekbones appeared higher, his nose straighter, his eyes blacker, and he was beyond ancient — I squeezed my eyes shut hard, hard, hard, but, when I opened them again, he remained regarding me with an expression of compassion and sympathy.

A voice within me hissed that this must be some clever trick — or had Minnie slipped something into my coffee? Still and all, a slumbering portion of my soul sprang awake in joy. Although I remained cognizant that my corporeal body was seated upon a chair with that modern traffic zipping back and forth less than 100 yards away, the person opposite me appeared to squat within a great cavern whose sole illumination was a small flickering fire. Adding to this mystical effect was a distinct scent of smoldering mesquite wood that nudged deeply hidden memories awake; I also realized that everything in that cavern was somehow familiar to me. My "rational mind" quickly interceded to warn this must be either an illusion or sheer lunacy. How could I "recognize" that which is only imagined? How could I presume that both Nino and I could exist in two separate time periods at an identical point in time?

In a heartbeat, I could not twitch nor so much as breathe nor could I think as I commonly perceived the act of thinking. In its stead, I "understood" without having to perform the usual task of logical progression that assimilates facts and assumptions until conclusions of sorts are formed. All the while, uncountable tiny gray cells commenced bursting within my physical brain to punch holes through those barriers raised by a socially imposed concept of logic that until now had denied me so much as a glimpse of this separate reality. I suddenly "understood" that these barriers exist only because of the limitations imposed on me by my five accepted senses — boom! In a nanosecond, a latent essence erupted within me in a flash of Zen satori. Somehow I clearly "understood" that Nino and I and every being great or small that ever existed throughout the entire universe remain alive in shifting forms and fashions that are forever linked — in that same moment, that ageless patriarch across from me began chanting ever so softly in a language I can only poorly imitate.

> Oh, hah lee-ee! Oh hah lee-ee!
> Hah wah-biszt hah-yee
> Schichi hah-dah-hee yagha neen-yee-yah.
> Oh, hah lee-ee, Ihidnan! Oh hah lee-ee!
> Netne-he ztah, Guy-nah-tay.
> Hi-dicho, hi-dicho, hi-dichooooooo.

I blinked but once and both the cavern and its singer vanished. Before I could speak, move, or perhaps escape into the desert night to drive fast and far away, the familiar form of good old brown-eyed, gray-haired Nino reappeared.

"Now, about that Yamprico," he yawned as if nothing had given him pause. "Let's see, it was about 1896 or so when old Taglito — that's what my mother called Tom Jeffords — showed up in Pahgotzinkay. Always a real gentleman, he brought her and my sister some fancy new woman-duds to wear and bags of that hard candy they liked so much — horehound, they called it.

"Know what he brought me? A spanking-new hunting rifle, that's what. Well, sir, this young buck was proud as Punch to tote around that besh-shea-gar, I can tell you! Then when he handed over some gold dust from his mine..."

"Excuse me, Nino, but weren't you — weren't we just in a cave?"

"Aw, no, by that time we'd all built cabins for the winters — it gets too cold for wickiups that high up. Anyway, my mother didn't have to ask me twice to take a pinch or two of that gold dust and go fetch her some store-bought pots and a big ration of bacon, salt, and flour and such. She knew I was just itching to get a load of cartridges for that new rifle and she wanted to take advantage of the ride.

"Besides, she wanted Taglito to herself for a little bit. You know how it is..."

"Wait, please! Who — who was singing by that fire? I smelled the smoke..."

"I think we all were there — everyone liked that Taglito, even my sister Nadina."

"No, no, I'm talking about that cave where you were singing."

Dismissing me with a shrug, Nino went on.

"Sasabe is a little-bitty town on the Arizona-Mexican border about a day's ride west of Nogales. It was safe for me to go there because white traders couldn't tell a Pima from a Yaqui, so nobody asked who was what. See, they still had an open season on Apaches back then. Come to think of it, it's still against Arizona law for a Chiricahua to be here in Cochise County at the Cochise Visitor's Center near the town of Cochise," Nino sniffed while flicking cigar ashes over Cleo.

"Okay, but what was that song you were singing?" I asked again.

"Oh, I'm always real quiet on the trail; it's a habit, you know. As it was, I threw in with a bunch of Papago Indians who were heading north for the San Xavier Mission. They get real Catholic when some saint's day rolls around because they get free food, don't you see? Anyhow, come nighttime me and them Paps bedded down in this big arroyo."

"How close was this to Sasabe?"

"I think I could just see the peak of that big mountain the Paps think holds up the roof of the world."

"Baboquivari?"

"That's the place," he agreed. "Now don't get to thinking us Apaches always ran around with Papagos. It just so happened we was all going to the same watering hole, so it made sense."

"Shame on you, Nino Cochise," Minnie said. "You've got some Papago friends. They're good people."

"Aw, were talking about how it was then, not how it is now." To me he said, "Back in those days the Paps and their cousins the Pimas never hit it off with us, don't ya know? They were the farmers and we were the fighters, so we figured it was up to us to hang around all those mountain passes to help guard 'em. Those fellows couldn't get it through their heads we were protecting them from those thieving Mexicans who always came sneaking in come harvest time, you see. By the time us Apaches did our job of fighting and such, them Pimas had the crops in. That's why we fighters had to sort of borrow from the farmers now and again just so we could stay on the job."

"I read where they said you just lolled around those cool mountains during the hot summer and then robbed them of the fruits of their hard work."

"See that, Nino? I told you Robert wasn't just another dumb white man," Minnie giggled.

Nino chose this moment to reach for his cookies but found the saucer empty. He scanned the floor, patted his lap, and even stared at mine — then he spied telltale crumbs surrounding Cleo.

"No wonder Kickapoos ate your pappy," he snarled with a cuff.

"Anyway, those Papagos set to boiling beans for their supper. That's why they are called Papagos instead of their real name, Tohono Oodham, don't you know? Papago means Bean-Eaters in Pima-talk."

"Doesn't the word 'apache' mean enemy?"

"Yeah, well, the white man got it screwed up lots of times by naming Indian tribes what the other tribes called them. Ain't that a hell of a note?"

Minnie scuffed in to plop an oversized gingersnap in between Cleo's paws as a treat of sorts. She had barely turned back to the kitchen when Nino had snatched it up and crammed it all into his mouth.

"Like I thaid, it wath thundown when we dethided to pith camp at the mouff of thith arroyo."

Minnie spun around.

"Are you having a stroke?"

"Wha?"

"You're talking awful funny."

Nino gulped the dregs of his coffee and croaked, "I had a frog in there for a minute." To me, he said, "I wanted meat, so I took that new rifle and went out looking for a deer or a javelina or even a jackrabbit or two. Now those desert jacks aren't as tender as mountain rabbits since desert critters eat all that prickly stuff, but any meat's better than no meat in my book.

"Well, sir, pretty soon I'd strung my way up a ridge that went along this big arroyo — I like high ground when I'm out hunting — but I wasn't having any luck. It was getting dark when I came to this drop-off; I made out pretty quick that it was too steep to go back to camp that way — all of a sudden, my scalp started crawling. I turned around to see this big black fella looking at me over the tops of some chaparral bushes. He didn't say or do nothing, but he gave me the heebie-jeebies!"

"It sounds just like them shivers you got up there in Washington, Robert," Minnie said.

"Now, I'd always thought our tribe warned kids about these Yamprico characters just to keep them close by the fire at night. Of course, when us bucks got older, we didn't want to believe all that woolly-booger stuff... or maybe we didn't want to know something's out there that's bigger than us. Yep, maybe that's it."

Nino yawned again and his chin drooped toward his chest.

"Hey, hello! Was this Yamprico about seven or eight feet tall, maybe three or four hundred pounds?" I asked in a loud voice.

Nino's head jerked up, his eyes flew open, and he said too quickly, "Oh, ahem, maybe so! I have heard those Yampricos up north get that big, but not this feller. I am about 6' 1" and, while he was taller, he was sort of wiry. Things go like that in the deserts, you know.

"It was his head that seemed the strangest; it was planted smack down on his shoulders. He wasn't furry like an animal, either, no, huh-uh; he had long and stringy hair all over. Know what else? He had the longest arms I ever saw pinned on a human being. Something more, he stood there with his hands held open like this, see, with his palms out front just like the one you'd seen. I think he wanted me to see he wasn't toting a rock or anything, or maybe he just wanted to calm me down. They have that way about 'em, so they say."

"Was he wearing anything?"

"Naked as a jaybird."

"Did you point your rifle at him?"

"I'd forgot I even had it," Nino snorted. "Hell, I'd even forgot my six-shooter and my Bowie knife, too!"

"Did he have a bow or a spear or anything at all?"

"Not a stick."

"Yes, he did," Minnie nearly shouted. "You said he was carrying a canteen of water!"

"How could he be carrying anything if he was holding his hands open like this?" Nino bellowed while flapping his hands at her.

"You said so!"

"Guy, go get my razor strop off the wall in the bathroom."

"You said it, you said it, you said it," she screeched while stomping her feet.

"Are you married?" Nino moaned while puffing his cigar like the Little Engine Who Could.

"Nope."

"Hear that, Minnie? I told you Guy wasn't just another dumb white man!"

Before I could ask who "Guy" was and why he called me that, Nino was shouting above the din of pots, pans, and spoons being banged around in Minnie's kitchen.

"That Yamprico feller started to back away from me real slow-like, but he kept his hands up where I could see 'em. When I saw that he was about to back off that cliff, I hollered at him. By golly, he just turned and stepped right over the side. Whoosh, he was gone!"

"I think he jumped because he was scared of that gun," Minnie shouted.

"How many times I gotta tell you he steppppppped!"

I could easily imagine a young Nino face-to-face with that open-handed Yamprico; I wondered too when or if I would ever face one again. Next time perhaps I should hold my hands out, open and empty.

"I trotted over to take a look," Nino continued. "I thought he'd be all banged up on those rocks in that wash. Instead, he —"

"Whoee! That boy was long gone," Minnie whistled. "Never found even a track. Never saw him again, either! Now tell us about when you went back, Nino! That still curls my hair!"

Nino covered his face with his one good hand and hissed through its fingers, "I ain't finished with that night!"

Slam, bang, crash, thump, bump!

Nino motioned me into a huddle; Cleo licked her fangs and inched forward. I hitched up my jeans cuff to present her an easy cayenne-hot target. Damn. She ignored the offer.

"See, Minnie always tells the end of a story first. It's in her hereditation," Nino whispered.

"But how was he carrying a canteen?"

"It was just an animal's gut he had twisted around his waist and looped up over one shoulder. That's how those fellers carry spare water when they're on the move."

"Maybe that's what makes them stink, too. Back East, in particular, they always talk about their sour odor."

"Naw! I'd bet they only stink when they're sneaking through human territory. Think about it: when Indians hunted buffalo way back in the olden days, they'd dress up in a buffalo hide and hunker down to shuffle around on all fours. Of course, they had to change their smell too, so they'd rub on lots of fresh buffalo poop. I figure that's how them Yampricos get close to animals they want for dinner, see. Doesn't it make sense that they would try that same trick to get past humans?

"See, every animal identifies each other by their poop and scent glands and stuff, so it makes sense the Yampricos might think if they rub ours on them they can slip past us... Waugh!"

We each wrinkled our noses as a rotten odor wafted up between us. I edged back in my seat, allowing that another whole day separated Nino from his traditional Saturday night bath, but why was he glaring at me?

"So you never heard of using guts to make canteens?" he gasped. "That's an old trick us Apaches used to beat the socks off the U.S. Cavalry. See, we'd borrow a string of some white rancher's horses, mount the worst nags of the lot, and ride like the dickens out across the desert. When we'd get to the first waterhole, we'd kill all the worn out horses — they were tuckered anyway — and strip out their main guts. Fill 'em with water, wrap 'em around the necks of the next-best horses, and off we'd go again."

"Cruel but smart."

"That's when we'd ride hell-bent-for-leather for the driest country we could find, swapping riding horses back and forth on the run. It worked every time because those cavalry guys always rode their best horses first and almost never carried spare water."

"Dumb as a box of rocks!"

Nino's laugh sucked air until he gagged. Making a pee-yew face, he snatched up Cleo and pitched her across the floor.

"Get the door, Minnie-girl! Cleo's gotta go potty right now!"

"Supper's ready," she announced while setting free her four-legged stink bomb.

"Did you ever do that?" I asked. Nino impaled me with his best eye until I added, "Use horse-gut canteens, I mean."

"Oh? Ohhhhh! Yeah, I had to do that sometimes when I had those doggoned Rurales on my tail," Nino said while hopping to the table. "Boy, oh, boy, look at that spread. Is that real butter? Um, boy, pass me a chunk of hot bread! Hey, this T-bone steak is done just right, Minnie. It still moos! You're a darned good cooker."

"Do you have any pet theory how that Yamprico disappeared?" I asked while sliding in beside him.

Nino flipped his butter knife sharp side up and his grin folded into a frown.

"Do you think I'm gonna say he got sucked up in a beam of light or maybe stepped off into another dimension? Or maybe you think I'd paid a visit to Mescalito first?"

"No, no, but he had to go somewhere and I'm asking your opinion, that's all."

"Don't get myths or monsters on the brain," he growled. "First off, too many folks think this is some hokey joke because they can't find 'em in their college books, they ain't at some zoo, and they ain't stuffed in a museum!

"You can bet your socks no true human being makes fun of this stuff because they know it would bring 'em real bad luck of the worst kind. The Yamprico or Sasquatch or Windigo or Ohmah-ah or Skookum or whatever name you stick on 'em, don't ever call 'em anything that don't mean some kind of people."

"That's interesting; I know the Kwakiutl tribe in Canada uses the term Dsonoqua when they talk about that legendary giant cannibal woman who supposedly ate bad kids —"

"Ha-hah! There you go, Robert! You just made my blasted point!"

"I did?"

"You said the Dsonoqua is a cannibal woman because she eats bad kids, right? Being a cannibal means you eat your own kind, doesn't it?

Where is my dictionary? Doesn't that prove the Kwakiutls know that Dsonoqua was human?"

That insightful argument would one day prove a cornerstone to my opinions; facts I would soon learn from the Kwakiutl's master carver, Lelooska, would further underscore these conclusions with a heavy stroke.

"Let's tell Robert what you didn't find the next day," Minnie said brightly.

"Where was I — oh, yeah, when I had skedaddled back into camp that night, those Papagos were stuffing beans down as fast as they could swallow. Don't you know they made terrible fun of me for coming up empty in the meat department? But after I told 'em about my brush with that Yamprico, you should have seen the bonfire they made. It was so big I had to sleep in the brush — pass the salt, please."

I heard a lone coyote yapping out beyond the mesquite grove that crowded around Nino's mobile home. I wondered if those scary dreams those Papagos had had about a Yamprico circling their camp might compare with what a certain cookie thief was feeling out there all alone and in the dark. Of course, I knew nothing for certain, so I said nothing... nothing at all.

"Yessir, Robert, it rankled me no end that those fellers sat back there stuffing their bellies while I was cold and hungry, so I got a big stick and whacked some bushes and hollered like a devil had me by my popo. The sun hadn't peeped over the ridge the next morning before those boys were hot-footing it to confession over there at the San Xavier del Bac mission," Nino said in between laughs.

Of course, I joined in quite heartily — especially when I heard that coyote yap even closer than before. Were those little paws I heard tap-tap-tapping at our chamber door?

"Did you ever catch up with them?" I asked, perhaps more loudly than necessary.

"Heck, no! I headed back up that arroyo to see what was what. I'm one of those fellers that needs to know what's smoke and what's mirrors."

"Shush, you two," Minnie hissed at us.

The most pitiful of all whines came oozing in from under the front door. Another coyote yap — closer now — and those little paws did some fancy clawing. Minnie barely cracked the door open before a four-legged cannonball scrambled in to leap onto the couch where it shivered and quivered among the crumbs of ill-gotten cookies.

"Aw, look at that. Sure must be cold out there for poor little Cleo," I cooed while smiling into her weepy pop-eyes. "More butter, Nino, hmmmm?"

"Why, thank you, amigo. Anyway, like I was saying, there ain't no better tracker than an Apache, but I didn't find so much as a smudge nowhere around the bottom of that cliff. That's when it was my turn to head for Sasabe, lickety-split. I was raised with the idea that if I was supposed to know something, Usen would show me. I had looked, and He had showed me nothing. Adios!"

" 'Usen' is an old Apache word for God-the-Creator," Minnie explained as she handed out slices of hot apple pie all smothered with cheddar cheese, the final treat from my gift of goodies.

After we all had cleaned our plates, I noticed the old man's eyes glazing over again as he loosened his belt three whole notches.

"Come on back tomorrow, son. We'll have breakfast about seven."

"Thanks, but I'd better scoot so I can get into the Everglades before the water level drops for the winter. Where I am going will take an airboat and that means standing water. Tell you what, I'll bring my daughter Riki with me next summer; I want her to meet you."

"Nino went back to look for that Yamprico again. He found good stuff," Minnie said while she cleared the table and fired up the coffee pot again.

"You went back?"

"Yessir, but it was a few years later when I was working as a bodyguard for old Colonel Bill Greene.[14] He was that big copper king down in Cananea,[15] you know. The Colonel wanted me to guide one of his highfalutin' geologists from the East to look for more copper. I started him off at that same arroyo…"

"Nino found a cave," Minnie said quickly.

"Yeah, see, while that kid went to poking around, I spotted a narrow little shelf tucked up and under the edge of that cliff. I left him to his rock scratching while I circled up to have a look, then let myself down onto a little ledge so's I could shinny over to where I found a sort of cave hollowed out nice and neat-like. That's why I hadn't seen that Yamprico when he stepped over the edge; he had already gone round the bend.

"Now I started singin' one of those sacred songs old Dee-O-Det gave me; it's not smart to surprise people what's bigger than you, he always said."

"He found bones," Minnie added with a nod.

"Yeah, but they were mostly javelina and deer, so don't get excited. It was that pile of cow bones that perked my ears because there wasn't a ranch for miles."

"Could it have been a free-range maverick?"

"Maybe so, but most cows in Mexico are accounted for. See, water is scarce and where there's water, there's people, and they'll corral a loose cow in a heartbeat."

"Jaguar?"

"El tigres don't sleep where they eat and he had made a big nest of twisted chaparral twigs; he had put a keep-out bar there, too."

"A what? What's that?"

"There was a saguaro cactus rib stuck across the entrance to let you

---

[14] William Cornell Greene.
[15] A corrupted word from an old Apache word for horsemeat.

know that was his place."

"Could it have been blown in there by a storm?"

"Naw, it was up and inside — that's only one of the keys you gotta watch for, Guy, because they'll leave pointers, too. You just gotta learn to read 'em; want to know how? Don't think with your brain; let instinct be your guide.

"Anyway, it looked just like a hobo camp without busted glass and rusty cans and no signs of fire."

"Did you collect any tools, a club, a spear, a metate, or maybe samples of hair?"

"What some call collecting, I'd call stealing. I don't touch what ain't mine."

I fetched a map while Minnie searched for his glasses. The old warrior stared, grunted, and stared again before tapping an area within a triangle formed by Nogales, Sasabe, and the village of Saric.

"Look for an old wagon trail first; there'll be a horse trail to the west of it maybe 100 yards or more. Bronco Indians[16] stayed off the main road, see?

"You'll dip down real sharp at the mouth of the arroyo I'm talking about. It'll look sort of narrow at first with high banks, but it gets wider as you go west. Unless a big gully-washer wiped out the banks and all, it might still be there."

"How far is it from Sasabe?"

"About a day's ride on a fast horse," he yawned while hopping to his couch and beckoning me to follow. "You know who could be a big help to you? An Indian archaeologist — too bad there ain't none."

His comment gave me something to ponder. Were any Native American scientists specializing in human remains? If not, is it because their cultures hold it disrespectful to disturb the bones of another human being? Certainly, Caucasian scientists have no qualms about digging up

---

[16] Indians who left the reservations without permission.

ancient Indian bones to study, but how would they react if Native archaeologists raided graveyards all across America for the bones of early Anglo settlers? How violent would be the outcry among Italian Americans if Indian scientists wanted to measure Enrico Caruso's chest cavity for clues to his wonderful voice or would Germans object if they dissected Martin Luther's brain for signs of extraordinary intelligence? It sounds ridiculous... unless one walks in moccasins.

Obviously, "wild" Native Americans held a respect and reverence for their ancestors that "civilized" men have lost.

Those fanciful images recalled my visits to London museums where E. A. W. Budge and his teams of Egyptologists displayed room after room of mummies from the Upper Nile valleys. Each cadaver represented an individual who had once laughed, loved, cried, played, and perhaps blushed with modesty in times long past. Now their bodies and private parts lie garishly exposed to hordes of gum-chewing gawkers who, on average, are uncaring for that individual's presumed wish for privacy after death.

On the other hand, sensible studies of such remnant bones grant insight to how each species past and present helped move our world toward its present state. The exacting science of comparative anatomy dictates we must not accept on faith alone either the reality or the denial of the Bigfoot, Sasquatch, or whatever term we use to classify these purported beings, nor should we hastily classify them as Hominidae, Pongidae, or perhaps something in between. Yet, because of their apparent uniqueness and reported similarities to humans, would we not be wise to err on the side of caution and remain objective and open-minded?

Wishes for such wisdom aside, I knew in my heart of hearts that I must accept that my concept of getting any living thing admitted to science without causing pain, death, or confinement to at least one specimen had but a slim chance of success. However — and despite personal aversions — if I could produce but a single bone, perhaps that might help protect their kith and kin — Nino, his voice softer now for privacy, cut short my musings.

"Maybe me and some other seekers I know can steer you around the potholes to get you closer to them big fellers. See, those darned soul snatchers got us true human beings thinking day is night, and learning the truth is like putting together a puzzle blindfolded — boy, you're gonna be mad as a wet hen once you catch on to all their dealings," he chuckled.

"Seekers, soul snatchers, Yampricos, true human beings; what a great list of mysteries," I laughed back.

Nino dropped the smile.

"You'd better be dead serious to take this on, son."

"Yes, of course I am. I'm sorry, but —"

"No buts! I want your word of honor you'll never try to kill or hurt or capture even one Yamprico, no matter what."

"Yes!"

"Yes, what?"

"Yes, you have my word of honor."

"What if I told you Usen is about to pull the plug on us humans because we've been so ornery? See, if we get knocked back to square one, the Keepers will have to use them Yampricos to start us up all over again. We'll be back in caves with spears and rocks, and we'll darned well deserve it!"

A cold-footed spider scurried up and down my spine. Dr. J. Schoneberg Setzer, a new member of my science advisory board, had once proposed that exact premise to me. Setzer, a highly respected theologian at Hartwick College in Oneonta, New York, had mused to me, "I wonder if these giants are God's stand-ins waiting in the wings should we destroy ourselves."

"Ever heard of a place called Gashpeta?" Nino asked.

"Huh-uh, no. What is it?"

"It's that sacred cave where some Tewans shut up a Yamprico who had gotten too old to hunt so she turned cannibal and was eating Tewan kids."

"Tewans, Tewans… Tewans — that's the Pueblo Nation?"

"This band is called the Cochiti."

"Do you mean they have a legend like the Kwakiutls about a cannibal giant who —"

"Legend, your aunt Ruby! Those Kwakiutls couldn't talk Tewan and they live a thousand miles away, so how could they dream up the same blasted boogey man? That's your white genes talking, son! It's high time you fess up and come home; you got some Apache blood, don't you?"

I gulped. How could he know those whispers had flitted among my mother's family tagging me as fractionalized Indian, a member of that mixed breed family that neither whites nor reds fully claim? Like my mother, I was born blond, blue-eyed, and fair-skinned. However, my father, from whom I had been estranged throughout my life, was quite swarthy with dark eyes and hair and he looked nothing like his fair-haired, blue-eyed sister Faye — wait! No wonder Nino seemed so familiar. There were distinct physical similarities between my biological father and the man hunkered across from me. How blind had I been these past two days?

"You know, I remember asking my father's mother, my grandmother Addie, if that was true and she admitted both my father and grandfather had been from Oklahoma and had had Indian blood. It had something to do with someone way back slipping off the Rez at Fort Sill and pretending to be Mexican."

"Fort Sill,[17] huh? What does that tell you?"

"We're related?"

---

[17] Fort Sill had been the last place where the Chiricahua people had been imprisoned by the U.S. Army. Geronimo is buried there.

"Maybe in times past. Looks like you took your mother's coloring, but you sure have the build of an old-time, bandy-legged Apache. I got my first clue when you came waltzing in here. I got a glimpse of your nagual too, you know. You're one of us."

"Nagual? What's a..."

"See, you're driving a white car this time around, but you still got a red soul behind the wheel and that's what counts.

"How would you like to see some bones of one of them giants?"

"What? *What?* Sure! Yes, certainly! Where? When?"

"Got a map of New Mexico?"

One flew out of my briefcase and I had hardly spread it over the coffee table before Nino snapped a spot along the Rio Grande River north of Albuquerque. It was the Cochiti Reservation.

"Gashpeta is there someplace — go find it. They say that giant woman is still shut up in her cave. You will have to ask permission the Indian way to get in. Just be real patient and respectful and maybe it'll happen."

"Who do I look for? Who do I call?"

"You'll know when you get there — or they'll know you."

"It's a desert up there, right? Bones last for centuries in deserts. This could prove they are real — has anyone been digging at that site? Do you think anyone has published anything yet?"

"Tzuh, tzuh, son," the old warrior yawned. "That cave was shut up way before those Jesuits told us good sex was all bad. Besides, if those universities heard about it, they'd write it off as another crazy legend."

The right side of my brain shouted yippee, wahoo, and let's boogie! However, when I factored the additional 500 miles out of my way to chase a legend, the left side of my brain moaned that I should be reasonable, practical, calculate every move, and count every dime.

"Maybe I could stop there when I head west again next spring?"

"Get the ball rolling now or forget it. If you get in a pickle, call me.

Yah-tah-hey, son."

This grandson of Cochise had been calling me son for over an hour. It had been the first time I had discussed the mixed blood question with anyone; it was good to be accepted for what I really am.

"Yah-tah-hey, Grandfather," I said.

Nino was smiling as his eyes shut once again, his hair curtain closed, and he keeled over. His rumbling snores told me that all was well in Nino-land so I gathered my briefcase and dared to kiss his forehead goodbye. I already loved him as a son loves his father.

I was exchanging adieus with Minnie when I spotted Cleo slithering into her favorite ambush spot just inside the front door. I turned just so to allow her a clean and easy shot at my peppered heels. When her fangs sank into my tender flesh, it hurt so *good*! Yes, yes, yes, I admit I was glad that nasty, sneaky little bushwhacker got a mouthful of gooey, sticky cayenne pepper that would fire her gullet for hours to come.

"Cleo, no, no, no," Minnie cried. "Bad, bad girl! Come to mommy, come, come."

Instead, Cleo snapped at her, snarled at me, and shook her head hard enough to rattle her pea-brain out through her ears. Moaning, whining, and sneezing, she scooted to her pink water bowl and I watched with sublime pleasure as her lizard tongue flicked in and out, zip-zap-zip to spread her richly deserved misery. I waited with a patience that would have made Geronimo proud until that pop-eyed shyster dove beneath Nino's couch. Hmm, I thought. Perhaps she was fetching Nino's pistol...

I slipped outside and let the desert night fold in around me like a dark blanket. Somewhere out and beyond the mesquites that lurking coyote gave out a string of yaps of hungry disappointment. I have always loved the sounds of wild things but, for some silly reason, I scrambled into my van and locked its door. Feeling foolish, I rolled the windows down — there it was again. Was it only another wispy breeze teasing the dry chaparral, or was someone out there singing? It could not have been

Nino for he was fast asleep; nevertheless, my imagination heard...

> Oh, hah lee-ee?, Oh hah lee-ee!
> Oh, hah lee-ee?, Oh hah lee-ee!

I spun my van out for that modern I-10 highway where thoroughly modern cars and trucks were about to be joined by an almost-modern van speeding east.

> Oh, hah lee-ee? Oh hah lee-ee!
> Oh, hah lee-ee? Oh hah lee-ee!

Why did I make a mental note to bring Cleo honest-to-God doggie treats next time out? Was I feeling guilty? Some Apache!

2. Phantom Lights

My mind was swimming with tumbling images of open-handed Yampricos, one-legged Apache bandits, horse-gut canteens, and gloomy caves filled with the dry bones of a giant cannibal as I joined a convoy of trucks heading east on Interstate 10. Chanting over and over in my mind was that eerie singing, *Oh, hah lee-ee! Oh hah lee-ee...* I may as well drive, I thought. Sleep would be impossible.

It seemed only minutes before I left Arizona and whizzed into New Mexico where signs marked the exit ramp to Lordsburg. That would be the shortest cutoff if I intended to take up Nino's challenge to find that mysterious cave they called Gashpeta. I needed to top off the gas tank, fill my thermos with the meanest coffee I could find, and make the decision to follow up on all this cave legend stuff or rush homeward to link up with my Miccosukee Indian pals for another adventure in the mysterious Florida Everglades. Indeed, another factor weighed heavily on me. I missed my kid to the point of pain. After all, I had the neatest daughter any father ever had. My Riki was bright, eager, curious, hard working, loving, and trusting to a fault. It was a delight to take her everywhere I went; she always made me so proud. She was not only my daughter; she was my very best friend, even if she was only eight. If she were here with me, what would be her choice, I wondered. It did not take long before I heard her cheering, *Gashpeta, Dad!*

In her echo Nino's voice came again as that exit ramp drew nearer, *You go now; if you get into a pickle, call me. I might be able to give you a little advice.*

Something else the old war-horse had growled in the very first hour of our meeting hammered at me, too. *This Apache's too old to lie, and I'm too mean to give one good hoot in Hades if any of your scientist dinks believe me or not. 'Member, that's the same crew that once went around telling everybody dumb enough to listen that the whole world was flat. Waugh! You think the Yampricos give diddley if white people believe they exist or not? Not on your life — and neither do I.*

Well, Morgan? Should I angle left on New Mexico's State Route 90 to Silver City where I could cut over on Route 152 to Hillsboro — I wondered if Blanche's Café was still there — to hook up to I-25 North? If I did, I could be in Albuquerque come sunrise. However, if I stayed my course, I would be in Florida the following night — something else pestered me. The facts were Nino Cochise barely had enough money to put beans and bread on his table, but the question of payment or reward for his information never came up. He had given me no reason to think he was deceiving me to his benefit. *"Waugh!"* I grunted in imitation of my new mentor.

My adrenaline shot ever higher at the thought of Gashpeta. Any sealed cave containing authentic giant bones could be the answer to all my prayers. While I had already persuaded newspaper publisher Roy Craft and County Commissioner Conrad Lundy to draft a landmark ordinance shielding the Bigfoot people from wanton killing in Skamania County, Washington, it had not been enough to trigger the chain reaction I needed for international protection. However, if giant bones were indeed at Gashpeta, and if they proved to be humanoid if not *Homo sapiens*, perhaps I could get federal laws passed to protect those existent North American Yampricos from being shot or captured by glory-hounds and idiots.

Old Nino had brought those bones up as if to bait me. "Hello, Robert. How would you like to find some real giant bones that would change history, shake the foundations of every major religion on earth, and shatter the Creationist crowd into smithereens? Pass the hot bread, please."

I yanked the steering wheel to the right and whipped down the exit ramp. Good-bye, Arizona, and hold on, Florida! Hello, Gashpeta! I sang a chorus or two of *Dem bones, dem bones, dem dry bones!* and angled north.

Gas tank filled, windshield cleaned, overcooked bottom-of-the-pot badass coffee in hand, I had time to reflect on the past two days. Some fellow, this Ciyé Nino Cochise. Truly, why did he seem so familiar to me and why did that itsy-bitsy inner voice inside me keep rattling on that indeed I did know him from somewhere long, long ago? Perhaps I was simply worn out from that summer's work and the letdown that always follows a near miss. Alternatively, perhaps I had suffered oxygen deprivation induced by Nino's incessant cigar smoking! Then again, were those strange eyes that had peered out through his hair curtain his own, or did they belong to some imagined specter? Moreover, how did his hair go from grey to white and back to grey again?

Oh, hah lee-ee? Oh hah lee-ee?
Oh, hah lee-ee? Oh hah lee-ee?

I hit Albuquerque shortly after dawn. After a lingering breakfast at Denny's, I invaded the library at the University of New Mexico where I boned up for several hours on the Keresan legends of Gashpeta. Nino had been correct; science had relegated it to a quaint legend and nothing more.

Next, I hunted up a good topographical map of the area, ate my fill of hearty tamales, tacos, and steaming cheese enchiladas at Poncho's before stocking up on a few provisions and some fresh water. The sun had set before I arrived at the Cochiti Indian Reservation midway between Albuquerque and Santa Fe. My eyes were stinging and bloodshot from the lack of sleep; all I wanted now was to find a secluded campsite away from the millions of broken glass shards and the windblown litter that marked the village boundary. I bumped past the slumbering little pueblo to follow a narrow dirt road out past the cemetery and into the lonely San Bernalillo National Forest. A few miles further, I came to a fork in the road where my headlights rounded a faded sign pointing southwest toward the distant Jemez Indian Reservation. Tacked below it was a dusty yellow and black U.S. Forest Service sign warning that the smaller animals in that area might have fleas carrying the bubonic plague. The Black Death, here in America? My, my. All this time I had thought the bubonic plague went out with the Crusades. So much for my medical knowledge.

Desperately needing sleep and longing to flop onto that soft, soft sand, I nudged my tired van ever deeper into the deserted Jemez Mountains. Within a few miles, the road narrowed into a mere lane as it twisted down into a small arroyo before crossing a dry creek bed. I gave up when I discovered that lane switched back again before it angled up a steep grade toward a gap in the mountains. I pulled to the side of the road and let the motor die. In short order, I was dragging a small tarp and my sleeping bag 20 yards or more up the slope and away from the road to pitch a hasty lean-to under a stand of scrub oak trees. Like an old-timey Apache, I made a cold camp — no fire, no lights, and more than one escape route.

As I settled down to rest in the chill of the night, I heard the plaintive *prrreep-poor-will* of a nocturnal goatsucker calling from somewhere down the valley. I sleepily wondered if it might be a Ridgway whip-poor-will. This rare desert bird is known as *the little sleeping one* among the Navaho because its winter slumber literally deepens into hibernation. My fading thoughts pondered how that beautiful little creature could be the only bird in the world that hibernates. Did the other birds believe it when they told of sleeping out the winter? I knew the Navaho people had taken a lot of scoffing from white scientists before those skeptics ate crow pie... my eyes flew open again at that thought. If only a single bird species out of hundreds of species around the world actually hibernates, why not one subspecies of primate? Perhaps that would explain the Yampricos strange disappearances each winter; besides, that is what the Russians claim happens to their Alamastis in the Caucasus Mountains, yes? Then I recalled those huge barefoot bipedal tracks I had found back in 1969 where they had emerged from a snow-bound stream some 16 miles from the nearest civilization. While I had continued upstream on snowshoes, the residents several miles *downstream* were reporting a sighting of a Bigfoot and then, and then, and then I... *zzzzzzzz*.

What first awakened me was not any particular sound. What awakened me was that an amazingly brilliant light bathed my camp... and *only* my camp. Not a speck of light was to be seen on the hillside or the trees, neither around me nor in the arroyo beyond; my camp was alone and perfectly circled as if it was at center stage.

I allowed my eyes to slit open, stupidly musing at the sheer pureness of that blue-white light. I was momentarily fascinated by the extraordinary sharpness of detail it produced within such a narrow beam. Leaf shadowed leaf complete with their notched edges and ragged insect holes, and the images of twisted twigs and clinging acorns were etched on the earth above me like paper silhouettes.

My first complete thought was that a sheriff's deputy was checking me out — wait! Perhaps it was a jacklighting poacher. Intellect intruded to argue that the distance from the road up to my camp barred any normal light from spotlighting me so precisely. This beam was so pencil-thin that it left the surrounding clusters of scrub oaks shrouded in utter darkness; my deep slumber exploded and I snapped awake. That light source was directly above and behind my lean-to — *but the road was below me*. Whoever this was had to be very close behind my lean-to — I held my breath to better hear. My world was silent around me. Too silent for comfort.

I patted around for my machete; was it to my right or my left... or did I leave it in the van? Worse, did I leave it *outside* the van? I released my breath when I saw it clipped to my canteen belt. I rolled over and *streeeetched* — the light began to move the moment that machete cleared its sheath. I stared dumbly at the lifting shadows while Nino's voice yelled inside my brain, *That light is being lowered, you dummy. Do something!*

I see it, I see it, I silently yelled back. Still, I had heard no car or truck engine, no crunch of boots, nothing. I gripped my machete to my chest and crouched on my knees in that eerie silence until I noticed that the light was dimming slightly as if it was going out of focus. I squirmed out of my warm sleeping bag to peek around the corner of my lean-to. I barely glimpsed the light fading to black in the sky above a distant cleft in the Jemez Mountains. Did I say fading? That pencil beam of light was not fading. It was as if a long, skinny tube of liquid light was being reeled in. "T-That's impossible," I stuttered while blinking and staring into that cold night sky. No matter, damn it! I knew that is what I had seen. That light did not blink out nor did it turn off, as one would expect. It appeared that something tangible and substantive had been withdrawn to its source. A retractable tube of light? Oh, I must be dreaming; I *had* to be dreaming. Still, how could that be if I was on my feet with my heart pounding like a trip hammer? I was as awake as ever I could be and had every faculty fully engaged through fear and sheer adrenaline! Okay, okay, calm down, I told myself; calm down, and think logically.

I took inventory of the situation. I knew for certain this light had not come from anywhere near my lane; it had to have come from something above and beyond the next line of mountains that were a mile or more in the distance — a helicopter? Yes — er — no. Any helicopter hovering that close would have been easily heard and its safety lights would have been clearly visible; but what else floats in midair? A sudden chirring sound to my left was answered by a timid peep-peeping sound. I had not realized until that moment that even the usual midnight bugs and varmints had been silent throughout that entire episode — *don't just stand there. Go track it*, Nino ordered from inside my skull.

You go track it, I thought back as I flopped back onto my sleeping bag. *You didn't go tracking your Mexican Yamprico at night, so why should I go looking for ghost lights?*

I imagined Nino's face glaring at me through my squeezed-shut eyes. He was right. I must try to find the source of that light before daylight. Within minutes, I was dressed and pouring over my topographical map while my van's engine warmed to the task of struggling up those steep mountain grades. I first located my campsite at a point where the narrow dirt lane began its ascent to that cleft where my mystery light had last been spotted. Beyond that point, the road curled down toward the Jemez Indian Pueblo and eventually linked into New Mexico Route 4, the highway that led through Jemez Springs to Los Alamos. Los Alamos? That name is synonymous with the Manhattan Project and the famous National Laboratory where the first thermonuclear H-bomb was developed. Perhaps they had developed a liquid light beam that is doled out and then reeled back into a totally silent helicopter…

Nino's voice rumbled into my inner ear something about this area also being infamous for UFO sightings. Oh, that's just hunky-dory.

Nino (*he got me into this*) and I roared up that cold, dark, and lonely road in a mighty cloud of dust. When I (*we*) arrived at the last possible spot that would provide a line-of-sight view of my campsite, I (*we*) slid to a halt and waited for the dust to settle. There was nothing there, so I (*we*) listened and watched and waited until it was obvious that I (*we*) were alone. Only then did I get out to study soft ground. It was clear that no vehicle had passed that way for at least a full day because every tire track was crosshatched by the wanderings of deer, coyotes, snakes, rabbits, bugs, lizards, and pack rats. I stared back down into that valley where my campsite awaited me. The angle bothered me because my initial calculations had been correct. The source of that light had to have been suspended at least 300-600 feet above where I was standing. It was clear that if some ordinary military helicopter from Los Alamos had somehow been involved in this spooky incident, the prevailing wind would have most certainly borne its fluttering sounds directly down the canyon to me. Even so, no spotlight existed in 1972 that could fire that powerful of a beam of light over that distance, maintain its perfect spot to a mere 10 foot diameter, and then "reel" itself back in.

I drifted back down and into the valley where I collected my rain fly and sleeping bag. I shivered my way back to the van and told Nino to take the first watch for any more of those phantom lights while I dozed inside my securely locked vehicle.

When I awakened, the stars were retreating within their indigo canopy and the eastern horizon was beginning its daily melt into that peculiar color of opalescent blue that sparkles but for only a few heartbeats before vanishing into the warming dawn. This enchanting scene usually is reserved for God's own wildlife and those few human misanthropes like me who manage to escape the veils of civilization while wandering strange and out-of-the-way places. However, I was not in an appreciative mood, and not even a frisky young coyote yapping after a speeding roadrunner managed to entertain me.

I wondered if Nino Cochise had ever had *his* camp spotlighted. I made a mental note to ask him... the next time around.

3. Rattlesnakes
& Cannibal Giants

My van crunched to a halt at the edge of the Cochiti pueblo just as the sun peeked above the giant cottonwood trees edging the banks of the Rio Grande River. Thin columns of new smoke drifting up from among the scattered frame and adobe homes told me that the tiny village of some 400 souls was awakening, too. I wondered if they suspected that a weird phantom light was lurking about in their mountains. They probably knew all about it; Indians seldom miss much about their ancestral homelands. Fat chance they'd tell me about it, though.

Perhaps that spotlight had only been a hallucination of some sort. After all, I obviously had been under the spell of Nino's tale of Gashpeta, that mysterious cave the books at the university library had described as "... that legendary place where the mythical Twin heroes of Keresan folklore had allegedly shut up a giant cannibal woman to save the tribe's children from being eaten." On the other hand, perhaps I had guzzled one too many No-Doz tablets of pure caffeine, or maybe I had been made delirious out of sheer exhaustion. Yeah, that's all there is to it, I assured myself. Gashpeta is probably just a plain old cave made spooky by another colorful Indian legend. Yep, yep, it all made rock-solid sense in the warming light of day.

I felt better after my sleep, fitful though it had been. In fact, I felt so

57

good that the odor of cedar smoke and baking bread wafting through my van sparked an urgent need for hot food and a half gallon of *very* strong coffee.

The nearby village of Peña Blanca is a literal wide spot in the road linking the Pueblo Indian village of Cochiti to Interstate 25. About thirty miles to the north sprawled Santa Fe; to the south was Albuquerque. When I had passed through this village the previous night, I could not miss the obligatory Catholic church that had probably once served as a mission, a dozen or so vintage adobe houses, one shuttered gas station, a concrete block bar with a dusty neon sign that blinked *Coors-Coors-Coors* through its smeared window, and a darkened eatery specializing in Mexican food. Thankfully, that eatery was open. I chuckled when I pulled in beside a battered pickup sporting a dusty bumper sticker, "I'm Cochiti and Damned Proud!"

Inside, I took the table closest to two young Indian men who were working over huge platters of *huevos rancheros* and beans doused with some mean-smelling salsa. The more slender of the two men wore his hair military short; the stencil above the left breast pocket of his faded Navy denim work shirt read "S. Lopez."

"What ship?"

Two pairs of black eyes flicked over to scan my dusty hiking boots and smudged face. The chubbier fellow returned to work on his breakfast as the stenciled one mumbled, "*Yorktown.*"

"Attack aircraft carrier, huh? CVA-10. Last I heard she was out of Frisco. How's she doing?" S. Lopez stopped mid-chew and his companion snorted before sucking his coffee mug dry. "I was an Aviation Ordnance man, Second Class," I continued. "Did my training aboard the *Yorktown* when she was called the galloping ghost of the Korean coast. That was before I shipped over to the *Princeton* for a cruise. Did the Hawaii, Japan, Philippines, Thailand, Okinawa, and good old Hong Kong tour."

"They gave the *Princeton* to the Marines for Helicopter Assault," S. Lopez sighed.

"Sorry to hear that. She was an anti-sub when I was aboard. I guess the Navy is getting rid of all the old carriers that still hoist sails."

S. Lopez's ripping laugh not only broke the ice, it made his partner drop his fork. While I placed my order with one very sour-dour waitress, AM-3 Sonny Lopez and I compared ships, skippers, harbors, and the sampan ladies of Hong Kong nights. Sonny had been discharged less than a month before and seemed glad to be back on dry sand.

"Ah, you'll go back to sea sooner or later," I said. "Blue-water is a disease."

"No way, man," Sonny said as he scraped the last dribble of chili pepper salsa from his table's pot. "The only white caps I want to see better be on my beer. So what are you doing way out here if you liked it so much? Slip your mooring?"

I waited to reply until after that bad-tempered waitress had slapped down my own pot of red-hot salsa along with a plate brimming with one humongous green chili omelet ringed with diced peppers and double-fried potatoes. "Gashpeta," I said as I passed my salsa pot over to Sonny.

He looked odd sitting there with that pot suspended above his coffee cup.

"Why do you want to do that?"

"Yeah, how come?" his companion burped.

"I had to come see if it was true. I mean, you know how legends go..."

"Ain't no legend, man," the chubby man growled as he snatched the salsa away from Sonny and dumped it over the remains of his *huevos*. I learned this was Sonny's cousin, Ernie. After we shook hands all around, I slid my plate onto their table to outline my mission. I was quick to admit that I had learned precious little since my first encounter with the Bigfoot. To date, the most I had experienced had been fleeting glimpses, wads of unidentified hairs, a few hundred giant footprints, lots of yells, hoots, and screams, snapping limbs, and those darned rocks they liked to zip past my skull. Worse, I was frustrated because every report I made had been jeered at by the news media and brushed off by most academicians. I also described my new Science Advisory Board and ticked off the seventeen names, and ended my monologue with my standard complaint. "It seems that every time I follow protocols that are used to study Pongidae — the Great Apes — I come up with blanks."

"That's cause they ain't apes, man," Ernie snickered.

"A year ago I would have argued, Ernie, but not now. In fact, I just left an old Apache who said he was sure the media deliberately uses the dumber reports just to make these creatures sound like a fantasy or an illusion of some sort."

"Be careful, man, those Apaches learn to lie swinging in their cradles."

"I don't think this old man would lie, Ernie. If you'd met him you'd understand."

"Oh, yeah? How old is he?"

"He was born in 1874."

Ernie blinked and his lips moved as he did some ciphering. "Yeah, well, maybe he is too old to lie," he nodded.

"Like I said, I came to see if Gashpeta was just another old legend to keep kids close to home at night."

Ernie's bark sprayed eggs and salsa at me as he sputtered, "You want to know the difference between our legends and your own dumb-ass history? History is what you whites make it; but what you call a legend is what us Indians know happened. You lie more than any Apache ever born!"

Sonny jerked a thumb at his pal. "He's studying anthropology down at Eastern New Mexico..."

"Was, Sonny, was!"

"You'll go back."

"Bat shit, too!"

"You go back or I'm gonna kick your fat caboose from here to Santa Fe. We don't need another ignorant Indian who can't do crap for the tribe." To me, Sonny said, "He gets one lousy grade in archaeology last semester and he's been torqued ever since."

"You didn't like archaeology," I asked as I casually wiped his salsa from my shirt. "You know, the more we know about the past, the better we can understand what's going on today."

"Had to drop it, man."

"Drop it, my ass. You *ran* out!" Sonny said while punching my shoulder. "See, Robert, good old Ernie here accidentally dug up some human teeth over where they found all those dinosaur bones — where was it?"

"Let's not go there, okay?"

"When he saw those old teeth, he was scared white."

"You don't know anything, Sonny, because you was out there playing sailor-boy in your little white jumpsuit. Man, you looked weird in those tight pants with your bubble-butt sticking out. The whole tribe laughed themselves sick at those pictures you sent."

"He dumped those teeth, the dirt, and the shovel and hauled ass; he probably dumped in his pants, too. Now I have to go all the way down to Portales to get all his junk out of his room."

"You don't have to go get nothing, man! Leave it! Let it all rot."

"Ernie, I'm telling you: you've been on the rez too long. You're too damned superstitious."

"Yeah, well, maybe you were gone too long, what about that? I don't see you out there picking up somebody's old teeth. Screw you!"

I tried to rescue the situation by asking, "Say, Ernie, did you know Dr. George Agogino? He is the Director of that Paleo-Indian Institute at Eastern New Mexico University. He was one of the first to join my

Science Advisory Board."

Ernie's snort sent bits of tortilla into my coffee cup.

"I didn't hang out with no directors, man. I was just another redskin fresh from a rez."

"Dr. Agogino gave me a copy of a picture he took down at Monte Alban in Mexico; it looked just like a stone carving of a Bigfoot. Maybe that is whom your Twins shut up at Gashpeta. What do you think?"

The mention of the famous Twins who had guided their culture back in the Tewans earliest history erased both Sonny's grin and Ernie's frown. The two Cochitis studied me for several heartbeats.

"This Doctor George, he thinks the Twins are just a bunch of legends, right?"

"Not necessarily, Ernie. I got the impression he considers most legends are based on some fact that is now related in some colorful way, like sort of a parable. I think you'd find him open to anything that had solid logic behind it." I nudged Sonny with my foot while adding, "You want me to go down with you? I'll be glad to make the introduction…"

Ernie scooped up their check and jumped to his feet.

"Yeah, right, and he'd have my big feet running over his face if I ever saw another dead tooth. I've had so many nightmares I won't even dig up Mom's potatoes. If it ain't up where I can see it, it ain't getting picked!"

"Okay, but will you show me where Gashpeta is?"

"Gotta go to work," Sonny said too quickly.

"We got jobs at the new dam so we can't be late. See ya."

"What dam?" I asked. "Don't tell me they are damming the Rio Grande."

Sonny's face fell ruefully. "I was overseas when our tribe voted to let the Army Corps of Engineers build one of the world's heaviest earthen dams just down the road. It'll give us all jobs we'd never have otherwise."

"They say it's going be the sixth largest earthen dam in the States and among the top 20 in the world," Ernie said with a belch.

"Good luck, Airedale," Sonny waved back at me as he followed Ernie to the door.

The screen door had barely slapped shut behind them before Miss Warmth flipped my check onto the table. It stuck to some of Ernie's dribblings. I counted out the toll. $2.35 was cheap enough — and my breakfast had been tasty. In fact, I tasted that salsa all day and all night, too.

Outside, I found Ernie's truck rumbling alongside my van. "Maybe we'll meet you at the overlook around 5:30," Sonny yelled as they spun out. That left me nine hours to kill.

Brimming with anticipation, I spent the morning reconnoitering the area where I knew the Thaánu and the Keres-speaking Indians had been dealt some rough treatment by the same early white invaders they had once befriended. It had all begun in the 1540s with the murderous Spanish conquistador Francisco de Coronado and his pedantic friars, Padilla and Escalona. Those two zealots had undertaken their missionary work among the Indians with such obnoxious fervor that they had quickly earned the honor of becoming the first Christian martyrs of New Mexico. By nature a gentle people when compared to the volatile Apache, Comanche, and Navaho tribes, the Pueblos had given their Christian invaders the false impression of being just good-old-boy farmers — and the arrogant Spanish had mistaken their kindness and generosity as a weakness. However, once those farmers had become aware that the true mission of the Spaniards was gold, gold, and more gold, the Indians had set aside their planting sticks long enough to whip the greedy white butts each and every year for two centuries to come.

It was nearing noon when I stumbled upon a tribal graveyard set upon a tall hill overlooking the Cochiti village. While all of the burial mounds were neatly kept, one new grave graphically displayed that curious blend of old and new faiths typical to many Native Americans. There, carefully placed between two opened cans of Coca-Cola, were the desiccated remains of a McDonald's Quarter Pounder. Heaped beside it were a handful of coins and some hawk feathers bound together by a rawhide thong. As many Indian traditions demanded, the deceased had been provided both food and drink, a little money for the journey, and the required sacred feathers to whisk evil from his path. Standing guard over it all was a white votive candle decorated with stenciled drawings of Jesus and Mary. I added some coins to the pile and left the graveyard as I had found it, neat and quiet.

Knowing that nights descend quickly over the desert like an impatient shroud, I decided to scout along an overgrown and unused trace for a new campsite that might be safe from white lights and wandering Wangdoodles. I soon found a circle of bare sand nestled at the base of a tall mesa directly south of Bandelier National Monument. Above my campsite rose a steep escarpment leading up to the ruins of an ancient Cochiti pueblo where long-ago Indians had hidden each night from marauding Navahos or the occasional Apache. I kicked the circle clean of sharp-edged fragments of quartz before tossing out my ground cloth and building a small fire ring. I gathered a supply of dry sticks from a nearby wash and stacked them close by, draped my sleeping bag over a tall bush to let it fluff out without offering haven to those nasty little scorpions that love dark places, and flopped down for a short siesta. This was perfect for me. Come midnight that mesa would serve as something big and solid between me and that gap in the Jemez Mountains; besides, I could see for miles in all other directions.

Gashpeta? On my first try? Fan-*tas*-tic. With my best Cheshire cat grin slitting my face, I let the repetitive, albeit unmusical, song of a cactus wren and the mesmerizing darting flight of a violet-capped Costa's hummingbird lull me into a sun-warmed snooze. I did not dream one bit.

I arrived early for my 5:30 PM rendezvous with Ernie and Sonny fully refreshed and charged for adventure. With one eye on the empty parking lot that overlooked the budding dam site, I wandered to the edge of a nearby cliff to take in the lay of the land. Some 100 yards below me, the broad expanse of the historic Rio Grande River flowed through a deep hard-rock canyon before it angled southeast where it served as a liquid border between Texas and Mexico. To the northeast and amid the distant Sangre de Christo Mountains, the Pecos River began its own winding journey into Texas. There it would blend its waters with the Rio Grande near Langtry, that whistle-stop ghost town that Judge Roy Bean had named for the famous English actress, Lillie Langtry, back in the rootin'-tootin'-shootin' days of the Old West. After all, Judge Bean had been the only law west of the Pecos and, with his law book in one hand and his six-shooter and a rope in the other, he could name any darned place any darned thing he chose.

With evening falling nigh, the Sangres assumed their bloody red tint and the air carried that sudden chill common to high deserts. A full hour had passed and I was getting anxious. What would I do if they had chickened out? How would I find them? Perhaps they would return to that café; maybe I could go into their village and ask around — Ernie's truck came skidding to a halt amid a great cloud of fine dust. "Better hurry," Sonny snapped as he trotted to the edge of the overlook and stepped over the cliff.

Ernie shot me a nasty glance as if it was my fault. He snapped "Yeah, better hurry, man," before he also dropped from sight.

I hastened after them along a hidden path that slanted down, down, down until it leveled out to parallel the river's edge. Without a word, we three dogtrotted north along the floor of a rock-strewn canyon. Upon rounding a sharp curve and entering a flattened area about the size of a football field, Sonny suddenly called a halt. I noticed that before squatting down, he took pains to turn his back to a strange red-rock cliff that jutted above the opposite bank. I noticed too that before Ernie sprawled to wheeze and to hack and spit, he also turned his back to that same cliff. Oddly, both Indians displayed a sudden interest in serious whittling.

I caught my breath while scanning the rocks around me. I saw nothing unusual... until I spied a stylized petroglyph pecked onto the face of a nearby boulder depicting a huge water snake undulating along the bottom of a river. Hammered into adjacent rocks were the zigzag symbols of lightning strikes erupting out of the wings of a great thunderbird — to my right was a deer hunt crafted with gracefully arched stick figures — to my left was a line of dancers poised beneath a falling star. I turned around to yell thanks to my guides only to face another artful depiction of planters bent low to the ground while rows of corn sprouted in their footsteps. Thrilled and fascinated, I darted from rock to rock until Sonny's whistle spun me around. He made a quick chin-jutting motion at a specific monolith set nearest the water's edge. Just as quickly, he turned his back again and resumed whittling. I realized something else, too. My hosts had begun singing in a language I did not know.

I found the target boulder was heavily caked with dried mud. Curious as to why Sonny thought it deserved special attention, I splashed handfuls of brown river water over it until five egg-shaped indentations appeared. More rinsing revealed the unmistakable image of a human footprint complete with its arch and our distinctive inside hallux, the great toe identified with the family Hominidae. More water revealed another set of peck marks nearby. I splashed and scooped until I had swabbed clean a second image that set my heart to pounding. It expressed a much, much larger footprint that showed a uniformly flat foot and the broadest heel imaginable. Most interesting of all, it had that distinctive human hallux.

I felt a chill skitter up my spine like a goosed mouse. I had seen this

Photo by Robert Morgan

Figure 2: Large flat Forest Giant print (right) versus smaller human (left). Note that both have the distinctive hallux of a hominid. Abo, New Mexico.

image before — but not in stone. I had seen its twins impressed by living feet into the mud of the Everglades, the pale sand of central Florida, the pulverized dirt of log drags in the Pacific Northwest, trekking paths amid the volcanic slopes of Mount St. Helens, and in the muck of McBride Lake in Washington State. I had followed the mates to this unique track many times over in sites too wild and too remote to allow fraud; I had knelt to measure them at over 18 inches in length and eight inches wide. Nino's voice murmured in my inner ear, *Yamprico!*

"You betcha, Red Ryder," I cried aloud. Yamprico, Bigfoot, Sasquatch, Windigo, Yeti, Dsonoqua, Alamasti, la loup-garou, or whatever else you wanted to call them, this track was theirs and theirs alone.

I nearly danced over the soft sand to sink down in between them.

"You ever been down to Abo, Sonny?"

"It's south of Albuquerque. Why?"

"How come you know it, white boy?" Ernie said with a rueful shake of his head.

"Oh, I'd stopped there a couple of years ago with my daughter Riki to see some petroglyphs I'd heard about. We found the clone to that one over there. Same big toe, same flat foot, same heel, and same size. Maybe it's the same artist?"

"Same giants, maybe," Ernie spat.

"Some people think they're all over North and South America. What do you think?"

"I know some Assiniboines from Canada who are scared crapless of 'em," Ernie grunted. "Knew a Muskogee, too, who said they have 'em down in those Looziana swamps where those coon-ass Cajuns think they are werewolves. I even heard about 'em from some Alaskan Aleuts — my roommate was Abnaki and Cree; he said his grandfathers have always traded with 'em in Quebcc. You act like it's some big news, man."

"The giant people are no mystery to us, that's for sure," Sonny agreed.

"So why not report 'em?" I asked. "It would make my job a lot easier."

"Nobody out there cares what we believe."

"I do."

"I don't get it," Sonny said as he flipped his pocketknife into the sand. "How come people can't see what's right in front of their noses? Do you know how many anthropologists come up here and ask us with straight faces if they can make recordings of all our myths and legends? Myths? Legends? Man, if they want myths they can start with that Bible of theirs! Water into wine; yeah, right on, man. A few hunks of bread and a couple fish feed hundreds... walking on water... aw, c'mon! Talk about myths! What makes them right and us wrong?"

"Yeah, but then they'd have to admit we know something they don't.

Photo by Robert Morgan

Figure 3: Giant's whistling mouth. Gashpeta, Cochiti Pueblo, New Mexico.

Fat chance," Ernie snorted. "Besides, if it ain't in the history books they write, it can't exist." He shot a nervous glance at the lengthening shadows. "Robert, you got time for one more quick look before we're gettin' out of here. I ain't staying here after dark, man."

I scooted off and had barely covered 20 yards before I was again stopped in my tracks. Staring back at me from another flat rock was the unmistakable image of two giant creatures with their mouths rounded into a whistling pucker — this was impossible! How could that exact same symbol of the dreaded Dsonoqua, the Cannibal Woman of Canada's Kwakiutl tribe, be reproduced 2,000 miles south among a nation of people of an entirely different linguistic group? There were few enough commonalities among the Salishan, Wakashan, Keresan, or even the Tanoan root languages, so how could they come to share this identical mythology if it was based solely on oral traditions? This had to be either a mistake or... one exotic coincidence... unless they each had seen the

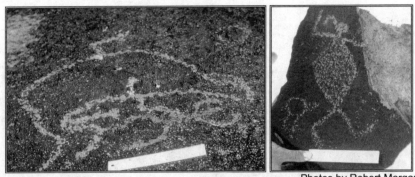

Photos by Robert Morgan

Figure 4: Cannibal giant woman with captured prey and after having eaten. Gashpeta, Cochiti Pueblo, New Mexico.

exact same type of entity!

The carving on the adjacent rock made my mouth go dry as a cotton ball. It was a frightening glyph of a childlike human figure whose thin arms appeared to flail helplessly in the grasp of a grotesque giant being. The next rock in line showed the same giant... its belly huge and distended. It was big enough to hold a —

"Time to go."

"In a minute, Ernie."

I stepped a few yards further to stand before the most powerful symbol in the entire gallery. Hammered into the patina of the largest boulder at water's edge was the figure of a raging giant poised ominously in the mouth of what appeared to be a cave. This giant's arms were held in mute fury as if striving to smash an invisible barrier. Below that figure and its imprisoning cave were mystical power symbols that made me shiver — Sonny startled me when he whispered close beside my ear, "That's the symbol for the sacred power our Twins created to guard Gashpeta. They shut the Cannibal Woman in there because she'd been sneaking into the old pueblo and stealing kids, they say."

Sonny's added "they say" was another of those typically oblique Indian statements. Just like Nino, he was hesitant to take credit for

Photo by Robert Morgan

Figure 5: Sacred power symbols to keep the cannibal giant in its cave. Gashpeta, Cochiti Pueblo, New Mexico.

information someone else had passed along.

Careful to keep his back to the river, Sonny used his whittled stick — I glimpsed fresh symbols cut into its stem — to sketch medicine arrows in the sand before he jammed it hard into the sand.

"You know the story, right?"

"Only what I read in the university library, but I did not see where anyone even mentioned these. Symbols are always so damned subjective; only your shamans can really interpret them."

"See that kid in her arms?" he whispered with juts of his chin. "See how thin she is? She was starving, man. Now look over where she's got a fat belly. Guess what's in there." His chin quivered when he turned to gesture at the last and biggest rock. "This is the one where the Twins put the power to hold her inside that cave. Look how mad she is because she can't get out."

Ernie pushed to his feet. There were no shadows left; desert nights fall dark and quickly. "We'd better get back."

"Is Gashpeta near here?" I asked Sonny.

"Look over my shoulder and straight across the river," Sonny whispered between clenched teeth. He urged me to concentrate on the area two-thirds of the way up the face of a solid rock cliff. Two oblong boulders slowly emerged into view. Even in that dimming light, they appeared to have been jammed into the mouth of a small cave. Indeed, this was not some mythical place that only special people could see under the influence of mescal buttons. Gashpeta must be real as rain! I gulped — could the bones of a desert-dried giant hominid lie just beyond those stone plugs? What if the DNA extracted from its skeleton provided indisputable links between *Homo sapiens* and *Homo… Homo* what? The impact of such a discovery would ignite a veritable whirlwind of scientific debate, not to mention a religious furor that would rock nearly every established religion in the world.

"Let's open it!" I cried.

"You are really nuts," Sonny groaned as he leapt to his feet and quickly put distance between us. I let them both go while I stood fighting the urge to plow across that river with or without their blessings. I wanted to claw my way up to the mouth of that cave, and… and what? Did I think I could tear out those huge boulders with my bare hands?

"I'll fix it so you can take it up with the tribal council, okay?" Sonny called back and Ernie added more urgently, "You'd better get your white ass out of here before it gets dark, man! I ain't shittin' you!"

Cursing myself for having no pick, no axe, no shovel, no crane, no ropes, no winch, and no cables, I trotted after them. The moment I caught up, I was instantly sandwiched in between them and hustled away.

Photo by Robert Morgan

Photo by Robert Morgan

Figure 6: The cave at Gashpeta as seen from across the river. Scenic view and a detail of the top picture. Gashpeta, Cochiti Pueblo, New Mexico.

"Are the Twins exclusive to the Cochitis?" I panted.

"Most everyone around here has stories, but they probably stole 'em from us," Ernie puffed as he kicked at my heels.

"Did the Cannibal Woman live at Gashpeta or is it just where she's buried?"

"They say we didn't exactly bury her; we just made sure she couldn't get out of that cave again," Sonny tossed over his shoulder. "They say there had been some big drought and the food got so scarce that the giants had to raid our gardens. When we drove them away and the stronger ones had to leave to find food, that old woman must have been left behind. At first, they say she just hung around that cave screaming and crying a lot."

"Sometimes even now you can still hear her screams at night," Ernie huffed, and then hastened to add, "At least that's what they say."

"It is told that our kids started disappearing out of their beds; that's when we lived up on top of that big mesa just west of here. We even went to using ladders to keep 'em safe at night, you know. At first we blamed it on those thieving Apaches; that is, until old people came up missing, too."

"How did she get at them if they were on top of that mesa and you pulled up the ladders?"

"They're great climbers, they say."

"That giant made one big-ass mistake when she started messing with our kids," Ernie growled behind me. "Steal our horses and we'd track you all the way to Arizona, but you go swiping kids or somebody's grandmother, us Cochitis will track your sorry ass to Hell and back."

"Our scouts followed her tracks right down this same path," Sonny said. "That's how they knew for sure what was going on. When they got back with the news, our holy men started singing to call in our sacred Twins for help. They chanted and sang almost a whole week without stopping, they say."

Ernie's poke hit me hard in between my shoulder blades.

"You think I'm chicken shit because I want us out of here, don't you? You gotta understand this is one place no Cochiti with any sense likes to come, especially at night. Nobody knows what would happen if a white guy was here, too. Bad luck, I'll bet!"

"But she's long dead..."

"Maybe her body might be dead, but that ain't the problem, man. It's this whole bad-ass place," he said with another poke.

"How can a physical place become evil? People, sure; but places?"

"See that? You white people go around acting as if the Giver of Life made the whole universe just for you. Talk about conceit, man! Native People don't mind accepting that everything is an equal part of our Maker. That means me, you, trees, deer, plants, snakes, rocks, dirt, that river over there, and even the Giants are equal parts of the whole. We're all related whether we like it or not. Me, I'm glad to have so many neat relatives in this world; if I thought the best there was in this whole universe was those poo-butts I see strutting around in big city malls, I'd ask the Maker to bring me back as a frog.

"I had a chemistry class where some turkey-faced professor thought he could impress all us dumb old rez Indians. He broke out some microscopes and started talking about atoms and neutrons and protons and electrons and all that pud-stuff you can't see. We laughed at him, man. All he did was confirm what our grandfathers had taught us while we still had crap in our diapers. We know that if you break everything down to its basic elements, you'd find the same copper that is in these rocks is what we have in our fingernails. It's like that same life force that is in you and me. Ever think that maybe that rock chooses to sit around to think stuff over while we're out running all around like headless chickens? Ever think of that? Ever talk to a rock? They have a lot to teach us if we'd just learn how to listen."

"I think there's a difference in that we —"

"Bullshit," he wheezed. "If humans have souls and if souls don't die, why can't my dog or your cat or this rock have souls? Or even Gashpeta?"

Ahead of me, I saw Sonny's head nodding emphatically as he threw back, "Maybe that place back there made the giant go crazy. I mean, maybe that old woman was okay until the spirit of that cave did something to her —"

"Okay, okay, I have no problem with places having their own ambiance, okay? Yet you don't have the corner on the market on this awareness. Millions and millions of people in India and China and Japan and Tibet and — surprise — even some dumb ol' white folks have long talked about the spirit of the place, okay? Yet, you keep referring to this Giant as a person, so you think the giants are human beings just like us."

"Why do you think we call her a cannibal?" Sonny shot back. "Don't cannibals eat their own kind? Wasn't she eating our people?"

"Yeah, I've been told that. So are you saying she was just a giant Indian, or what?"

"I said she was more like us than *not* like us, understand?"

"But was she human?"

"She wasn't what we'd call a True Human Being — let's not go there, okay? Right now, you'd better watch your step. Come sundown you'll find our rattlers go on the move to look for warm spots; they can't take fast changes in temperature, y'know."

"I'd sleep in your van, if I was you," Ernie gasped as we entered the steepest part of our climb. "Our little brothers just love to crawl down inside sleeping bags with you hot-blooded white boys."

"Nino said something about those True Human Beings you mentioned. Exactly what does that mean, Sonny?"

Ignoring me, he said, "We call snakes little brothers because they were made to share the desert with us. See, a Cochiti never gets bitten unless they forget — *whoa!*" he exclaimed while freezing almost in midstride. We piled up like Three Stooges as something dry, brittle, and gray came rasping over the stones less than a yard ahead of Sonny's left foot. My heart skipped beats as the largest rattlesnake I had ever seen came slithering directly onto our path. When my adrenalin kicked in, I accidentally knocked Ernie off balance and, when he scrambled to stay on his feet, that snake sprang back into a tight defensive coil and whipped his rattles around like a runaway buzz saw.

"Holy... that's the granddaddy of them all," I whistled.

"Don't do that," Ernie yelped.

"I'm not moving and snakes can't hear."

"I mean whistling at night, you jackass! You'll call in every ghost within a hundred miles!"

Too fascinated to argue, I watched Sonny spit into the palms of each hand before he gently extended his arms out from his sides in the four-and-eight o'clock positions. Was I wrong or had that rattling slowed a beat or two? Palms wet, arms extended, my Cochiti friend spread his fingers even wider as he began chanting ever so softly. Within a scant minute or two, the rattling began slowing little by little until it stopped altogether. However, the snake's forked tongue continued to flick out nervously as if to taste the air.

"He knows Ernie and me, Robert; maybe you'd better tell him you won't hurt him."

"Huh? Do what?"

"He tastes a white man, see? You scare him. Just tell him you won't hurt him, okay?"

"Yeah, sure, er, I... er... I won't hurt you..."

Ernie's salsa breath poured over my shoulder like a bad wind. "Don't say it, dummy! Think it! Will you hurry up? I want outta here!"

I did the best I could to project reassuring thoughts to that snake and, in good measure, I sent snake-loving thoughts to all its friends, neighbors, and kissing cousins within a hundred miles. Nothing happened. That stubborn little brother remained unconvinced and unmoving. Sonny closed his arms a bit as if to better focus his energy. For my benefit, I suppose, he spoke in English.

"Come, little brother, let us pass. You were kind to warn us that we were sharing the path, and we thank you. Now go your way so we can go ours. We are *Cochiti*! We have a white friend with us. Is that what makes you unsure? His name is Robert Morgan. Remember how he tastes so you can tell all your people that he is a guest of the Cochitis. He means you no harm. Let us go home to our families and you can find someplace where it is warm and safe."

I felt my jaw drop when that snake uncoiled and slithered away to disappear down the slope. Was this because we all had ceased motion and that threat seemed removed or, perhaps, had that snake sensed a greater peril because of the deleterious effect caused by the continuing drop in ambient temperature? That seems somewhat logical, right? In fact, I do not know its reasons. What I do know is that North America's most feisty snake had been coiled into a perfect fighting position, yet it had crawled away without so much as a backward rattle the moment Sonny had ended his plea for peace.

By the time we were all happily hopping up onto the overlook, my mind should have been filled with a myriad of questions about snakes, spit, and kind words, yet I said nothing of those concerns. There was something much more urgent on my mind.

"What's the chance of you taking me back down there in the morning and maybe I can —"

"Tomorrow is a holiday at the pueblo," Ernie said as he slid into his truck, slammed the door, and cranked the engine to life.

"Wait, Sonny? You said you would talk to the council for me. Will you?"

"I said you should talk to them, not me. Come on in for breakfast and I'll see what I can do," Sonny yelled above the engine's roar.

"Same time and place in Peña Blanca?"

"Not tomorrow. We'll all be in the pueblo. You'll see everyone going around from one house to another and stuff gets pitched off the roof at you. Be careful you don't get brained by a can of soup!"

"Where will you be? What time?"

"Don't worry, we'll find you, white boy," Ernie laughed as he sprayed gravel over my boots and roared out of sight.

As the desert silence folded down around me and I shrank in size amidst that vast desert, I knew I needed some advice. I looked up at all those stars that were emerging in the black New Mexican sky and wondered how early old Apaches fall asleep.

4. Shaman Waters

Cochiti Pueblo & Gashpeta, 1972

Nino's anger fairly crackled through the telephone line that linked Peña Blanca, New Mexico, to Willcox, Arizona. "Listen here, Guy, anytime those fellas catch up with you like that, don't you dare look at that light — don't go following it, neither. The next time they try that..."

"Next time, hell," I bellowed back. "There isn't going to be any next time."

"... Don't even think of following them. That's what they want you to do, don't you see?"

"They? They, who? Who they? All I saw was —"

"Are you sure they never pinned that light on you?"

"I'm sure. But who —"

"Keep it off your skin and never, never look into it. You gotta stay cool and calm; you gotta make yourself like one of those robots. Tell them with your mind; you tell them no, no, *no.* You got that? You tell them you know who they are and what they want and that you ain't buying into their game. Make a big thick thought barrier like a cloud between you and them, you got that? And never-ever look them boogers in the eye unless — now get this — unless they're real tall and sort of blondish. Those are Star People; they're the okay ones."

My mind raced. Maybe I am just plain goofy from the lack of sleep and have a hangover from all that caffeine? Here I am out in the middle of nowhere looking for some prehistoric giant no levelheaded scientist would dare believe in, and now I have some screwball spotlight beaming down at me from what, the Starship Enterprise? I took a deep, deep breath and began again.

"Nino, please, will you just tell me who was behind that light?"

"I don't think you gotta ask."

"Yes, I do! I haven't the slightest clue."

"Stop wasting time asking about stuff you already know because I know you know it even though you might not think you know it, see? We all know it, but you are covering up with all this stupid stuff. Just don't ever go out on them like you did or they'll clean your clock in a hurry. Now listen, go find four jars or bottles that'll hold water, see? Then…"

"Nino, Nino, Nino, you're not listening to me. If you don't tell me who —"

"… fill them with water. Put one at each of the compass points around your camp, but not true north. Use your compass to line up with magnetic lines because that is what those boys operate on, don't you know? Come to think of it, from now on you'd better start packing jars everywhere you go. Remember, if you're roosting for a while, you'd best bury them — but don't drink that water or even wash your hands in it once it's been set out overnight."

"*NNNNNNNino*! Just tell me —"

"Are you getting everything I'm saying or not?"

"You're going a mile a minute so how can I —"

"Whenever you pull up stakes, don't leave those jars behind 'cause they could hurt somebody if they don't handle them just right — and don't dump that water out in no creek or river or lake, either. It's best to dribble all that charged-up stuff over some hot rocks. Oh, yeah, don't breathe the steam, either. You got all that?"

"No, I do not!"

"And be sure to put the head of your bedroll to magnetic north every night, too, no matter where you are. You'll dream better."

"But I don't want to dream," I yelled, but the line had gone silent. "Er, hello?" Moments later, I heard the scratching of a match followed by wet mouthy sounds. Oh, that's just great. Here I am in a quandary and asking for advice and Nino spends time sucking one of those stinkaroo cigars to life. Before I could ask my next question, a Lily Tomlin-like operator cut in to demand every nickel, dime, and quarter I could scrounge out of the ashtray of my van. When the *ding-dings* stopped, Nino took off issuing more orders.

"Tonight you'd better use the water from the Rio Grande in those jars; you'd better scoop it up in front of that Power Rock at Gashpeta because it might have some *gudiyingo* powers that could help you. See, the Supernaturals must've taken a liking to you or those Cochitis wouldn't have helped you and that snake wouldn't have accepted you so fast, see?"

"I don't know anything about any Supernaturals but Sonny was a Navy Airedale like me and that's what brought us —"

"They were late meeting you because they were with some medicine men."

"Huh? How do you —"

"They showed up because they were told to."

I was definitely out of my element. Everything I had taken as a reality with clear, crisp, and logical edges suddenly had hidden facets I could not see.

"You got all that?" I heard him ask.

"I set four jars of Gashpeta juice at four points of a magnetic compass."

"Right."

"Is this supposed to be some sort of offering?"

"It's something Dee-O-Det did in times like these. All the old *diyin* know about it."

"The what? The who?"

"The *diyin*. You know. The shamans!"

"Oh, yeah, right, uh-huh," I replied as if I knew what he was talking about. A sense of foreboding suddenly injected me with a coldness that poked my soul about as hard as Ernie had poked my back with his big, fat fist. To my narrow-minded way of thinking, the mere mention of shamans meant things mystical, odd, strange, and, perhaps at times, maybe wonderful... or quite mad or evil. Since my youth, I had studiously familiarized myself with everything from the mumbo-jumbo of Cuban Santeria to the deadly hoodoo of voodoo. I had also delved into the roots and philosophies of both white and black witchcraft, the mystical secrets of Cabbala, and the inferred cannibalism of the sacred transubstantiation of Catholicism. I had learned enough to try to remain within those boundaries set by things tangible, explainable, and soundly scientific — whatever that meant.

"What do these *diyins* know that I should know?"

"I had a dream about you last night."

"What did Dee-O-Det tell you, damn it!?"

Suddenly, I heard Minnie yelling something about his kicking all the covers off her all night long as he shouted, "Just think about what this Sonny fella did to get that rattlesnake moving. You got that?"

"I don't give a hoot about Sonny or —"

"And keep an eye peeled for big black cats; big as jaguars, y'know?"

His statement struck me as an absurd way to dodge my questions; somehow, it transmogrified into a grotesque image that made me chuckle, "I just saw two such cats cruising the main drag in Albuquerque. Do they count?"

Nino did not reply for a few heartbeats — I visualized his face turning a deeper shade of crimson — and then he said smoothly, "I'll work with you only if you take it seriously. You're fooling with stuff that can do some real good for the Clan, but if you can't stay on the beam, let somebody else take over."

"Er... sorry."

"You'd better keep your eyes peeled when ravens start following you, too. If they do, you'd better not take chances of any kind or you might have some real bad luck. You'll know the jig is up if you get a strong notion to do stuff that your *nagual* tells you is cow-dumb. Listen to your *nagual*, son, and remember that nothing out there can really hurt you... but there are things that can make you hurt yourself. Got it?"

Psst! the nasty side of my gene pool hissed. This is the perfect time to break into my best shower-stall imitation of Sinatra's *That Old Black Magic's Got Me in Its Spell* before I drive away to the east at 70 mph!

I almost got my mouth open when Nino cut Frances Albert off at the pass. "By the way," he said innocently. "Minnie wants me to tell you that Cleo sure must miss you. Minnie says she ain't eating much since you left. She just hunkers under the couch and growls at the door."

I pocketed that grin for later; instead, I amazed myself by asking, "Okay, okay, but before I do all this, please tell me why the water, why the black cat stuff, why the ravens, and why should I —"

"Deposit $1.35 for three more minutes, puh-leeze..."

Out of change, I barely shouted goodnight before the line went dead.

I stood in the dark at Peña Blanca's only public telephone holding that dead receiver in my hand and staring into nothingness. I probably looked like some runaway kid who had just called home to discover that everyone had moved. What to do, I asked myself over and again. I was seriously considering driving down to Albuquerque to hole up in some brightly lighted motel where no snakes, jaguars, or ravens would dare to tread when a battered truck with a single headlight wheezed up. Two big and four little Indians piled out to surround me. The littlest Indian pointed at that dead receiver in my hand with a glare that accused me of murder. "Busted again?" he asked.

"Nah, but it sure talks funny," I said as I handed over its body. They gaped as I jumped into my van and swung her westward-ho toward that lonely mesa where my desert camp was awaiting its drink of shaman water. Yes, indeed, I vowed to sleep with my head to the north — magnetic north, of course — and I would keep a careful watch for all lurking black panthers and midnight ravens that might come tap-tap-tapping at my Volkswagen's door.

"Good evenink," I sang out to no one there. "Pear-mit me to introdooze mein-zelf. Mien name ist Count Yamprico von Gashpeta! I haff come to shine mein evil light upon you," I giggled. Yes, sir, it's all just superstitious aboriginal nonsense, I assured myself as I picked up speed. After all, did I not demand cold logic based upon laboratory science and backed up by multiple blind tests? Did I not require all results to be documented with footnotes and cross-references? Don't give me this woolly-booger crap about things that go bump in the night. No-sirree-bob! I've fought too damned hard to get a solid education and I demanded rock-solid proof based only upon three-dimensional logic. Take last night's light, for instance. Why, it was probably only a, uh, an, um... er... it was as if that pencil beam came from someone — no, no; that beam came from some*thing* that hovered a couple of miles away without making a sound and maybe that snake uncoiled because... because why? Why, why, why?

I had nearly crossed the bridge that spanned the Rio Grande before I remembered my orders from General Nino. My van and I roared up the rise to the top of its hill and curled back onto the overlook. Finding it deserted at that time of night was no surprise, so I took my time grubbing around until I found my tattered old canvas water bag that old-timey desert travelers like to hang around car radiators for emergencies. My air-cooled VW sneered at it, but I kept it because, because — I riffled through my trash bag and luckily scored four waxed paper coffee cups. These would suffice for this one night to hold my *diyin* water.

I had only starlight to guide me because that sliver of a dying moon had not yet arisen, but I hopped over the edge of the guardrail anyway. I dogtrotted halfway down to the canyon floor before I realized I had forgotten a flashlight. I cursed in six languages but did not break stride until I hit the warmer river bottom — warm sand? Rattlesnakes! I skidded to a halt and froze in my tracks. I strained to look along the river's edge but could spy no squirming tubes in my path. Who knows, I tried to laugh, perhaps only alien snakes guided by night-flying ravens were out waiting to ambush my heels with more malice than even Cleo possessed — that moment of pause did me no favor. I turned to gauge the distance back to the top of the overlook and the safety of my van. I was trapped midway between my target and my refuge; I also felt damned stupid. What had I been thinking? I was alone, no one knew I was down here, and this area was not exactly a tourist attraction. If I was hurt I could be stranded for days if not weeks or months... Nino's voice came to whisper in my inner ear, *Listen to your* nagual, *son, and remember that nothing out there can really hurt you... but there are things that can make you hurt yourself.*

I spat into both palms and spread my arms out just as Sonny had. I felt weird sending thought-lovies out to rattlesnakes — *Waugh!* As opposed to being cooled by the chill night air, my wet palms had become hot — wait! They instantly cooled the moment my attention switched away from all those goody-good thoughts. Baffled, I wiped my hands dry, spat again, and repeated the sequence. Initially, the moistened parts of my palms chilled just as they should... until I again projected warm and fuzzy thoughts. Once again, the centers of my palms grew hot. Yeah, right. To hell with this mumbo-jumbo stuff; I dashed headlong toward Gashpeta. A snake would have to strike at sonic speed to hit these flying feet!

The moment I rounded the bend to enter the gallery of petroglyphs, I angled straight to the river. Gasping for breath, I stumbled to the water's edge and plunged my canvas bag into the roiling current. It seemed to take forever for that *gudiyingo*-wet stuff to start filling it. Heart pounding, my gaze was inexplicably drawn across the river to the opposite cliffs where Gashpeta waited. I could see nothing; the shadows were too thick, too dark, and too secret — a bizarre thought hit me like a boiling snowball: what if that cannibal giant could magically set itself free to creep out in the dark of each moon? The noise of the river slurping and slapping and lapping suddenly seemed deafening. An entire army of giant Yampricos bent on avenging their dear old cannibal ancestor could march up on me without my hearing a single tramp — was it because I was listening so intently that I felt instead of heard it? Was it because my senses were so keen that I felt that riffling wind as something... something tangible... whisked just above my head? Ready to brawl with devil, demon, or saint, I whirled around.

I saw no one.

I heard no one.

I smelled no one.

Nevertheless, *something* new was out there lurking in that blackness. What — who — where?

I twisted and turned to peer this way and that while those hulking cliffs on both sides of the river seemed to swell up around me like prison walls so grotesque and so ominous; but no giants, panthers, or ravens leapt into view... damn it! *Something* had changed; my *nagual* said so — wait! That something twitched a scant few feet to my left. I felt more than saw eyes peering straight at me from the darkest of those thick shadows. Whatever it was, it was surely watching every move I made, counting each breath, and listening to every banging thud of my heart. Standing stock still, I forced my eyes to the edges of their sockets. It was not good enough. An inch at a time and as if in slow-motion pantomime, I swiveled my head until I did not need to imagine a dark figure squatted atop a great rock nearest the water's edge. That shadow and I stared at one another until it dipped its head ever so slightly — *oh, god; don't let it be a raven.* I forced my slow-motion movements until my entire body was square and set. My eyes burned like fire because I did not dare blink — but I blinked anyway. I fairly melted into my boots when two huge eyes blinked back. Oh, lord! It was only an owl, a huge, downy, beautiful, big old great horned owl that had drifted just above my head to light upon that rock.

We stared at one another, that owl and I, and so calm was he that he did not move a feather even though I fairly danced in relief while hoo-hooing at him in greeting. Shifting from fear to folly, I laughed and shouted raucously until the walls of the canyon echoed with the joy of my release. Why so happy? All my life owls of all sorts have enamored me. No matter that my Indian friends whispered that these night predators were sent to gather the souls of the dying, I had always found the presence of any owl quite comforting. I borrowed Nino's Apache salutation for my new owl friend. *"Yah-tah-hey,* little brother." With that, the owl solemnly dipped its head again before pushing off. In a few silent flaps, it disappeared down the canyon as if reconnoitering the same route I must follow to the overlook. Hah! Owls eat snakes, don't they? I snatched up my dripping water bag and followed in *my* owl's wake.

Wearied by a week of short sleeps and long drives; I was trudging my way up the path and was nearly safe at the overlook before something dawned on me. Every single apprehension I had had about returning to that sacred gallery had evaporated with the appearance of that owl. Even more startling was that owl's choice of perches: it had been the power stone of Gashpeta. That did it. I fairly shot out of the canyon, slammed into my van, and peeled out like a teenager who had just experienced his first French kiss.

Within the hour, I had planted cups at the magnetic cardinal points to my camp. I had not the slightest clue what I was doing, but I filled those little beggars to their brims with *gudiyingo* water. *No más por esta noche.* I had no strength left to worry about anything else, to be sure. At the base of that big mesa where that ancient Cochiti pueblo had once stood, I got a little fire going for some good old western desert at-mos-phere. I fished out salty sardines and cold spinach from cans and munched tortilla chips doused in Old El Paso salsa, hot-cha-cha-cha. Feeling the need, I broke out my emergency ration of *Three Finger Jack* golden tequila from my sack of secrets, chopped a withering lime into halves, whitened the back of my hand with salt, and slugged away for one, two, three, four, five long liquid punches to the gut. *"Aeeii, yo soy Beto,"* I cried as I stumble-danced about the fire. *"Yo soy uno hombre con poco pelo, y estar vivo y coleando."* Killer lights can kiss my royal popo; this hombre was still alive and wagging his tail. Life, sweet, sweet life was now ever sweeter. So, what? I had a full belly so warm and happy that I just had to imitate Cuco Sanchez's heartbreaker "Lloren Guitarras," a Mexican love song about guitars that weep for that one special lost love. Ah, if only to hear Cuco's "Guitarras a Media Noche" out here in the wilds! It would be the most romantic sound in the whole wide world if only… time for another tequila-punch in the gut and a lick of salt, wham-bam-thank-you, Jack! Suddenly… I felt terribly alone. I missed my kid, my Riki. I always missed my best friend in moments like this.

Nothing else for it, I brushed my teeth, spit on an ant hill, snapped out my sleeping bag in case some scorpion had learned to climb bushes, and flopped down — head to the north — for what I hoped would be a good, long rest. Overhead, stretching from horizon to horizon, was that same magnificent buttermilk sky that must have inspired good old Hoagie Carmichael to song:

> *Oh, buttermilk sky, I'm keeping my eye peeled on you*
> *What's the good word tonight?*
> *Are you going to be mellow tonight?*

Smug and snug at finding Gashpeta so quickly, I watched my little fire ebbing into embers while the quiet side of my brain began to muse all over again. After all, my mind mused, what if that once-upon-a-time-long-ago cannibal giant had actually passed by this very spot. Mightn't that starving old woman have paused just here to sniff the air, her toothless mouth drooling thick slobber as the murmuring of sleepy Indians drifted down from the mesa that loomed overhead? Would she have softly padded up some secret path to grope through a paneless adobe window to snatch away a sleeping child or a dozing old crone — did she shuffle this way again bearing her grisly meal in her gaunt arms?

My mind's eye flitted back to the canyon and magically hovered just outside those solid rock plugs that sealed the entrance to Gashpeta. Had the intervening centuries of dry desert air preserved some trace of her macabre feasts? Better still, were her own giant bones lying there awaiting discovery? I settled deeper into the soft down of my sleeping bag with my trusty machete clutched to my chest as my brave shade slipped in between the rocks. As it flitted about in the blackness of her tomb, my shade sent back the sour scent left by those terrible feasts — my eyes flew open and I sat bolt upright. How dumb could I get?

Sonny's rattlesnake had been coiled to strike, yes?

No matter: Sonny had stretched his arms out, palms open, and I had watched that snake uncoil and quietly crawl away, right? Well? Didn't my own palms go hot when I had tried it? I recalled my own amazement as a young boy when I had witnessed the effects of magnetic induction on cold steel. Within moments of placing an ordinary bolt within odd-numbered coils of copper tubing that were charged with electricity, the bolt became white hot. So why would it not be theoretically possible that the wetting of one's palms might facilitate thought-projected magnetic energy into a closed loop out and around any chosen subject, but always returning to the alternate palm? Was this scientifically possible — or was it just fanciful speculation? Crafty old Nino had told me twice to "think about it." Only now did I remember how he described that exact same posture being aimed at him by his desert Yamprico.

Now here's something I thought was funny: he stood with his hands held open like this, see, with his palms out front. I think he wanted me to see he wasn't toting a rock or anything. He had big hands with long fingers. Thick 'n strong.

Again, I flopped back down to consider my own encounter back in 1957. Was it merely shock that had prevented me from pulling that trigger even though a Bigfoot loomed an easy mark in my rifle sights, or had that giant held his hands out the same way behind those bushes? Had I unwittingly been his target and had fallen within the magnetic loop of this unmeasured force? I have no idea how long I lay there considering all the possibilities of projecting magnetics in a laboratory, Kirlean photography, thought projection, universal body language, and just plain voodoo. I last remember cinching up the drawstrings to my sleeping bag to keep out cold snakes while vowing that with or without my two Cochiti friends, I was going to look Gashpeta straight in the eye, come the morrow.

My first dream that night came in the form of a skinny giant woman chasing the Twins around my camp with a laser gun — I was amused to recognize they were twin Ernies. One Ernie finally tossed a cup of my *gudiyingo* water on her. She melted. I enjoyed that dream. However, as I drifted further down and down into a deeper slumber, I experienced something Freud and Jung would have loved to debate. I dreamed that the same rattlesnake that Sonny had calmed came slithering into my camp where I lay sleeping. As if separated from my own body, the shade of my second self calmly watched as that rattlesnake oozed in beside my left cheek. Through the eyes of this other self, I could clearly see that snake's long forked tongue tasting the air that ebbed and flowed with my slowed breathing. "What are you doing?" I whispered down from my separation.

"Tasting your soul," the snake hissed back.

"Did you come to kill my body?"

"You know better that that," the snake hissed just as the owl from the

Power Stone drifted down to land between my resting body and the dying fire.

"What is your verdict?" the owl hooed to the snake.

"He is not afraid. I must go tell the others," the snake replied as it slithered off to disappear into the night. The moment the snake was out of sight, the owl hopped onto my body's chest to hoo something my separated shade could not understand. Still, my sleeping body began smiling even before it opened its eyes. I gulped when I saw that my eyes were huge and round and blue and as shiny as two new marbles — the howl of a wolf wavered out from among the brush and an eagle screamed from somewhere atop the mesa above me. My physical body closed its big eyes again. Satisfied, the owl drifted off into the night as silently as a passing shadow. Somehow, I knew my owl really would never be far away. Neither would the snake, the wolf, or my eagle.

My shade gently drifted down to disappear within my body. We slept together warm and safe until the next fiery dawn.

5. Haunted Tombs
& Sleeping Fools

I stood straight, naked, and strong in the first rays of the rising sun. The dawning rays, the longest ones, are healing to body and soul, so the Old Ones say. I stood there until the coolness of new dew set me to shaking. It felt so good to be alive! I puffed my fire's embers to flame beneath my coffee pot and waited for cold water and brown grounds to bubble, boil, and brew. After my morning ablutions — for me that's a canteen birdbath limited to face, hands, and all pits — I drained my coffee of its last drop, peed the fire to death, and prepared to beat-feet toward the Cochiti pueblo. Wait, wait, hold it. I had almost forgotten those cups of *gudiyingo* waters. Let's see: Nino had said I must carefully dribble them over hot rocks and not breathe the steam. Three yielded to the torture, but not the fourth... the one I had placed to magnetic north... because that cup was empty. I held it to the light but saw no holes, so I refilled it and sat back to wait. No luck; no leak. I knelt to examine the soft sand around that cup's burial place but found not so much as a mouse track. I smashed and burned them to ashes.

I arrived to find the entire village swarming with laughing and shouting Indians. Each person, large and small, young and old, was lugging a sack while dashing between houses. They encircled each house in turn and commenced jumping up and down — it was easy to spot Big

93

Ernie because he didn't jump; he just bobbed a lot. Transfixed, I watched as one gang laid siege to a neatly kept adobe house made distinctive by its large rose trellis. While the crowd chanted and screamed, adult Indians followed by a swarm of little tykes emerged on its roof. As if by signal, they began pitching cans, bags, and boxes of foodstuffs down upon the cheering crowd below. It seemed to rain everything from macaroni to spaghetti to chili, beans, potatoes, and bread! I watched in wonder when another family, sacks bulging, sneaked into an adjacent house. Within moments, they reappeared on that roof where they too commenced waving their arms and yelling at the crowd. Big Ernie was the first to bob over to where food again began raining down. Once again and as if by some secret signal, yet another family group broke away. Up on another rooftop, quick as a wink, and the same food was parachuted again into different sacks — it was a daisy-chain food fight!

"You need to meet someone," Sonny announced as he slid in beside me and slammed the van door shut.

"Does anyone eat all that food… or do they just like to beat it up?"

"Anyone can keep what they want, and that includes you, if you're low on chow. Want me to stop?" Sonny said with a strange little smile.

I wondered if he was pulling my white-boy leg, but about what? This food-fight or my presumed needs? Oh, well, I thought. Keep your secrets. You have every right and, truth be known, I would respect you more if you did. White boys don't need to know everything; it's your culture and I hope you keep it forever.

"I'm fine, thanks," I smiled back as if I believed every word.

Jutting his chin this way and that, Sonny guided me through the center of the village and past a crumbling chapel topped by a weathered Christian cross. Directly across from the church steps, twin poles of a wooden ladder spiked up to mark an underground kiva, the traditional center for Pueblo councils, law, and learning. Soon we entered a long sandy lane. Sonny spoke again as if there had been no pause.

"Lots of people take out whatever they need before they reach their own roof. That way nobody knows who needed what, you know. That way everyone keeps their pride, the pueblo gets stronger, and everybody has fun."

"Those bags must get skimpy pretty quick!"

"Not in this pueblo, man. They get bigger all day long, 'cause people who have more than their neighbors always add more than they take out," Sonny said with obvious pride. "Watch real careful and you'll see some families run inside with three or four bags but by the time they show up on the roof they'll have six or maybe even seven. No one notices either way; it's not polite to count, you know."

I followed another jaw-jut toward a neat adobe house set back from the road. Its four battered trucks, two cars, and one new bicycle each bore a bumper sticker proclaiming, *I'm Cochiti and Damned Proud!* While stepping out of the van, I was greeted by the odor of baking bread. It was easy to spot its source; set in the backyard was one of those remarkable adobe beehive ovens that are traditional in the American Southwest. Sonny led me through the open door and into the kitchen where a leathery Indian elder sat at a table devouring a rasher of bacon and eggs. Sonny nudged me onto the chair opposite; still, the old codger gave us no notice.

My butt had barely hit the seat before a matronly lady was ladling out a generous bowl of the best green chili stew I have ever tasted. I was instantly ravenous. Adding to this remarkable hospitality, a graceful maiden dressed in too-tight jeans and a razzy cowgirl shirt, darted in, arms filled with hot bread. "Hi!" she chirped as she dropped the largest loaf beside the elder's plate. "I know who you are," she smiled at me. "I'm Sees-Far Woman! Want some coffee?"

"Woman? Hah! You're Sees-Far *Child*," Sonny snorted.

"In thirty-eight days, two hours, and fifteen minutes, I'll be 18, and then I'll be Sees-Far Woman, sailor-boy!" With more smiles for all, she filled our mugs to their brims, bagged the remaining loaves of bread, and then slapped back out through the screen door. "I'll be on time, Sonny, don't worry," she tossed back as she hopped on that *Damned Proud* bicycle and peddled furiously toward the village.

Sonny said something in the Cochiti language to the older woman. She turned off the gas burner to her stove and left the room without a word. In the heavy silence that ensued, that elderly gentleman solemnly sliced hot bread for each of us with his pocketknife. I was halfway through my chunk when he leaned closer as if to inspect me through milky webs of cataracts.

"This is Juan Cornplanter," Sonny explained. "He's our, uh, he's one of our holy men."

"A medicine man?"

"Don't say that, okay? That's a term we try to stay away from now because of all those stupid movies. Our *curanderos* are people who know how to make medicines of all kinds to help sick people; it's hard to explain in English. That's not Juan; he is the holy man who keeps our history and he —"

"I keep... our sacred flame... alive... in here," the old man said in soft tones while tapping his heart.

I began the customary amenities by thanking him for inviting me to breakfast before Sonny corrected me. This was not the holy man's house; it was Sonny's. Our hostess was also Sonny's mother, the bread baker was his youngest sister, and Juan Cornplanter was there as part of some special routine. Untraditionally, this holy man came directly to the point.

"No one should ever... open Gashpeta. It would be bad... for our pueblo."

"Mr. Cornplanter, if there are giant bones in there it could be so important to science —"

"Some bones in there... belong... to our ancestors. If we disturb them... we would call back... Cochiti spirits who might be doing...

other things. That's not... a good thing."

I felt my face flush prickly red. I had been selfishly considering only the boon of finding that giant's bones while ignoring that many folks believe that souls sometimes choose to remain attached to their earthly remains or possessions, especially if they had died a sudden and violent death.

"May I at least take a closer look? I promise not to touch anything."

Juan Cornplanter allowed the tiniest of smiles. "Yes, you may go to look but only... if Sonny is there. Something else for you... to think about is Gashpeta... is not... all you came for," he said in that curious speech pattern. It was as if he tasted words before letting them loose.

"Our traditions say... I should wait before... I speak of certain things that... we hold sacred. I know you must... go away soon. Times change, so maybe... our traditions should keep up... as we enter... the Darkness before the New Dawn."

Chancing being rude, I studied him in return. I wondered if he was playing that old routine, "I'm the big honcho on this Rez, Bubba, and you're nothing but another damned uninvited white-boy guest who wants some quaint-ass stories to laugh about over some beers, so I ain't telling you diddly-squat! Instead, let's play mumbo-jumbo and see who wins."

So there we sat; I stared at Juan Cornplanter while he peered back at me through his trammeling eyes. The longer we sat peering and staring, the more my hope ebbed. Somehow, God help me, I knew this elder was speaking from his heart. His speech impediment, if that is what it was, seemed to lend more weight to his remarks because he tasted every word before allowing them to join the sounds of the universe.

"A brother rattlesnake... came to see me last night... while I was thinking... about you and... Gashpeta."

"He dropped into the kiva through the smoke hole," Sonny added with a nervous giggle.

"Wha, wha, wha..." was all I could choke out as my dream of

talking owls and hissing rattlesnakes came flashing back.

"Brother Rattlesnake reminded me that... only True Human Beings... can find Medicine Helpers... to share in their powers. Some True Human Beings are lucky... to have more than one Helper. You sure are... lucky. You have... three."

I jammed my mouth chock-full of hot bread; I needed any excuse for silence until my paralyzed brain kicked in. I kept repeating to myself that I had no clue as to his meaning, but that was a lie. I well knew that such beliefs linger among people of knowledge who are rumored to dwell within all races of Man. These special persons accept that both benevolent and malevolent natural powers — seen and unseen — continue to be active on this earth. They believe the better powers are seldom approached of late because modern humans have allowed themselves to be blinded by truly evil angels whose lies drip honey. This complicated belief system teaches that once discovered and recognized these natural powers can be called upon to reveal the true origin of all human souls. They may also assist the unveiling of each soul's long-ago crime that caused them to be cast down among these hordes of evil angels. Excepting the circumstances that sometimes follow long periods of personal meditation and preparation, such as those demonstrated by Siddhartha and each Dalai Lama, communication between truly benevolent natural powers and a living individual is limited to encrypted dreams or flashes of spontaneous genius. These problems are compounded because accurate deciphering of these communications is only possible by that specific individual, and no one else. Of course, no conventionally educated person exposed to Freud, Jung, or Menninger ever bought into this. For instance, I had been taught that dreams are either wishful or fanciful thinking, or are manifested when parts of the waking brain expunges symbolic gibberish. I once likened dreams to the awakening of an inert computer system that must clear out lingering and unconnected fragments before it can function. Of course, professional analysts proclaim that the only proper, logical, and safe dream interpretation is to be found on their couches at $200 an hour...

In any event, I sniffed within myself; *I* certainly did not have any Medicine Helpers. I am a rational, well-read, and decently educated person who — *liar* — something hissed in my inner ear. While that part of me that was rational sat there in clueless wonder, Juan smiled and nodded as if he had been following my every thought.

"The visit from Rattlesnake was... a good sign. He too is my... little brother. He taught the Cochiti that... there are forces from far away that fight to control us... in ways we cannot see. It is a war that will go on... for all our time here."

"Why do they want to control us?" I heard my voice ask.

"To serve... them."

"Are they winning?"

"Yes."

"Can we ever win?" I asked as though I believed every word.

"Only when we choose to awaken... and... to see."

I had to fight responding to him in kind because it might appear that I understood him. I could not — *I would not* — even pretend to understand. I wanted to get back to topics I could see, smell, hear, touch, or taste, so let's get back to those big-bad bones that might or might not be in that cave.

"Perhaps part of the answer lies in Gashpeta? If I could just take a peek inside; a photograph or two —"

"Look, but don't touch anything," the old man said as he shuffled out, pausing only to toss back a few words in Cochiti. Sonny laughed. I ripped off another chunk of that delicious bread and kept chewing until Juan's truck had sputtered away.

"Wanna know what he said?" Sonny asked.

"Not particularly," I lied.

"He said you went away from the True Human Beings a long time ago to learn the ways of the Others. He said the Others don't want to let you go home. He said you'll have to kick them in their cajones to get free."

"Can we go now, or do I have to kick yours?" I snarled.

It took the better part of an hour before Sonny and I reached the gallery of petroglyphs across from Gashpeta. As before, Sonny turned his back to the river while I broke out my gear.

"How exactly did the Twins shut her up, do you know?"

Sonny broke up cigarettes and scattered tobacco in a circle around us. Selecting another stick, he sat down and began whittling as he spoke. "I can tell you the story Juan's grandfather told him; it's been handed down a long time. They say that after our warriors followed that cannibal's track down from the mesa to her cave, they went in to kill her. It was dark inside so they could see only human bones and skulls laying all around in a big mess. They say the smell made them sick and all those bones scared them. It was like a graveyard where everybody is buried on top of the earth, you know.

"Then that old woman started screaming from somewhere in the back of the cave. The warriors ran away because they couldn't see her so maybe she wasn't real. When they got back to the village and told what they'd seen, our chiefs decided to make a big ceremony. We needed to ask the sacred Twins for help, you know? We got bad luck right away, though. We lost an old man that same night. After that, everybody was told to build a big fire where everyone could dance, sing, and beg for help all day and all night. On the second night, the giant came and took a little boy. Some of the people got so scared they wanted to move far away, but most everybody wanted to stay. What if our ancestors came back and couldn't find us, you know?

"They say what made everyone really scared was on the third night. This time she took our most powerful shaman. They say that is when the Twins appeared. They said that shaman had sacrificed himself so he could get inside the giant to make her sleep. He was brave, you know.

"That night, the Twins went to spy on her. When they came back, they said she had eaten up all that shaman. They said she would sleep for three days and three nights. They made a big speech to make our men work like crazy to find three big stones — one for each day she would be asleep. While the men dragged those stones up above her cave, our women cut their hair to make a net and some long ropes. That's how they lowered the rock plugs, they say. Our kids got into it, too. They gathered all the wood they could find and piled it just inside the mouth of that cave."

I looked across the river through my binoculars. "I see only two stones. Where's the third?"

"It's there. Anyway, it was the dark of the moon on the last night when the Twins went in. They woke up the giant by shooting sacred arrows at her. She got mad when she saw all that wood blocking her way out. She started screaming and howling but the Twins drove her back with arrows until Lightning came down to set the wood on fire. They say all the women and the children and the old people lined up right here where we are standing to sing the power songs the Twins taught them to keep her inside…"

"They were here where we are now?"

"While all that wood was on fire, our men used the ropes and the nets to swing those rocks down to plug up the cave. The Giant really got mad when the Twins slipped out through the cracks to get away. Then the Twins chinked up all the holes so she would roast quicker. We were lucky that someone saw smoke pouring out through her secret escape-hole way in the back of the cave. We covered that one up, too."

"That sly dog had two entrances?"

"See that stone over there? That's the one the Twins gave all the power to — that's what they say."

"That's a better story than what I just read down at the university library!"

Sonny shot me a sly grin.

"We always keep the real stuff to ourselves." Leaning forward, he added in a whisper. "They say she screamed a long, long time after that, maybe for years. She finally stopped, though... except for certain times."

"Certain times? What certain times?"

Sonny's whittling picked up speed.

"Sometimes she screams in the dark of the moon. Maybe that's why we play our radios too loud."

I did a fast calculation; we were entering the dark of the moon this very night. Oy! Well, like it or not, it was time to look while trying not to touch. I heard Sonny muttering a chant the moment the bottom silt of the Rio Grande began sucking at my feet. As I crossed, I wondered how many centuries had passed since any Cochiti Indian had approached Gashpeta head-on.

The cave entrance was a round hole located some 50 feet below the canyon rim and about 100 feet above a talus slope that angled down to the river. I looped my climbing line and my camera over my shoulder before stashing my daypack directly below the cave entrance. I made my way south along the riverbank; within a half mile, I found a way to scramble up to the top of the ridge. Doubling back, I soon spotted my daypack. Anchoring my line around an outcropping of stout rocks, I took a deep breath and rappelled down the face of the rock cliff, cursing even the slightest noise. It was silly of me, but the closer I came to that cave entrance, the more I expected a 6,000-year-old mummified arm to reach out to grab my foot.

Up close now and swinging freely, I was amazed to discover that this cave entrance was a whopping four feet wide. Moreover, Sonny's description had been accurate. The two larger plugs were augmented at the top by a third yet smaller and flatter rock not easily seen from the far side of the river. In addition, every possible orifice above, below, and in between those solid plugs appeared to have been solidly chinked. I tried to swallow, but my mouth was as dry as a 1,000-year-old pile of — I twisted around in midair to make sure Sonny had not scooted off on me. Why, I didn't know. He would not do me any good even if — what if that was not true chinking after all. What if that myriad of stacked and stuffed rocks just happened to have been naturally fractured around those three bigger ones? That could happen, couldn't it? So why not yank out one of those chinking rocks and see what was behind it? If this was a natural occurrence, I would probably find a solid wall of stone that would expose Gashpeta as only another colorful legend — but what if I was wrong? What if that giant's spirit could seep out and all those bad luck things began happening all over again — oh, good grief! What nonsense! I looked over to make sure Sonny had his back turned before I reached out to get a grip on one squarish piece of the chinking... a breeze puffed against my ear and I heard — or I thought I heard someone sighing... or singing? I twisted around again. Sonny had not moved and the river flow barred anything less than a shout. The breeze puffed harder and I would swear I heard scant snatches of a voice... above or below me?

I yanked my hand back faster than a kid caught in his grandma's cookie jar. Feeling foolish and ashamed, I dangled there like a pale spider to search around those plugs for any obvious evidence of fire that I did not have to touch. I saw not a single charcoal fragment, nor even a hint of smoke residue. Knowing that fierce desert winds can scour paint from a house, I began searching for pecked petroglyphs formally sealing the cave. Drawing another blank did not surprise me. When I added Sonny's gory story to the extreme reverence displayed by these modern Cochitis, it was reasonable to assume that the moment that old hag was safely shut up inside, the entire tribe had probably scrambled back across the river to peck all their fears, furies, and prayers into rock faces well out of her scrawny reach. Searching for shards, too, would be useless. Desert scavengers would have devoured any fragment of bones she might have

Figure 7: The rock plugs in the cave at Gashpeta. Cochiti Pueblo, New Mexico.

tossed outside long ago.

Determinedly, I pushed over and again out from the cliff face to look for a faint trail leading upward. Again, there was nothing certain, nothing clear; however, when looking down from this extreme angle, I could see where an expert rock climber could make that climb both ways, albeit with effort. Out of breath, I allowed myself to swing freely while I rested — there! There those sounds came again as if to tantalize and tease me. Damn it, I could get closure to this mystery only if I could pull out one of those chinking rocks... but any promise is a promise that must be kept.

Sweating outside and cursing inside, the rising midday heat made pessimism blossom. Perhaps this is all just another quaint legend, a cute myth — or a big juicy lie aimed at jerks like me. Maybe fat Ernie and skinny Juan and even that Sees-Far brat had half the village hunkered just over the ridge where everyone is laughing their tails off at this ridiculous dummy! They might even have a TV crew up from Albuquerque to show the world how gullible some idiots are — I was getting cranky. The sun had reached its zenith; it was hot and getting hotter and sweat was stinging my eyes — I *hate* to sweat! I angrily kicked out from the cave a few more times to take some last-minute photographs of Gashpeta. Satisfied, I dropped down below the lip of the cave for one last look. If only I could find just one small hint of hominid intrusion. No luck, no luck.

I swiped sweat away before checking my camera's frame counter: I had one frame remaining on that roll. I kicked out again, but this time it was too hard and I swung out too far. I had barely snapped my picture before I crashed against the cliff and sent loose stones clattering down the slope below me. I was unhurt; nothing destroyed; no big deal — except that when the noise had ceased, my heart leapt into my throat. It was not my imagination; I heard a faint but unmistakable sound of chanting somewhere... above me?

Hey-ya, hey-ya, kok-oi, kok-oi ge-ee

That was *not* Sonny's voice!

Chi-pi-dag kok-oi, kukpa kia, kia, kia!

Or was it? Yes, sure, maybe — no — I cursed as I twisted round and round in mid-air. Sure enough, good old Sonny was blithely sitting across that river. He had his back to me and, although the sloshing and the bubbling of the river swept his voice away, I could see his body swaying as if keeping time with his private little song — but that burbling river had no effect on that phantom singer who was surely *above* me.

Hey-ya, hey-ya, kok-oi, kok-oi ge-ee
Chi-pi-dag kok-oi, kukpa kia, kia, kia!

Feeling less like a spider and more like a trapped fly, I tried yelling above the dull roar of the river, "Sonny? Sonny! Do you hear something? Can you see *anny- body* up there?" But good old deaf Sonny just kept a-rockin' and a-swayin' back and forth while I kicked out over and over again, shouting for all I was worth, "Hey, hey, hey! Sonny-Sonny-Sonny-boy, you dirty rotten, no-good, lousy swab-jockey! Annnnnswerrrrrr me!" I was coughing, hacking, and spitting dust to clear my dry throat for one last bellow while that chanting kept wafting down to fade in and out with the wind. Anger overpowered fear. I inched up the rope. Inches became feet. I climbed one yard. Two yards. Three. The more I rose above the lip of that cave, the louder that chanting became. Okay, that solved, I inched back *down* the rope. The chanting faded accordingly. I cannot tell you how long I dangled there until I found the guts to inch up again until I heard so clearly...

Hey-ya, hey-ya, kok-oi, kok-oi ge-ee ...

"Sonnnnnnnnny," I bawled but that sucker didn't so much as twitch. Now my imagination kicked in big time. After all that noise I'd been making, if I lowered myself down and past that cave mouth, anyone who just might be inside could bash out some chinking and reel me in like a bloody fish — oh, get a grip! That giant's been baked, broiled, burned, and dead for more years than I could count! Besides, even if her spirit is in there, spirits don't get hungry, right? Right?

So, what's she chanting, "Double the white meat, hold the mayo?"

Nino's voice spoke hollowly inside my throbbing brain, *Spirits can't really hurt you, you know. They can only make you hurt yourself...*

Okay, right, sure, uh-huh! So why not try again? I carefully secured my camera and unsheathed my trusty Uncle Henry knife to clench in between my teeth like a miniature Tarzan. I made a promise to myself as I adjusted my climbing gloves; if just one of those rocks around the entrance to that cave became unchinked; I'd slash the line and take my lumps on the rocks below. I was *not* doing battle with a giant, even if she was a thousand years old. At the last moment, I decided to ascend the rope just a few yards for one final confirmation. Taking a deep, deep breath, I again moved up that line like an inchworm with a firecracker up his behind. Sure enough, fragments of words, strange words, foreign words came ever closer, and my bam-bam-bamming heart kept the beat.

Chi-pi-dag kok-oi, kukpa kia, kia, kia!

That voice seemed so clear and enchantingly delicate that I flashed on poor old Odysseus and his test by the sweet-singing Sirens — could the river separating me from Sonny perhaps hold a hidden whirlpool for evil Charybdis. Should I call to Crataiis for help so I could scoot past Scylla's new cave? Even mother Circe had warned, *Scylla is not mortal; she is savage, extreme, rude, cruel, and invincible. She sits and howls with the voice of a hound... but in truth she is a dreadful monster.*

Aw, crap! That something just yelped above me! It could have been a coyote, a fox, or a wild jackass stuck in the bum by some cholla cactus or — I rammed my Uncle Henry back into its sheath and rappelled down so fast that the friction scorched my gloves. When I hit the talus slope, I tumbled backward into the roiling currents of the Rio Grande. I came up spouting brown water like a mini-whale while plowing toward Sonny and safety — halfway across the river, I realized that my daypack was still on the bank below Gashpeta! Like an idiot, I paused long enough to allow the river's silt to begin sucking me into its murky clutches. In a blink, I was up to my calves — maybe the daughter of Charybdis did live in New Mexico after all! It took all my strength to pull free. I plowed ahead, cursing at the ridiculousness of it all.

"Don't need the pack! Don't need the binoculars or that expensive climbing line or the emergency kit... aw, crap!" What about all my money and my credit cards? Worse, what about the only set of keys to the van? Snarling like a waterlogged cougar, mean enough to tangle with any singing giant who would dare to cross my path, I circled back against the current. I slogged onto the beach to snatch up my pack — forget the line! Proud of myself, I hummed the "Colonel Bogey March" from *The Bridge on the River Kwai* all the way back to Sonny's side of that haunted river. Reaching land, I pitched a rock in his direction before squish-squishing my way toward the overlook. Sonny didn't catch up until I had nearly reached my van.

"What happened? Where's your climbing line? Man, you're soaking wet! Where are you going in such a hurry? Heading back to Florida?"

"I'm gonna open Gashpeta and yank that bitch out!"

"You wouldn't dig an inch before our tribal police would be all over you. Nope! Not possible!"

"Oh, yeah? Well then, I wanna talk with Juan Cornplanter! You take me to him, you hear, or I'll rip those plugs out with my teeth!"

We drove back to the village in silence while I calculated my moves. I'd first head to the nearest hardware store for diamond bits to drill into those stone plugs; I'd set steel rods inside; I'd hook those rods to a winch and yank the plugs out and I didn't give a toss if I came up with a live monster or a pile of dry bones. Yes, of course, I'd call Dr. Agogino and Grover Krantz to give them the option of being my witnesses because I wouldn't know an eyetooth from a shinbone! Me, I'm just the finder, not the keeper.

Ah, yes, I could see it all so clearly; as the dust would then settle old George, Grover, and I would find the great skeleton of that mesquite-smoked giant. Better still, she would be desiccated and in perfect condition. Behind her and in a pathetic pile we would find the bones of her victims. These should be buried according to Cochiti custom — except for my Scylla! Her carcass would provide all manner of answers through DNA and carbon dating tests, X-rays, and scores of laboratory mumbo-jumbo examinations — maybe she could be cloned?

I had to call Nino very soon… "Watch out," Sonny shouted as I swung into the central plaza. I barely missed hitting Ernie and that big sack he held against his bouncing belly.

"Hi, guys! What's the rush? Hungry? Wow, Morgan you are a mess! Fall in the river or did the giant chase ya, hardy-har-har!"

"Guess what Robbie-boy here wants to do," Sonny said grimly.

Ernie's face blushed a darker red and his lips pooched and pursed like a fish out of water, but he could not squeeze out a single word. Instead, he stalked off looking like a wounded bear.

The light was fading fast as I paced amid a grove of cottonwood trees that crowded the riverbank below the Cochiti village. I felt like a naughty schoolboy made to wait outside the principal's office. Nearby, Juan and Sonny were huddling with a knot of tribal elders, some of whom I assumed were shamans. It made quite a picture; this ad hoc committee of traditional holy men was dressed in full Cochiti regalia for the dance that night. Interestingly, they had not bothered to gather in the kiva, they didn't beat drums, and they didn't smoke pipes like in the movies. The only sign of any sort of ritual was the cigarettes they kept tearing open and scattering about as they spoke in hushed tones. Make up your minds, I thought. What's the big deal? Ding-dong, the witch is dead; her bones can be useful, damn it. You aren't using them, so c-c-cut me loose!

A flicker of movement on the far side of the grove caught my eye. It was Sees-Far Child peeking around the trunk of a huge tree. In the waning light, she looked like a Sees-Far Woman to me. In place of that razzy shirt and her too-tight jeans, she was fresh and beautiful in the traditional dress of her tribe. Her squash blossom necklace flashed as she leaned out again to beckon to me. I barely made two steps in her direction before Sonny called out. He patted a spot in the sand beside him. It was time to talk. I saw Sees-Far Child stamp her foot when I veered in his direction.

Juan again broke tradition by cutting to the chase.

"If we... allowed you to open Gashpeta, bad luck... would come to this village. None of us here... is powerful enough to stop it. The best thing is to... leave things as... the Twins had left it. We wish you... well."

"Why are you all afraid of some old curse?" I asked, perhaps too boldly.

"We choose to follow the ways and path of Those Who Walked Before," a man with crooked hands snapped. "They always lived in peace with our Giant brothers. This old one was... different."

Regretting my challenge, I tried reason instead. No matter how eloquent my argument about the fallacies of ancient curses, their response remained united. I then related my own encounter with a Pacific Northwest Bigfoot. I admitted to having felt haunted by an overwhelming urge to look again into those knowing eyes. Unmoved, the Cochitis averted their faces with hardly a shrug. I went on to recite why I was adamantly against taking the life of anything — even a worm — if it was only to prove its existence to the white man's science. However, I said, if the Cochiti people materially helped prove these giants did exist simply by allowing science to examine the bones of something already dead, it could bring new respect for other Native American opinions about how True Human Beings came to be, and how the world should be run.

"I can't hear your words," an old man with crooked hands shrugged.

I heard the drums and singing beginning in the village so I knew my audience was nearly over. I spoke more loudly to say, "Look, I would really like you to consider —"

Crooked Hands cut me off with a curt wave and another shrug.

"The wind blows your words away."

"I-I am sorry, but I'm not sure that I understand..."

Sonny hissed in my ear, "If he hears your words but disagrees with you, you might be offended. That's why he is telling you he can't hear you. He is being polite to a guest."

The squat man with one eye blinded with cataracts cleared his throat. "Juan's ally says you are a brother to us. This ally says you went to sleep in times long past. If you are a sleeping brother, the wind will let you hear these words: why should we bother with people who care only how they look on the outside if they stay empty on the inside? These are people that only care what kind of car they have, how big their house is, and how much money they have in the bank. They all have ugly souls; they cram too much food into their bellies while the next person is starving. They won't believe us because we have no big cars or fine homes. These ugly souls just shout big words every Sunday and then go back to sleep again."

I borrowed Crooked Hands' shrug and replied, "Wisdom not shared is made hollow. A True Human Being is not selfish with such wisdom... even if the wind blows his words away."

I looked over my shoulder. Who said that? Did I say that?

"That is true," Crooked Hands nodded solemnly, "but I still cannot hear your words about Gashpeta. Our ways respect everything the Creator gave us, including the Giant people, yet we see white men looking everywhere for gods of gold. They are like sleeping fools who don't want to know truth. Instead, they talk about some other person dying to pay their soul debts and try to scare us with all that hellfire stuff if we don't do everything they say. I never heard their words. It's all baloney."

It was Blind Eyes' turn to nod.

"I think maybe the Others — the true evil ones — first came down to earth way across the oceans just to mix with Sleeping Fools. I think it was those Others who told the Fools they could take everything from us. They told them they could kill us without sinning. They told them the Cochiti and the Children of the Blue Corn Woman or White Corn Maiden had no souls to worry about, anyway. Those white people in black robes saw us not as human beings but as animals and slaves. You know, even when I was a boy those Black Robes were still arguing if we had man-souls or dog-souls."

Juan Cornplanter sighed with sadness, "I think... some of our young people allowed those Black Robes... to put them to sleep, too. They pretended to be white so that person who died... might pay their debts, too. Everyone who had a red heart knew... that was wrong, so those who walked away ended up hiding their shame... with whiskey and stuff. They are off... the path, I think."

A tall man of many angles spat onto the sand and rubbed it in, saying, "Those Sleeping Fools can't hear the words of True Human Beings because they are slaves to the Others. That's what I think."

Juan, Crooked Hands, Blind Eye, and Many Angles made me want to ask more questions; instead, I heard myself replying as if I had an answer or two of my own. "Grandfathers, even a sleeping mind can hear wise words. Who can say that one day every sleeper might not awaken and remember them? Maybe ten of their lifetimes or even a hundred will pass... maybe those sleepers might even think those wise words belong to them. Does that matter? What matters is we accept that those who deliberately put people to sleep are not True Human Beings. Perhaps it is the Others who make fools of us all."

The thinnest shaman among them who had sat among the deeper shadows now cleared his throat. This Thin Man spoke in a voice equally thin, "Maybe you should come live as a Cochiti. Maybe then you'll know why we must leave Gashpeta alone forever."

"But if she was so evil, why..."

Thin Man corrected me. "Do not think she was evil in the way you mean; she was only crazy because she was old, sick, and hungry. Even her own kind left her behind. We have always lived in peace with the Giants; they came before us and will be here when we have all gone Home."

Crooked Hands wagged a knobby finger under my nose.

"Maybe you are being led by the Others, and *you* don't know it! Look around us. Tonight our children play outside and no one worries about bad luck. What if you let that one crazy Giant out and we can't put her back? Maybe the Twins would refuse to help this time."

"But, my friend, if we change our minds about opening Gashpeta, you can do it," Blind Eye promised.

Oddly satisfied by their honestly and wisdom, I played my last ace.

"Were the Cochiti asleep when they agreed to have this big dam built on their sacred land? Maybe the rising water will loosen the chinking at Gashpeta; maybe the rock plugs will fall out; maybe the spirit of the crazy Giant will swim down to your village again. Now, that would be bad luck, don't you agree?"

"We did... a big joke," Juan Cornplanter chuckled. "We knew the whites... would build their dam even if... we didn't want it. So, we... outfoxed them! The River Spirit promised... he'd stick his tail under the dam. If it brings us bad luck... he'll pull out his tail! Whoosh! No more... damned dam!"

While everyone laughed heartily, Juan lit a cigarette, puffed a ball of smoke into the night air, and said with a smile, "I can see you are... waking up, my brother, and that is good. This prayer... is for you."

Blind Eye took the cigarette to repeat the act before passing it down the line to Crooked Hands, Thin Man, Many Angles, and Sonny, too. Then they arose together as if drawn up by a common string. I knew the meeting was adjourned, case closed, request denied. As everyone except Sonny hurried toward the distant drumming, I heard someone chuckle, "Those whites mess with those giants, and they'll end up dealing with the Keepers."

Nino's initial comment about "Keepers" flashed through my brain: *Then chew on this,* he had said. *What if I told you that Usen is about to pull the plug on us humans if we don't start toeing the line? If he does, and if we get sent back to square one, maybe the Keepers will have to use those Yampricos to start us up all over again. We'd lose everything we worked for up to now; we'll be back naked in caves, and we'll darned well deserve it.*

Thoroughly confused, tired, and disappointed, I was trudging to my van when Ernie appeared. He looped one heavy arm around my neck and wheezed salsa in my face.

"Wanna fight?"

"Get off! You outweigh me by two hundred pounds," I said while frantically maneuvering upwind.

"Not with me, you jerk! It's Saturday night, man. We always go over to Peña Blanca to pound the crap out of those Santo Domingos. It's fun, ain't it, Sonny?"

"We'll even make you an honorary Cochiti!"

"Oh, sure, and with my pale face and baby-blues, guess who's the first target!"

Ernie gave me a Dutch-rub on my shaven pate, "What are you worried about? You're already scalped!"

"I think I'll take a pass, thanks. Besides, it's time to head east."

Ernie dumped a huge sack of food into the van before giving me a final bear hug. Sonny winked, grinned, and flipped back a military salute as they peeled out in their *Damned Proud* truck to roar away to their version of fun and games. Left alone, I sat listening to the distant drumming, the singing, and to fill my lungs with the fragrant scent of wood smoke. Part of me wanted to stay forever; after all, the souls of True Human Beings had returned to this village for thousands of years to live life over and over again among their forever-friends and family. For me, there was no such place; I had no feeling of permanence, or even of belonging. I could only assume that my path for this life was as a wanderer.

Such lonely thoughts rattled around in my weary brain as I drove away from the village and twisted down toward the bridge that spanned the Rio Grande River. I switched on the radio to search for any signal that had an upbeat sound. I was in no mood to hear about anyone else who felt lost, misplaced, or out of reach. Ah, good! Neil Diamond's "I Am, I Said," came through as a prayer answered. In a heartbeat, I was anxious to get back to my kid; after all, my Riki was my best friend in the whole world. Soon she and I again would be hanging out in Miami's Coconut Grove Park where she would do her ethnic dancing with the other kids (and adults, too). Later we'd talk about philosophy, the arts, animals, the mystery of life, and who shot JFK. Yeah, I'd take her to an outdoor seafood lunch at Monty's Conch or maybe a steak at The Taurus. They had some fine folks there, all golden brown from the Florida sun. Lessee, would Ann Black or Ann Swain still work there — or maybe Riki and I would find out where Teri DiSario was playing a gig. What a voice that child had. Clear as a bell and sexy as... Teri had a special song I first heard when she opened for the always-tardy Jimmy Buffet. It had a line; *It feels so good, good, good, to be with you!* I liked to imagine that Teri meant me whenever she sang that song. Ah, boy, and yes, ma'am; I am Florida-bound.

I hit the gas and twisted up the volume — whoa! Standing smack-dab in the center of the bridge was a dark form, a female form... a tiny voice hissed in my inner ear, *Sometimes she screams in the dark of the moon. Maybe that's why we play our radios too loud.* I veered hard to the right until I nearly left paint on the railing; I aimed for that narrow strip of pavement free of that dodging wraith. As my headlights washed past, I saw — Sees-Far Child? Was that a snake draped around her neck and over her shoulders... or my lost climbing rope? I skidded to a howling halt on the far side of the bridge, yanked on the emergency brake, and bailed out. I ran back shouting, "What are you doing out here? Where did you get that? Are you all right... I damned near killed you!"

Startled by my wild approach, the frightened girl threw my missing climbing line at me and danced out of reach.

"Hey, wow! Wait! Jeez-oh-man!"

"How did you get this? When? Where? Who told you where it was?"

"I-I-I pulled it up after you and Sonny left!"

"Pulled it up? When did you pull it up?"

"Right after you fell in the river and got so mad and stuff. I waited to see if you would come back again but you didn't, so I saved it for you."

"You were at Gashpeta?"

Sees-Far Child clapped her hands over my mouth.

"*Sh-sh-sh!* Don't ever-ever-ever say that word out here; not now, not at night, and never-ever when there's no moon! *She* might hear you!"

We stood together like two scared monkeys staring up river with big, round eyes. Its colors lost to the night, the Rio Grande shimmered back at us like some monstrous wet snake. Sees-Far Child sucked in a breath, held it, listened, and then breathed out again.

"Sonny didn't tell you he'd throw his loop of protection around you from where he was while I threw mine from up above?" she whispered. "We both sang prayers to the Twins for you, too. Sonny can be such a poop! I'll bet he and Ernie are having a great time right about now! They didn't tell you I had your rope, either? Those double-poops!"

"That was you chanting up there? You scared me silly!"

"Yeah, I have an awful voice so I sing kind of low, you know. Sonny didn't tell you, honest?"

"Not a word."

"I have to get back to the dance before Mom starts looking for me. Want to come?"

"You go."

"In 37 days my name changes to Sees-Far Woman."

"Come on, I'll give you a ride back."

"Just walk me to the end of the bridge; my bike's in the bushes. I really get scared out here."

"You mean because of..."

"Hush," she cried as she towed me along. Reaching the end, she pecked a kiss on my cheek before plunging into the brush.

"Thank you," I called after her. "Thank you very, very much, Sees-Far... Woman!" I heard giggling above the squeaking of her *Damned Proud* bicycle as she pedaled away toward the distant village.

I was nearing the center of the bridge when I was startled by a woman's shrieking scream. Although it came from somewhere distant, my blood still turned to instant ice. But had it come from the road to the village — or from somewhere up the river toward Gashpeta? Was it Sees-Far Woman? Had she had an accident — maybe it was only Sonny and Ernie playing another little joke.

I whipped my climbing line into a coil while listening, listening, listening... a hundred heartbeats later another weird and wavering shriek came skipping down the river at me. This had *not* come from the village nor from the road in either direction. It came from the gallery of petroglyphs. Perhaps the cannibal giant felt my departure was cheating her of freedom...

I yelled back until my throat hurt. When I could yell no more, I headed home.

6. The Lost People of the Everglades

Coral Gables, Florida, 1972

To keep the lights on at home, I had returned to working in the entertainment business as a writer and a director-in-training. The first thing I learned was that filmmakers keep some mighty long hours and I was grateful if I fell asleep before 1:00 AM. Therefore, I was not happy to be shaken awake by the insistent ringing of my telephone. Before the receiver reached my ear, I heard Robert Tiger's scream, *"Victor just shot himself!"*

All vestiges of sleep vanished when I learned that Victor Osceola was in an ambulance and on his way to the nearest hospital. He had swallowed a bullet... the hardest way possible.

I fumbled around for clean socks, splashed cold water on my face — to hell with shaving — lightly kissed my sleeping daughter, and crept out of the house. I knew Riki would be sorely disappointed when she awakened and I was gone again. It seemed like I was always going somewhere I couldn't take her. I had this dread that one day I would walk in and she would ask her mother, "Who is that stranger?"

It was easy to spot the clutch of Miccosukee Indians huddled in one corner of the hospital waiting room. Their satin jackets laced with line upon line of bric-a-brac gave color to the gloom. I thought I glimpsed the puffy, tear-streaked face of Victor's wife, Virginia. The others closed in around her before I could be sure. Only Robert Tiger stepped away to greet me. In his late teens, he looked much older now.

"Is that Virginia? I should go —"

"Not now!"

"Is he —?"

"Let's get some coffee," he said while shepherding me to the nearest coffee shop.

The hands of the eldest son of Bobby Tiger, a world-famous alligator wrestler, were shaking too hard to hold his cup. He couldn't manage those thimbles of cream, either.

"I can't understand why he would try to commit suicide," I said. "He has a beautiful wife; he's young and healthy! What the hell happened?"

"Victor's tried this crap before. Tried to drown himself in wine and whiskey all through school and then hit the drugs. Sliced his wrists, too. This time he stuck a stupid gun to his stupid head and pulled the stupid trigger."

"But when we spoke last week he seemed just fine."

"He's been talking about killing himself since we were in the fifth grade," Robert muttered as he slumped back in his chair. He looked like a disjointed stick figure. "Don't take it too hard, Mister Morgan. It ain't all your fault."

"Why would it be my fault?"

"Don't take it personally…"

"Whoa! Tell me what you mean!"

"Well, he was the first to talk outside the tribe to people like you about stuff he shouldn't have. Lots in our tribe think he got this bad luck because he broke the rules for you."

I was fast learning that many true Native Americans take seriously the notion that "bad luck" is a wholly earned and sometimes an instant punishment for breaking tradition. That concept remains an integral part of many of those reservation born-and-bred folks I have met. To their minds, bad luck stems from violating a code of conduct that I had not heard totally defined, yet they could be punished with something as simple as a broken finger to insanity to instant death; worse, certain types of bad luck could make you linger in agony for years. There was one specific and common thread: whenever such a thing struck, it was always in consequence to something the victim did that broke tribal etiquette or custom. After all, as Nino once explained, those tribal beliefs and customs had developed over eons of time and provided a matrix that enabled native peoples to survive, flourish, and to accept why they exist.

Fighting waves of guilt, I kept reminding myself that I had not badgered Victor to reveal even a single secret tribal belief about their version of the Apache Yamprico or the Canadian Sasquatch. However, I hadn't turned a deaf ear, either. It was true that I had also paid him for all he did share with me, but my coin had not been silver or gold but with a sincere friendship. Besides, I had kept my end of the bargain: I had not exploited anything that he had told me. Moreover, he had initially contacted me a few years back during a WKAT radio interview on Miami Beach — either the Bill Smith or the Larry King show — and I had returned his call out of courtesy. Victor's sincerity had convinced me to accept his invitation to visit him, albeit clandestinely, on the Trail Reservation west of Miami that lay in the heart of the Everglades. He had invited me; he had offered help in my research; but I had not asked for it. Technically, I was off the Hook of Guilt, but that didn't help. After all, if I claimed to accept certain Native American ways as true, the cause of his bad luck could have been either my presence or our topic of conversation.

Regardless of the cause, Robert Tiger and I were now hunched over hot coffee while one very young Indian lay naked and still on a cold slab with lead in his head.

My mind drifted back over what he and I had shared. "Sha-wan-nook-chobee": the Big Shawnee; "Ewash-shak-chobee": the Big Lost

People; "Ewah-shak-koochi": the Little Lost One. These were among the whispered names the Seminole and Miccosukee tribes had given "the lost giant people of the Everglades." What harm could come from my knowing these? I recalled my first visit to where a group of the once mighty Miccosukee Nation had been corralled on a reservation the size of a postage stamp. A handsome lad with a rugged face, Victor had rushed me inside their new mobile home while Virginia locked the door, drew the window shades, and removed the telephone from its cradle. After all, most reservations maintain a quasi-communal lifestyle, and its residents lead a fishbowl life among their surrounding relatives, friends, and peeping neighbors. All visitors from the outside — especially if they were non-Indian — were suspect.

I had barely finished my slide presentation that showed lots of footprints and handprints and many of the people who had borne witness to encounters with the Forest Giants, when he blurted out, "I never saw 'em, but I know they're around here."

"You said you did see them," sighed Virginia.

My nervous host splashed Old Crow whiskey into a glass. "I said I'd seen where they'd been, but I *never* said I saw 'em," he sputtered. "Nuh-uh, not me." He pushed the bottle my way. "You want a shot, Mister Morgan? Beer? Some gin? I got gin for my Genny, but she'll share with you."

"I'd better not, thanks. I saw Smokies hanging around down by Earl Shiver's Barbecue Hut. And please, the name is Robert."

"They won't bother you, man. Those Smokies are waiting for us Indians," Victor sniggered and tossed off his whiskey. "I know all them guys, that's for sure. One time me and another Robert — he's a Tiger — and a bunch of the Billie boys were heading for Miami. When the cops saw us coming, they turned on all those lights and —"

"Stop bragging and tell Mister Morgan what you want before someone comes to check," Virginia said.

When Victor poured another shot of whiskey, I began wondering how this evening would end. I had been around too many people who were nice and friendly until alcohol frazzled their brain; then they would get mean enough to pick a fight with God. I remembered Frank Johnson, my old Navy boxing buddy. A moody Kiowa-Pawnee from Oklahoma, Frank would get so drunk that he'd get lost in between bars. Worse, when he'd call me to come fetch him, he couldn't tell me exactly where he was. Once I searched over an hour before I spotted him squatting in a telephone booth. In the first moment, he was glad to see me; in the second, he took a swing at me for being late! I liked Frank in any situation, although I learned to keep a sharp eye on his right cross if he had whiskey on his breath.

Victor snapped me back to his home by saying, "I'd get in some serious-ass trouble with the tribe if they knew I even mentioned any of this stuff."

"I'll never do anything that will damage you, I promise."

He belted down even more whiskey before he whispered, "I've known all about Lost People hanging around our camp ever since I was a kid. Lots and lots of times I've heard 'em walking around, calling out, yelling back and forth to each other — I've heard that stuff ever since I was no bigger'n a minute."

With her eyes glued to that crack in the window shade, Virginia tossed back, "Victor's family has a camp up toward Big Tiger Swamp; that's near Alligator Alley. Almost everyone keeps a camp somewhere in those glades."

"You sure knew it when they came around, too," He said. "See, my Dad's kept his camp for years; my granddad had it before him. They say it goes back to when the whites were chasing Osceola and Coacoochee around. Anyway, it's nice out there because you can't even hear trucks at night. You just hear bullfrogs and some old gators whompin'. I'll take you out if you want."

"Has your mother and father ever seen those giants?"

"My dad saw 'em; I know my grandfathers did, too. They looked just like that picture you showed us of that big hairy woman."

"That was a slide Roger Patterson gave me from the film he and Bob Gimlin took in northern California."

"Are they still around?"

"Gimlin is, but Roger died fairly young."

"See, Genny?" he said. "Didn't I say it wasn't just us who has bad luck with them Chobees!?"

"Patterson died of cancer," I said.

"But he died, right?" he sneered. "That old cowboy got to see a Chobee so he thinks he's got the world by the tail. *Bam!* He's a goner, right? And I'll bet something else; none of those scientists believed him, either. I'll bet they even called him a liar and a fake, right? How much you wanna bet everybody at his church told his poor ol' wife that he'd been out messin' with the devil 'cause God didn't make no such thing as Bigfoot."

"I don't know, Victor."

"Yeah, but *I* know, and I'll bet this Patterson guy kept saying that he saw what he saw to the day he died." Victor threw his head back and shouted, "This redskin believes ya, Roger-Dodger!"

"I spent an evening with Patterson some months before he died," I said. "His story didn't change a bit. For what it's worth, I believed him, too."

"A dying man ain't gonna keep lying," He agreed with a sly wink and a nod.

"Think about this," I said. "Roger's partner Bob Gimlin is half-Apache. Gimlin held their horses throughout the entire episode; he saw what Roger saw and he backed up his story, so why do you think he is still alive and seems to be doing just fine? Where's his bad luck?"

Victor took a pull straight from his bottle before sniggering, "I'll betcha he was smart enough to haul ass to his medicine man and got cleansed and then got protection from his shaman. Yessir, he knew he had to set things right with those Lost People, you know? He had to have some medicine to get him clean!" Victor paused to belch before he went on. "Ya'know, when my Dad saw those pictures in the news, he told me our Chobees look just like 'em except they're not so big. Ours are skinnier. Don't need to pack on fat down here."

"Can I meet your father?"

"Oh, shit, no, no, no! He'd kill me if he knew I was even talkin' t'you."

"They say it's awfully bad luck to even talk about the Lost People or to do anything that might hurt 'em," Virginia whispered again. She hesitated as if she wanted to say something more but at that moment chose to use the bathroom instead.

Taking advantage of her absence, I asked, "Have you heard them yourself?"

"Hell, yeah. Sometimes they make like birds. Wanna know how you can tell when it's a bird or not? Birds have daytime calls that are different from nighttime calls, see? When you hear a night heron calling its night call and it's still daytime, you can bet it ain't no bird! They can imitate everything from a dog to a baby crying to a woman screaming... and they'll fool you every time.

"I'm serious, Mr. Morgan; I'm definitely serious. See, one time I had my hound out at our camp and that old boy had this dumb way of barking; he sounded like he was gagging on a bone because somebody had kicked him in his neck when he was a pup. He was pretty quiet around the Rez, but there were times when you couldn't shut him up out in the glades. Sometimes he'd walk around all stiff-legged with his hair standing up like a brush-cut and doin' like this: *gark, gark, gark*!

"One night we heard his dumb-ass barking comin' from all around our camp; hell, we thought he was out there runnin' around all crazy-like.

First, he'd be in one place, and then he'd be in another. Mom got sick of it so she got out the shotgun. She made me call him in; I think she would have shot him just to shut him up. But when I'm standing there yelling into the glades, that old boy came slinkin' out from under our chickee! He was so scared that he couldn't squeeze out even one *gark* — yet those others kept coming in closer and closer from every direction."

"Wait, wait, wait a second, Victor. Are you telling me they were imitating your dog?"

"Damned right! That's when Mom made Dad crank up the airboat to get us out of there. He couldn't get her to go back for a year. Come to think of it, that darned ol' dog ran off, too."

My mind kicked into passing gear. The possibilities were overwhelming if this could be proven. Talk about adaptation with a purpose...

"Yeah, but what really scares me, Mr. Morgan, is when a Chobee cuts loose with that jabber-scream of theirs! They use it sometimes if you happen to get in between two of 'em. Man, do they get mad!"

"A what-scream?"

"It sounds like someone screaming and jabbering all at the same time. It's spooky when more than one does it at the same time."

"How many have you heard?"

"Two, three, and sometimes even a bigger gang. Most of the time, they use birdcalls, catcalls, and gator calls, see? First, you'll hear one. Just listen, you'll hear 'em calling back and forth from way, way off. See, they never, never, never move around by themselves like people think. They ain't never alone, man. Makes me laugh when I hear white people talk like there's only one. That's as dumb as you can get."

"It's really weird at night, too," Virginia said as she returned. "I'll go out to that camp sometimes, but I don't really like to. I'm scared enough when Victor and his dad would go to that one burial mound to give 'em gifts. That's when the Chobees came around the most, but it got worse when they're followed back by those sky-lights —"

"Shut up!" he shouted. "You crazy bitch! You trying to get us killed? Stupid, stupid, stupid!"

Virginia rushed into the back bedroom; I heard the door lock snap into place.

The bottle was empty so he slammed through the cupboards looking for another. His bottle hunt proved successful but his hands shook so hard that he spilled more than he poured. He shoved one slippery glass at me while draining the other. When his breath returned, he croaked, "Genny's a city Indian who thinks she knows more than us Rezes. But I love her so much…"

"And I know enough not to go messing around on burial mounds," her muffled voice barked.

"I told you we never got out of that damned boat," he yelled back. To me he said, "Dad and me would just go close enough to some places we'd pass to toss some of our fish in to those Chobees, and that's all we'd do! Lots of the old people do that and then they don't get bad luck. In fact, they say good stuff happens."

"You talk as if Chobees deliberately hang out around your burial mounds," I said.

He scrubbed sweaty palms over his jeans, his voice became hoarser, and his words began to slur.

"Some of the old people think they guard our dead; all I know is they use 'em whenever they pass through. I know that for sure. One day my Dad and me had been out gigging frogs and doing a little fishing. All of a sudden, he got real anxious to get back to camp but wouldn't say why. He was in such a hurry that he took a shortcut that would take us close to this one old burial hummock. Tha's when we heard some mud-sucking sounds somewhere up ahead. As we got closer, we could see where something had just left a dripping-wet trail that went straight up the bank. Man, those bushes were still shakin'."

"Alligator?"

"Hell, no! I've seen gator drags all my life. Besides, we were already so close that we could see big, *big* human tracks with toes and all. Tha's when Dad started making birdcalls and hollering it was just us, the Osceola family, that we were sorry that we'd scared 'em, and that we were jus' passin' by. He was talking to them just like he'd talk to you."

"In English?"

"Wha-wha? Oh — er — Miccosukee. Anyway, Dad took the biggest fish we had — that bass was four-five pounds for sure — and heaved it over the bushes. Then he tol' me to pole my ass off and to not look back. I didn't, either... that same night we started hearin' a whole bunch of birdcalls and whistles, you know, the kind you hear in the morning time. Then things came creepin' in real close — I could hear 'em goin' *stepppp, stepppp, stepppp* behind our camp. Tha's when one let out one of them jabber-screams, and 'nother one laughed from 'nother way."

"Then what?"

"Tha's all, tha's... all, tha's... all..." he murmured as his head fell forward and his chin fell to rest on his chest. I could see his eyes were closed and his jaw was going slack. His wife slipped in quietly to remove his shoes, toss a cover over him, and we said our goodnights.

With each succeeding visit with Victor — never again at his home or on the rez — I learned more about how the Miccosukees who still inhabited the Everglades accepted an encounter with the Chobees as a matter of course. In fact, he claimed there was a small hummock that lay just south of their reservation that was a sacred burial place for certain old-time shamans. Moreover, it was a resting place and haven where the "Lost People" would stay when they were in the area. He promised more than once to take me there on the sly, but never did.

I learned too that the Lost People are given a wide berth whenever possible; yet certain items of medicinal herbs are routinely shared as gestures of respect; other gifts were exchanged to acknowledge presence and brotherhood. Victor claimed too that each consults the other via dreams or visions. In addition, he claimed that most Native Americans accept that the literal existence of giants demonstrates the realities of many other ancient beliefs. I found it refreshing that his ego did not mind being an equal child of the Great Spirit with every other living thing from mice to bears to eagles and even to grasshoppers and the lowly worm.[18]

However, I soon developed scars on my tongue. I steadfastly refused to be associated with those ridiculous tales of sightings of monstrous "Skunk Apes." It was tough enough to remain silent in the face of those weird concepts boon-dock rednecks circulated. These were the soulless creatures who thought they were demonstrating their manhood by mashing through the Everglades with giant swamp buggies while destroying wildlife habitat, polluting its waters, and shattering its calming silence with the roar of engines. To make matters worse, after lecturing at Barry College, Florida Atlantic University, the University of Miami, and for the Florida Zoological Society at the Miami Planetarium, I was introduced to the character "Buzz" who bragged that he had single-handedly created that odious term, Skunk Ape. This pretend archaeologist had somehow wangled in to head up the local South Florida chapter of the highly respected Florida Archaeological Society. He confided to me that he had also solved the riddle as to why the Florida Bigfoot — his "Skunk Ape" — smelled so badly. According to this screwball, their stench was due to their habit of traveling clandestinely through sulfuric-smelling caves and tunnels that he claimed webbed the entire coral base of South Florida. I later discovered that this same character had used the banners of his society to allow him to conduct what he claimed would be scientific digs on ancient Indian shell

---

[18] Their reverence for life in general could be a carryover from when their most ancient ancestors, perhaps from the original Buddhists, migrated to North America from Nepal and Mustang.

mounds. Far from being scientific with numbered grid lines, sieves, trowels, and brushes, this lunatic used dynamite because he was convinced these mounds held pirate treasure! Fortunately, the legitimate members of his society discovered his shenanigans and he was canned and banned.

Unfortunately, the term Skunk Ape stuck, probably because more newspaper reporters could spell it properly.

Along with my daughter Riki — who never failed to charm everyone in sight — Victor and I made plans to visit his family's private camp. As a result of our growing mutual respect we were introduced to his most trusted friends, the children of the respected Bobby and Louise Tiger. We were introduced to and instantly bonded with Robert, Donna, and feisty Spencer.

Robert's *"Psst!"* snatched me out of my somber reverie and back inside the hospital coffee shop just as the gang from the waiting room came filing in. However, instead of joining us, they sidled to the far side of the room and pointedly turned their backs.

"Don't let 'em hurt your feelings," Robert whispered. "They're not really mad at you; they're just scared."

"Who wouldn't be after this kind of an accident?"

"What accident? He pulled the trigger! Something he did surely got him bad luck this time."

"Oh, for crying out loud! What about Virginia? Why didn't this 'bad luck' crap get her?"

"*She* didn't call you; it was all him! He should have gotten permission from a shaman or his *hillis hiya*."

Robert's voice trailed off as the Miccosukee gang came shambling over. One fellow with a pockmarked face and tattooed fingers grumbled something in their language.

"Have to go," Robert sighed. "I'm their ride."

My cup was empty; the coffee urn was empty, and, truly, I felt empty.

For a fleeting second, I felt sorry for poor, pitiful me — *"You jerk!"* I shouted to myself. All such feelings should be directed toward that kid who probably had spent his last heartbeats in some puke-green operating room with steel tweezers probing around inside his skull. And, if I had any feelings left over I should direct them toward Virginia and Victor's mother and father, not to mention sorrow for all those grand Osceola kids who would never be born. Talk about bad luck — *NO!* All this "bad luck" crap was wearing thin. I knew that my Jewish and Muslim pals would stoically explain this event as "God's or Allah's will" while charismatic Christians would proclaim this the work of Satan who could only be defeated by throwing fistfuls of cash into the pockets of their bad-breathed preachers. Of course my Buddhist comrades would remind me to chant about karma, contemplate lessons to be learned, and the turning of the Wheel of Many Lives. Everyone in between would relegate this to a desperate act by another drunken Indian and would change their TV channels to some vacuous game show while passing popcorn.

After all, that's the easiest way to deal with someone else's bad luck, now isn't it?

Those thoughts drifted back to the previous weekend when I had helped Victor tune the engine to his borrowed airboat. We were preparing for a secret excursion to his father's camp. Now, only two days short of our adventure, he lay with lead in his brain.

"Are you Robert Morgan?"

I looked up and into the drawn face of an exhausted ER nurse.

"That Indian boy's luck ran out, didn't it?"

"I don't know anything about that, but you have a telephone call at the desk. It's your father."

My father? What father? Certainly, she had the wrong person. I hadn't heard from my biological father in ten years — or was it twenty? I took the call anyway.

The first words Nino spoke were in the form of a direct order: "Get up to that Big Cypress Rez and find a holy man that sometimes goes by the name Round-Bear. Tell him I sent you; be sure to tell him all about that sky-light stuff, too. He'll tell you a thing or two about 'em."

"Er, how did you find me here? Who told — ?"

"Don't waste my nickel! Just saddle up and get on the road while you still can."

"Let me hang up and call you back —"

"You gotta have eyeball contact for important stuff like this — don't go telling anybody where you're going, ya' hear! Don't go talking about Round-Bear *after* you meet him, either!"

"I think I have the right to —"

"Get going!"

"All right, all right! I promise to go after my lecture —"

"Lecture, my fanny! Cancel it!"

"But, but…"

"Dang it, you sure are one slow learner! Your friend there just got terminal bad luck and unless you want a taste of it, you'd better get cracking! That sky-light came looking for you once and, from what I'm hearing, it'll be back real soon. Ol' Round-Bear is the only real honest-to-God *hillis hiya* I know who's close enough to give you a fighting chance."

Something pinged deep inside my brain; I was astonished to hear myself say, "I'll take off first thing in the morning."

"He's waiting! You go *now!*"

"Nino, I — Nino?"

Click-buzzzzzzzzzzzzzzzzzzz.

"Hello? Hello, hello, hello!!!!"

Ingram Billie

7. Round-Bear

Lost in the Florida Everglades, 1972

I knew it was my imagination and an overactive ego to which I had no right, but I could not shake the feeling that the fresh ghost of Victor Osceola was prodding me onward as I barreled up Florida's Route 27. Resenting Nino's imperious commands, angry with myself for meeting with Victor in the first place, and, yes-yes-yes, also angry that he had the bad luck to die so young, I was determined to make the Big Cypress Reservation before dawn. What did I have to lose? What if Nino was (again) right?

Ripping through sleepy old Andytown, I veered due west on Florida Route 84. Nearly an hour later — or was it only half an hour — my headlights rounded a bullet-riddled BIA boundary sign that advised of a nearby Indian settlement. Turning north again, the pavement ended and my VW van's tires mushed onto a sandy roadway that paralleled one of those drainage canals that leach the life's blood from the suffering Everglades. Curiously, the roadway appeared to be edged by a random scattering of abandoned railroad ties. How odd, I thought. Who would want to build a railroad in the middle of nowhere — *whoa!* I dodged a torpedo-like shape that bolted out from beneath a palmetto bush — I felt one wheel jolt over its tail.

I slid to a halt and leapt out to glimpse a knobby black body slamming into the nearby canal. Hoping to gain a better view — that bad-boy alligator had to be at least seven feet long or better — I hurtled over those railroad ties... until one rose up with an angry hiss. I skidded to a halt and froze as those "railroad ties" transformed into a beached flotilla of alligators. Suddenly wanting to urinate, I danced, dodged, and pirouetted back to the safety of my van while those giants made the canal roil with their diving bodies.

My van and I continued our trek, albeit more cautiously.

It was dawning when I found a tiny Indian settlement with a single light burning. Lucky for me, it belonged to a convenience store. I filled my tank and paid the bill.

"I'm looking for an elderly gentleman named Round-Bear," I said to my yawning attendant. "He's what I think is called a hilly-hiyah.[19] Know where I can find him?"

Sleepy no more, the young Indian glared at me, slammed the till shut, and vanished into the back room. He didn't reappear until another customer came in. The moment we were alone again, I said, "Excuse me? I don't mean to bother you, but can you help me find Mister Round — hey!"

Slam!

Cussing under my breath, I helped myself to his telephone book but came up blank for anyone named Round or Bear. Feeling unwelcome and spied upon by unseen eyes, I went outside to lurk for fresh prey. After waylaying an even dozen Indians who stopped for gas, cigarettes, coffee, and the remains of yesterday's donuts, I had my routine down pat.

"Excuse me, I'm not a cop; I'm not a reporter; I'm not selling anything or working for any collection agency. I've been sent here by Nino Cochise who is a friend of Mister Round-Bear who is some sort of a hilly-hiyah… hello?" Without exception, I was impaled with startled looks before each victim scurried to their cars and I was left to dodge flying gravel.

Tiring of bashing against red walls of silence, I flagged down the first BIA car that hove into view. How did I know it was BIA? Who else would buy an expensive new sedan in such dull colors?

---

[19] Chris Kimball, once curator at old Fort Morgan and currently at the Collier-Seminole Park outside Naples, Florida, advised me the proper term was *hillis hiya* (Medicine Maker).

When the pudgy Anglo driver with a ruddy-red face rolled down his window, dull gray smoke plumed out of his dull gray car.

"Can you tell me where the Bureau of Indian Affairs has its offices, please?"

"It's a little ways yet. Ya'll can jus' foller me," he said with more smoke poofing out from a mouth filled with dull gray teeth.

"You're with the BIA, right?"

He flipped one cigarette butt past my ear and lit its brother.

"That's why they let me drive this here guv'mint car. If ya'll lookin' for the Cultural Center, it don't open for a spell yet, but it's nice to hang out in the shade." Jerking a stubby thumb toward the angry red ball that was rising in the east, he complained, "Gonna be another scorcher. This place makes the Miss'ippi Delta seem right cool, now don't it?"

"I'm looking for a man by the name of Round-Bear. Ever hear of him?"

That guv'mint man rubbed his chin with orange-stained fingers and drawled, "Wal, I heard one of ol' Josie Billie's names used to be Roun' Pooma or somethin' like that? They's got so many names, I cain't keep count. You sure it's a bear?"

"Who's Josie Billie?"

"Oh, he's one famous herb'list, ya know. That's an ol' fella what uses swamp plants to treat the miseries, so's they say. Ol' Josie, he got hisself writ up in the papers one time when he was a-working with some big ol' drug company and he gave 'em digh-ee-tallis for the heart. Seems I heard his brother Ingram was called Round somethin' or other, too, but I wouldn't swear onna Bible t'it."

"Maybe I could talk to someone at your office who could go over the Tribal Register?"

"Used to be a few of the real old ones was named Round this or Round that when ol' Motlow and Tommy Doctor was alive; they was what they called *ayikcomis* — somethin like an ol' medicine man. None of them ol' boys left anymore. The rest took up civilized Christian names now t'get along."

"Maybe my man is a Miccosukee instead of Seminole?"

"What'd you do, root that name out of some old history book? I know the Berts and Billies and Bowlegs and Cypresses and Fishes and Gophers and Johns and Tigers and —"

"Is there a cross-reference between Indian names and Christian names?"

"Aw, shoot! We cain't keep track," he snorted. "They change names every time they get a bad dream. How'd ya'll come to hear of this fella, anyway?"

"An Apache I know out in Arizona wanted me to look him up to see how he's doing and all that."

"I think you're being put on, son. Indians do that a lot. Gets to be a pain in the dairy-air. But sooner or later we'll bring 'em all to Jesus. You wanna tour of our tribal museum? It's got nice-an-cool air. Cornhusk dolls are great this year, and them Seminole jackets are on sale, too. Stop on by when ya'll git tired of chasin' somebody ya cain't catch," he chuckled and then drove away in a dull gray puff.

Forgetting the time difference between Florida and Arizona, I plugged a fistful of coins into the outside telephone and pecked out Nino's number. Nino answered on the first ring as if he was waiting for the call and wasted no time on even one how-dee-do. He ordered me to tackle the smartest looking Indian I could find and drag him to the phone. I barely had time to turn around before a dusty pickup pulled up behind me. A burly Indian sloped out of the truck; he looked like a bricklayer who was running late.

"You here to use the phone?" I asked.

"Coffee."

"This call must be for you."

The bricklayer gaped at me until I had moved beyond easy reach. He listened tentatively at first, but then his face shifted from suspicion to amazement.

"What? Oh, yeah... what? *What*? Oh, yeah, yeah, yeah," he kept sputtering while eying me up and down. "Yeah, sure, Grandfather, you bet. Here, *Guynatay*, you talk until I get back." He slapped the receiver into my gut and trotted to his truck to rummage through crushed cans, candy wrappers, and old mail.

Guynatay? What's that mean? Probably "dumb-ass white dude who is always in trouble," I thought. Suddenly, I realized that Nino was apologizing to me. I listened more attentively while he explained how he had neglected to warn me that those few who actually knew Round-Bear would always protect his privacy with the greatest of zeal. The harder I might press, the more they would deny his very existence unless, of course, I could be separated from the usual outsiders.

"By the way, that young fella you just happened to ask for help didn't show up by accident, bub. That's Round-Bear's great-grandson." One of those mind-spiders with cold, cold feet was scooting up my spine again while Nino added, "You'd better get this straight: in this game there ain't no such thing as a coincidence." Then he said something like, *"Onendi mba stiz n nalti gui-nah!"*

"Yeah, right... what's that mean?"

"You're like some loco coyote that pops in and out of holes like a dumb gopher!" He let that sink in before he warned me that his Bear pal had a peculiar habit. He liked to scoot off on secret treks into the outer reaches of the Big Cypress Swamp. The problem was he might linger days or even weeks to gather his plants and snails and little alligator tails and lots of the other secret goodies that shamans and healers are prone to covet. Regardless, I was not to leave this rez until Round-Bear and I had come face to face.

"You're talking as if my life depends on all this, Nino."

"Now you're getting the picture."

"Oh, yeah? Maybe I should just take a break —"

"He's hard to find because there's nuts running around who want to rub out people like him."

"Why? What could one old dude do from the middle of a swamp?"

"He's a Wisdom Holder; he's the guardian of a Wisdom Shield."

"Er, is that some sort of shaman or a…"

"*Waugh!* I keep forgetting how long you've been gone!"

"*Waugh,* yourself! I just left Arizona!"

"I'm talking about from the Clan."

"What clan? Whose clan?"

Nino dropped back into his *Me teacher; You, dummy* voice. "Your clan, my clan; *our* clan! Look, Guynatay, Round-Bear is way beyond a shaman. He's a high shaman, don't y'see?"

"How would I know that?"

"Do you know what a Cabbalist is?"

"Round-Bear's *Jewish*?"

"Is it sunny there?"

"Yes."

"Maybe you'd better get a hat on because something's burning your brains out. Round-Bear is a Wisdom Shield Holder for those True Human Beings who are living in *red* skins this time around. If he wanted to be a Jewish Wisdom Holder he would've been born wearing a Jewish skin, now wouldn't he?"

"Then Wisdom Holders can be of any race or creed or whatever?"

I spied Round-Bear's great-grandson hustling toward me as Nino spewed a string of nasty-sounding Apache words that ended with "… and dumb questions like that is why you'd better find Round-Bear before you go chasin' that sky-light again. Now get going!"

I slammed the receiver into its hook and stalked to my van. Determined now to return to Miami, I found my keys and twisted at the ignition switch. Before I could drop into gear, the bricklayer waved a scrawled map inches from my face. He snatched it back when I reached for it.

"Just look at it!"

I suffered to glance at it; I was too angry to care.

"Look again, friend. It's easy to get lost out there," he said with an easy smile.

I took the longer look before he stuffed it into his pocket.

"Don't go as far as the next village," he said as I patted around for a pen and a pad. "You only pass one-two-three-four houses; take the first trail to your left that's marked with a beer can set against the base of a tree. Go maybe a mile or so before you take a left and then make the first right; don't miss those turns or you'll have to start all over."

"Hold it, hold it; go slower, please," I said while trying to scribble every word.

"Okay, that's when you should start watching for a clump of three — one, two, three saw palmettos growing together to your left. Across the trail will be an identical clump; we call them the six brothers — you'll see why. Look for a shack that's so overgrown with vines that you can hardly see it. Drive around back — watch out for busted glass — and in the weeds you'll find a bridge over a slough; don't worry, it only looks rotten to keep nosy people away. It'll hold if you drive slow."

He waited patiently until I flipped to a fresh page.

"After you're over, go around what looks like a big trash pile. Now you'll be on a trail you can barely squeeze your van through. In about a mile or so, you'll come to another split; stay left for sure even though you'll want to go right because it looks easier. The one to the left looks like nobody ever goes that way; that's the only one you want. Keep going until you see a big mound that looks like it blocks the road. See that and you'll know you're on target. You can get around it by driving over the bushes on the right. Once you're back on that path just keep going until you can't go any more. He's probably waiting for you."

"You going to call him for me?"

"Can't. No phone out there."

"Then how will he —"

"You'd better hurry; he goes out a lot to gather plants this time of the year. See ya!"

Before I could sputter another question or even offer a thank you, he had jumped into his truck and roared away. He didn't hear me yelling that he'd forgotten to get his coffee.

Returning inside the store, I scooped up the two leftover sandwiches — one with curled bologna, limp lettuce, and mushy bread — filled my thermos with fresh coffee and plunked down cash for my invisible attendant.

I checked my Florida county road map before setting out. The route I was to follow would take me through the heart of uncharted areas of the Everglades where no roads were recorded. However, certain names piqued my imagination such as Little Lard Can Slough, Cow Bone Island, and Kissimmee Billy Strand. Had to be some stories there, eh?

Spotting that beer can marker was easy, but when I followed all those bewildering turns I found myself being swallowed into an expanse of murky waters and tangled tropical undergrowth. Finally, after stand after stand of gumbo-limbo, tamarind, and bottle-stopper trees, I finally spotted the ruins of the shack with its collapsed chickee out back.

"*Waugh!*" I grunted (just as Nino might).

As that bricklayer's directions had indicated, behind that shack was a saggy old bridge. I held my breath as it groaned with the weight of my van; it felt as if it dropped a good six inches closer to the brackish water before I muttered onto the far side. Daring to breathe once again, I took each turn as instructed while I crept along a trail that was only inches above the oozing waters of the Everglades. Every vestige of human habitation had petered out and the sand was getting deeper. I was about to let air out of my tires to give them a better grip when I spied the final

split in the trail — one could not call this a road — that I had been
warned not to miss. Once again, I angled left until everything seemed to
end against a mound of crushed limestone. So far, so good. Gingerly, I
brushed the van around that mound to pass hand-scrawled signs that
warned, "No Trespassing. Dead-End."

My van and I tunneled through the mother of all tangled scrubs for
sunless miles. I was convinced that no one could possibly live this far
back when that tunnel took a radical right turn and dead-ended at a small
clearing. Centered in this clearing was a quaint cabin, quite small, made
of hand-hewn cypress wood that had been weathered to a soft and silvery
satin. To my left was a large open-air chickee complete with a thatched
roof and a wooden plank floor set above the ground by six sturdy stilts.
Spreading beyond that chickee was an enchanting lagoon dotted with lily
pads and arrow plants and floating dabs of green and yellow algae.

I switched off my van's engine and stepped in a quietness that folded
in around me like a heavy blanket.

"Anyone here? Hellooo?"

No one appeared at the open door of the cabin; no one stirred behind
its windows; no one came out to stare, to frown, or to ask who in the hell
was I? Where were the yapping dogs that traditionally mark Indian
homes? Where were the shards of broken glass, the broken appliances,
and the hollow TV shells? Moreover, where were tire tracks other than
my own? Was this a deserted movie set — a boat-tailed black-and-white
grackle boldly flapped down to perch on the roof of my van. A cocky
creature, it fixed one golden eye on me as if to consider impaling this big
white bug. Perhaps to intimidate me, it tested my van's roof with its
beak.

"Who comes tap-tap-tapping along my roof, dear Mister Poe?" I said
to that feathered beast. When it flew away, a strange stillness descended
all around me and my gut drew taut. Maybe the old fellow had gone off
on one of his hiking binges; the prow of a beached dugout canoe allayed

that fear.

"Mister Round-Bear? Anyone hommmmme?"

A flicker of movement — what exactly moved I knew not — drew my attention to the darkest corner of that great chickee. There I spied an elderly man squatted among strange plants of all sizes and shapes that were scattered about like a potted jungle. It was made more fascinating by its canopy of dried twigs, leaves, flowers, roots, and stalks that dangled from every rod and rafter; its boundaries were marked by uneven rows of jars and jugs, each stuffed to overflowing with seeds, feathers, critter skulls, bones, snake skins, and desiccated animal parts.

The man moved again and a knife blade glinted through the filtered light.

"Hullo," I whispered. Realizing no one could hear that croak but me, I upped the volume. "Er, hi there, sir…"

I moved closer. That old man's clothing seemed limited to a flowing cotton shirt that draped over his folded knees; his exposed feet were shoeless, scarred, and callused. He wore no hat, no jewelry, and no trousers. His wiry body appeared as hard as last year's jerky; his hands were slender, his wrists small, yet each tendon seemed to tense, flex, and tug like living wires. Unlike the tresses that were in favor among young Indians in search of an identity, this fellow's hair was hacked short. He held a quick little knife in the palm of one gnarly hand; in the other, he cradled its small victim.

Uninvited, I stepped up and onto the rim of his chickee.

"Excuse me, sir? I'm looking for Mister Round-Bear. My name is Robert Morgan…"

He ignored me. Perhaps this wasn't Round-Bear. Even if he was, perhaps he was hard of hearing; perhaps had never spoken a word of English.

My good humor was flagging. In the past 24 hours I'd lost a friend and had been blamed for his death, I'd spent a sleepless night driving over lonely roads, I had played leapfrog with pissed-off alligators, and my only mentor had hung up on me. Now, with the sun getting hotter by the minute, I was in no mood to be ignored by this gnome in a dress!

I considered stomping hard on the chickee's planks to see how high a holy man could jump — instead, I tried tact... one mo' time.

"Sir, please, are you Mister Round-Bear? Nino Cochise of the Chiricahua Apaches sent me. If that doesn't make any difference to you then either I am in the wrong place or you don't give a damn. Either way, maybe I should toddle on back to Miami."

Still no reply. I was feeling like an unwanted stepchild. Perhaps I should go back to my van where I could stretch out for a quick snooze — soft footfalls spun me around to spy a tall woman with sad eyes gliding down the path from the cabin cradling two horse conch shells in her hands. Without a nod or a word, she placed the larger shell on a wooden holder beside that old coot. With averted eyes, she thrust the other shell at me before pad-pad-padding back to the cabin. My shell was brimming with a cool but very strong tea of some sort. I sniffed it. Whee-ooo! Strong stuff, indeed!

"Er, thank you," I called after her. "Thank you, too, sir," I also said to the old man but he didn't seem to give a rat's patoot; he just sat there carving and sipping, sipping and carving. I may as well have thanked that damned grackle.

Strange drink, this. Bitter and biting with conflicting scents of licorice and leather rubbed with Christmas holly and sprinkled over with ashes of burned cacti — or was that chaparral? Why did it have a deserty taste instead a swampy one? Whatever it was, it had a lingering tang. Still, it was so wet and so cool that I chugged it all. Hmm! Look at that! The bottom of my shell had residue akin to pieces of cork and hairy strands of — whoa! Talk about a quicker-picker-upper! My mouth prickled as if microscopic needles were attacking my tongue before they slid down my throat — when I chanced to turn my head, I saw itsy-bitsy sparks of red, yellow, and orange dancing inside my eyelids. I tried hard to contain my urge to spit — *spit*? Me? I never spit, I lied to myself. That's disgusting, that's rude, crude, uncivilized and, and, and no one has the right to spread their personal germs in public…

I spat anyway.

Oh, I'm just overly tired, I thought within my speeding brain; however, I was indeed feeling stronger. In fact, I felt so good that I wanted to talk, but no, no, no, no. Respect for elders was best shown by strictly attentive silence, my grandfather had always said. Yes, he had said that often. Um, boy, did he ever — and sometimes not so politely, either.

"More tea?" a thin voice asked. It took a few heartbeats before I realized that voice belonged to the Indian I thought to be Round-Bear.

"What? No, no more tea, thank you. Do you remember Nino Cochise? He said you'd remember him. He told me I should come to see you. He's an Apache…" How strange, I thought. My voice also sounded thin. Maybe something is wrong with my ears. I let my newly thin voice trail off because Round-Bear did not appear to be listening or, perhaps, he didn't give one hoot what I said. Ha-ha! I tried not to laugh aloud at my great joke: Round-Bear didn't give a hoot? Bear's can't hoot! Maybe he should change his name to Round-Owl, I thought to my private amusement.

This time I know I laughed aloud but it sounded as though the chickee was an echo chamber. Still, good old Round-Bear didn't blink an eye. Perhaps he was deaf after all; maybe his two little words "More tea?" was meant to fake me out?

Um-um-*um*! Why was my brain sizzling into such a hyperactive gear? Dunno! Didn't care, either, because I had 'portant stuff to discuss, right?

"Nino told me to come to see you, but I couldn't find anyone who knew you and even the BIA guy blew me off and that jerk at the gas station locked a door on me and if it wasn't for your great-grandson I would have never found you — alligators sure look like railroad ties sometimes, don't they, hmmmm?"

Damn! Lookit! Not even a condescending nod was granted to acknowledge my highly informative and highly entertaining accounting of such highly important events. Well, hell's bells and cockleshells, since my host had been the first to break the silence — and for no other good reason, I assured myself — a second flood of words burst out of me like someone had broken a damned dam. Get it? Damned *dam*. Jolly good joke, eh wot?

Thusly, I began to inform my new pal, good old Round-Bear, things I was absolutely certain that he was dying to know.

"Nino's living outside Willcox, Arizona. He wants to move to Tombstone soon so when he dies the last thing he'll see is the Dragoon Mountains where he was born. His wife Minnie is white. I think she's number seven. Nino had a lot of fake Anglo names because all the Chiricahuas were supposed to be in Oklahoma and he was afraid they'd put him there or kill them like they did to his dad Tahza, so he pretended to be anything but Indian for a long time and I think now he's ashamed that he did that. I think he changed his name every time he got into trouble, too, because he's still a wild ol' dog, if you know what I mean. That might come back to haunt him, I'll bet, because in time people will think he's someone he's not. Hell of a mess, I think."

I looked more closely. Was ol' Round-Bear wearing a stone mask? He didn't even blink at my information! Aw, well, let's talk anyway! Swoosh, the floodgates to my newly acquired motor mouth widened to flush out thoughts that had never tasted the freedom of sound, rat-a-tat-tat!

"Why do people deny being what they are? I'd love to salute everyone in my ancestry for giving me my turn; I want to go home to my true home, but I can't find it. Never could. I don't think I belong here. I can't think of anywhere I belong. I ran away a lot when I was a kid because I didn't fit in; I was always the outsider even within my own family. I didn't see anything the way they did. I had a hundred answers to every question they asked, but somehow I couldn't choose the one they wanted.

"Sometimes I wonder if I had been dropped off on this earth by accident — or someone had a sick sense of humor. See, I thought sports were games that were intended to be fun for all. But, if games are played by true sportsmen, how can they hunt and kill animals and call their victims 'game'? Then there are all those people who are born blind or crippled or into cruel circumstances. Where is that Loving God everyone chants about? If that's His love, I'll take vanilla, if you take my meaning!

"Life can be such a cruel jokester — oh, crap, what's that; look, look! Oh, lordy-lord-lord," I screeched as I watched my words sliding out of my mouth to roll across the lagoon like floating marbles on the run. When they reached the far side, they magically expanded into huge balloons that shot up into the sky — poof, gone! The instant they were out of sight, I felt strangely free of rotten things that had been gnawing at my guts for years.

I stuck my finger into the conch shell to scoop out more cork. It was awfully bitter but I chewed it anyway. It made me spit. Such bad manners… suddenly, the dominant only-tell-'em-what-they-ask-for side of me reawakened to grab the switch to my oral floodgate and shut 'er down. Damn, I shouted within myself. Damn, damn, double damn! Why was I ladling all this goop over that poor old geezer who won't even talk back? Why should he care?

I licked the rim of my empty shell. It cut the tip of my tongue. I didn't care, after all, that blood belonged to my physical body and not to my soul, so it was not that important.

Strangely, instead of pain, I felt pleasure because I knew I was alive.

"Waugh, waugh, waugh!" I grunted Nino-like. Yes, I really must

shove all those bitter thoughts back into their dark holes and leave them there to rot, I thought.

Then, some small voice within me spoke ever so softly to say, "Every word and thought and deed is meant to be shared by the entire universe; each takes wing and flies away to exist forevermore. Once they are gone, they will never haunt you again but will be reabsorbed by other realities."

I snorted aloud to no one there, "Aw, c'mon! I doubt that big old universe gives one good diddly-damn about my peanut problems!"

Another voice, smaller still, replied, "The Maker of All Things cares about what happens and even that which does not happen; each is as important as the other. It is all equal in the end, you know."

Expecting that Round-Bear had finally deigned to speak to me, I whirled around only to find him still absorbed in his damned carving. It was then that I realized that those small voices I'd heard had spoken in the strangest of languages where words were not separated one from the other by enunciation, accentuation, and minute pauses for emphasis. Yet they had maintained a smoothly modulated tone that magically changed within its own envelope into an intelligible sequence — what language was it, anyway? Those voices that had spoken to me were not natural ones that begin with sucked-in air being forced back out through a fleshy larynx where vibrations were transformed into syllables by tongue, palate, and lips, oh, helllll no! Their communications were more akin to thoughts that I *felt* — who speaks this way? Was it a someone... or a some*thing?*

I looked for the culprit high and low among the tangle of potted plants but lost my balance and slipped onto my rump with a thump.

I felt so foolish! Now all those secret thoughts would be secrets nevermore — ow, ow, ow! My exhaled breath had seared my throat as if I had just run a 1,000-yard dash and flashes of blue, gold, and red dots zipped this way and zapped that way like miniscule comets.

I squeezed my eyes shut and blink-blink-blinked until they went away. It was then that I noticed that every plant in that chickee had magically taken on a pulsing glow as if they were electrically charged. I was mesmerized by these plants and wondered why some were amberish while others ranged from yellow to blue to a golden-green. I studied one in particular, a slender thing with smallish leaves that I assumed was a rue of sorts, or perhaps it was a mint? Why had I not noticed these wondrous differences before? To be sure, I knew there were serrated and pinnated and lobed leaves and some leaves were opposed one to the other while others were alternate, yet all were shaped to their particular wont and need from oval to ovate to deltoid — how was it that I could also see that those plants were moving? There was no wind, no breeze, and no vibration, yet they really were moving.

Enchanted by it all, I sank down to watch as one grew a single millimeter at a time while its buds were being fed juices that drew sustenance from the soil that bound its roots. No, no, not just "juices." That was its life-blood. My god, it's so alive, I thought — wait, wait! That was such a stupid thing to say. Of *course* it's alive! Still and all, I had never before had the privilege to see a plant grow... and it was singing in a soft sort of rhythmic hum. Similar species nearby hummed along in harmony one with another, while clutches of dissimilar species were a bit disharmonious. It was as if similars reassured one another while dissimilars caused cacophony — nah! Plants can't sing or even hum... yet *something* was. A swift glance proved that my human host was still mute, yet I plainly felt and heard these mellifluous sounds.

"This is madness! What's happening to me?" I shouted aloud — zap! A tiny bolt of light appeared to flash out from a nearby plant. Too late to move, it struck my forehead dead center and I fell off the platform to thump onto the grass. I heard myself grunt — did I also hear tiny shrieks from the broken blades of grass I had mashed? Impossible! Terrified, I leaped back to the safety of the chickee to stand with trembling knees.

"You are thirsty," Round-Bear said matter-of-factly.

"W-What?"

"You are thirsty," he repeated while nicking away at the tiny object in his hand — *nick-nick.*

Overjoyed that he had at last spoken, I searched for a common ground — any would do — while wondering if I had left my keys in my ignition. No, forget that. I was in no shape to drive out of there... yet. I didn't want to die. Hell, I hadn't told anyone where I was going. My kid might never know what happened to her dad. I had to act as normal as I could before I could scoot.

"Er-um, Nino Cochise told me about his personal experiences with the Yamprico — that's what the Apaches and the Papagos call the Bigfoot. I've heard that you folks call them things like the Ewash-shak-chobee," I offered. "He said you'd know all about them."

"Oh?"

"Yes, sir, he did."

"Sit."

My bum had barely hit the boards before that woman reappeared with fresh conch shells. She placed one beside Round-Bear and handed the other to me. As before, she padded back to her cabin.

I viewed this new brew warily; it appeared different from that last bit of grog, didn't it? More clear, maybe. No floating fibrous filaments, either. Nevertheless, cold caution fingered my heart. Had she drugged me once before with some secret shaman's potion that nearly turned me into a blithering idiot? Boy, was I green to that subject! I had never taken so-called "recreational" drugs of any sort. Moreover, I don't smoke tobacco or weed; only natural and normal air goes into these ol' lungs, and the fresher the better. Excepting a plethora of vitamin supplements, this old dog sticks with select organic foods, healthful wines, and an occasional darkety, dark-dark beer.

"Was that your wife, sir?" I asked to be polite.

"Who?"

"The lady who brought the tea."

"Ummm," he said before draining his drink.

Um, my *toches*, I thought angrily. I didn't come all this way to dance! Come on, come on, I want to know who she was because, because, because — why was I thinking in a language I had never spoken?

Acting on impulse (and perhaps an idiotic show of pseudo bravado), I sucked my conch shell dry, too. Wow! This new brew slammed into my stomach like a blowtorch — but only for a moment. In a flash, I felt much, much better all around, albeit a bit more sociable.

"I have some Apache tea in my van," I announced for no particular reason. "Nino dream-taught[20] me to ask the spirit of each chaparral bush for its gift of certain leaves — not just any leaf — because only those that it gives up willingly will do good. He said too that I should give them gentle tugs. I should try others if the plant holds on too tightly. In fact, I should never bruise or needlessly damage any plant that I have asked to help me. He said that they cry out, but only special people can hear them."

"Ummm," he murmured again.

"Nino didn't say it, but I'm sure he meant that gentle process of harvesting their gifts applies to any leaf, flower, fruit, root, bark, or berry whose life force would be absorbed when we eat it."

"Ummm."

"Nino said too that the wisest of True Human Beings always speak to any animal whose life they have taken. They introduce themselves before its spirit leaves its body. That way it knows that its death is not in vain or just for human vanity. He said those who kill only for heads or horns or claws or skins are weaklings who pretend to be macho. Most are cowards

---

[20] Nino was appearing frequently in my dreams — usually "waking dreams." Was it my imagination or only wishful thinking? No matter. The lessons were clear.

at heart who are nothing without their weapons. He said none would battle their victim mano-a-mano; you know, hand-to-hand."

I cranked up my volume when a scant suggestion of a nod accompanied another "Ummm."

"He believed too that no part of any animal should be wasted; before the white men came, the red man wasted nothing; oh, look-look, there they go again," I exclaimed. Those marble-like words were again flowing out from my mouth, but this time they went straight into Round-Bear's ear! Perhaps it was coincidence, but he chose that moment to lift his head to peer my way. His black eyes glittered and his stare burned through my skull and into my brain. As strange, he spoke not with his mouth but with his mind.

"Victor Osceola made his own bad luck, you know."

I was astonished to hear my own mind-voice reply, "How do you mean, Round-Bear?"

"He trusted a Deceiver."

"No, sir, I did *not* deceive him," I thought-yelled back. "He'd invited me to his home! We'd planned to do lots of stuff together; good stuff, damn it!"

"It was before you," his mind-voice replied soothingly.

"Well, he was a troubled young man; he was suffering. It's not fair that he was driven to that!"

"No one can escape their problems, not ever. So now, he must wait for another body before he can try again. Next time he will have more tests; he will have more problems to learn from."

"I don't understand, sir."

"We are all born equal in our First Life. We are now what we have earned to be, both good and bad, after many tries. Our fate is in our hands alone."

"How can that be? What about little babies who are born without arms or legs or are blind and starving? Those are not equal opportunities!"

"Maybe those bodies contain souls who in times past had cut off arms and legs from others or had blinded them. Now they are what they have earned to be. We all are. Our faraway brothers call this 'karma,' " he said before grunting "Umm, yes!"

My mind was spinning too fast to make even the smallest retort, so he continued.

"If the gift of a strong body, intelligence, and good health are wasted or do evil, the next life brings bad limbs, slowness of thought, and sickness. If you are vain and arrogant, you must learn what it is to be unhandsome. However, if you are kind to all things great and small, you are on the Path that leads Home. This is the way of truth; it is a turning of the Wheel."

"Then deformed and crippled people deserve to be that way?"

"What better way to teach understanding than to experience the pain and sorrow that you have caused? Life is a mirror of unerring clarity; you become what you have been; you receive what you have given."

"But what if people are insane when they do cruel things? Certainly, Hitler and Stalin could not be considered normal!"

"Insanity is a lesson in and of itself, is it not?" he said smoothly.

A flood of tumbling thoughts flitted through my mind. I recalled the eyes of inmates at an Ohio state mental institution where I had once worked as an attendant. Most were frightened at their situation, but others were furious and thus dangerous; and yet all — each and every one — had a lingering sadness.

"What is a Deceiver, please?" I asked to change the subject.

Always frugal with words, Round-Bear began to recite his version of our genesis and our destiny. It went something like this: the Early People[21] had lived on this earth uncountable years before we came.

---

[21] The uninformed call them the Sasquatch, Bigfoot, Yeti, etc. They are better called the Giant Forest People.

Being large, hairy, and strong, those Early People did not require fire or clothing to survive. They lived in harmony with nature's cycles of life, death, and rebirth. No life — no matter how lowly — was taken for pleasure; nothing taken for food was wasted or disrespected.

This changed when the souls of the first True Human Beings were brought here by our guardian Keepers.[22] Those souls had been banished from their faraway home because they were disruptive, covetous, mean, and violent. They were sentenced to remain in exile until they earned the right to return through being kind and peaceful. Being slow learners, their numbers have swollen into the billions while others earned their passages home.

Upon arrival, the soul of each new exile is given an earth body that mimics those of the Early People. However, not being so big or hairy, the exiles had to clothe themselves in the skins of animals; they also tamed fire. Some chose to wear differently colored body-skins to signal their clans of origin, their crimes, their punishments, and their rewards. None was superior to the others.

Both violent and prideful by their flawed nature, those first True Human Beings made weapons for war and conquest. When not attacking one another, they murdered snakes and insects for daring to crawl within their reach, fish for being bold enough to swim nearby, and birds brave enough to fly above their heads. They also ravaged plants and neglected to thank them for providing sustenance.

Keepers seldom interfere. Thus, each exile must stay on earth until they choose to love and respect all things great or small and to live in peace one among the others. Only then might they hope to return to their true home, each in their turn.

As is the natural way on earth, the vessels to all things great or small live and die, including the physical bodies of humans. However, the soul-

---

[22] Both Nino and the Cochitis used this term. They also referred to Keepers as "Star People."

spirits of True Human Beings are destined to linger in a sort of limbo while awaiting another "body-car" that fits their destiny.

However, the Pretenders also made their appearance in the earliest of times. These tricksters possess no souls of their own and they are devoid of the emotion we call love. When their body-cars die, they vanish into nothingness. Angry that they have no future and no past, they have little cause to be kind, generous, or truthful. Instead, they exploit everything to its maximum no matter the cost or consequence to themselves or to others.

While some Pretenders flaunt their evilness to strike fear in their victims, others are masters of deception. To deflect suspicion of their true nature, some artfully imitate human emotions while others conjure false gods, demons, or devils while preaching empty love; they intimidate the weakest among us while luring the hopeful with phony credos to worship, obey, and to serve them... or "burn forever."

Round-Bear added that True Human Beings are often duped into serving the Pretenders while others follow them by choice. In return, they are permitted to bask in the reflection of their master's power. For their perfidy, they pay a heavy price. The warnings about "An eye for an eye, a tooth for a tooth" are true and prophetic.

I cradled my spinning head. Early People, Keepers, True Human Beings, Pretenders, and Deceivers; my skull wanted to explode.

"Okay, okay," I blurted. "But how can I tell a Deceiver from a Pretender?"

"Pretenders express greed rather than kindness; they ignore the pain of others. They smile with their lips but never with their eyes; they gather more earthly things than they can use."

"And a Deceiver?"

"They imitate their masters, but sometimes they slip and show true caring." Round-Bear pinched my arm. "Remember that this is not the real you. This is only another body-car your soul drives through life to take you another step closer to going home."

"But I would not want to go without my daughter. Also my family; oh, hell's bells, I'd want the whole world to go with me. And what about you? Would you go alone?"

Instead of replying, Round-Bear returned to nicking that mysterious little object he still clutched in his hand. It didn't matter now. I was forced to close my ears and seal my mouth because the effects of his magical tea were again mastering my physical being. Increasingly numb, I sat staring at the magnificent patterns and grains of the wooden planks upon which I sat; they chronicled that tree's entire life. If read correctly, they reflected its struggle through wet, dry, cold, and hot times until it was felled — murdered — at a woodsman's hand. Why must it die before its time? Was it only so we could sit upon it? If that was so, then I was sad. How it must have screamed while the woodsman cut it down. Deaf and ignorant, he probably never heard its pleas for mercy.

Was in seconds, minutes, or hours before I heard a human voice — was it my own? — asking my host the why of it all. It was odd, so odd, to listen with my new awareness to an apparatus that required the inhalation of air through nasal passages that were lined with bristly hairs and mucus and into those blood-lined sacks we call lungs; it seemed so animalistic! I became conscious too that my exhaled air must pass through thin rubber-band-like chords in my human throat that quivered like tiny vanes until they created sounds, basic sounds that we were taught were vowels and consonants. I was fascinated to watch those sounds fusing together into words that formed sentences as each entered the outer world through my rubbery lips. It seemed so strange and bizarre to hear my voice bleating, gagging, and gurgling, and my skin felt akin to the confining folds of a deep-sea diver's wet suit.

Yes, yes, of course I knew that I was still seated in Round-Bear's chickee. I knew it because I could see him gazing at me with those soulful eyes, but why was his body changing? It was all in my imagination, I was sure, but I could see through his clothing and my gaze penetrated his flesh. I saw his skeleton supporting his organs, muscles, and tendons. I watched his stomach contracting to send his nearly digested foods deeper into his intestines where it was massaged and absorbed; I saw his heart pumping blood through arteries that fed veins and capillaries; I saw where teeth were missing and a bone or two had been broken, and I watched him swallowing his excess saliva.

Too weak to move now, I wanted so much to close my eyes to sleep it off, but my mind would not shut up. Murmurs, mutters, and garbled screeches issued out from the wispy shadows that encircled me — but then they stopped and an unnatural silence fell like a smothering wing and somewhere deep below I felt an all-powerful humming. I forced my eyes wider to find that I was on a hillock overlooking a deep valley that stretched toward a faraway line of sharp red cliffs. I sensed too that I was amid a vast crowd but, before I could turn to look about, I glimpsed a distant figure darting, scrambling, and clawing its way through the thick brush, bushes, and brambles that lined a maze of crisscrossing coulees. Why was that figure familiar to me? Could that be the newly dead Victor Osceola? No, no, of course not — *yet it was*! And all along his torturous path — no matter which way he dodged — hordes of grotesque figures popped up to reach for him, to snatch at him, to frighten him back toward those faraway cliffs. Just as fantastic, three shiny orbs shot up and over the horizon as if to follow behind him like shepherds. From time to time, they would fire light balls down. Each barrage turned him left and then right and then left again as if to herd him away from the larger packs of demons.

I leapt to my feet, shouting, "Victor, Victor! This way, this way!" until my throat went raw and hoarse, yet he didn't hear me… somewhere behind me I sensed but did not see some great and beautiful beacon beginning to pulse as if to light his path toward sanctuary. With it came a great cheer from that unseen crowd. "This way, this way! Come home, come home!" But, dear Victor, confused Victor, sad and weary Victor gave up — in less than a heartbeat, it all dissolved into a billion shattered shards.

I awoke from my dream amid the lengthening shadows of Round-Bear's chickee. Drenched in sweat, I tried to stand but couldn't find my legs. I lay staring up and into the rafters. Through the dusky darkness I saw mullein, arrowroots, clusters of saw palmetto and cabbage palm berries, sprigs of chicory, strips of bark and pods of seeds, prickly nettles, and many more that I did not recognize. However, instead of being dry and lifeless, they seemed so very kind and their glowing spirits — then plants do have spirits — sort of smiled down at me. I was content to rest there.

Was it moments or hours later that I was roused by the sound of a turtle shell rattle, the scent of smoldering sweet-grass, the whisking of my body by an anhinga feather fan, and a familiar voice saying, "You go now?" I turned my aching head to find a different Round-Bear squatting beside me. His face was streaked with white, green, black, yellow, and blue paint, a brilliant yellow scarf encircled his neck, and his head was crowned with a bonnet of white egret feathers. The tea lady knelt at my feet, as aloof and elegant as ever in her velvet blouse and her long skirt of many colors. Keeping time with Round-Bear's rattle, she echoed the rhythmic heartbeat of Mother Earth on a small water drum. Perhaps it was by suggestion — it didn't matter — but I felt stronger with each thump of the drum as if it was teaching my heart how to beat again in harmony with life.

Placed beside me was a low wooden stand that had been carved in the shape of a crescent. Its twin points were joined by a single curved groove. Within the fold of that crescent lay a bundle of fresh cypress sprigs cradling the tiny object that Round-Bear had been shaping. The greatest of its three images was a fierce face with pursed lips; the one below it was more humanlike. The third and last face was perfect and beautiful.

The drumming halted and Round-Bear set his rattle aside to help me to my feet.

"I dreamt that I saw my friend," I said as he nudged me to my van. "He was trying to run through a valley of mazes but all sorts of things wouldn't let him get out. Was that true?"

"Did you see it?"

"I think I did. I don't take drugs, not ever, you know. I don't drink all that much, either. I can get meaner than week-old cat dirt when I drink."

"Good idea," he said while pushing me into the driver's seat. Tapping my chest over my heart, he said, "This never lies if you know how to listen." Then he tapped my temple. "This lies a lot."

He tucked that tiny carved figure into my breast pocket, saying, "No one can hurt you now — except you, my brother. Maybe *sukee-tommasseh* will send *Eh tey hah'-ta* to show you where to bury her until it is time to go Home again. Until then, beware of the Pretenders."

I looked down the pitch-black tunnel of tangled vines and brush that marked my way home. "Maybe I should stay tonight. Maybe tomorrow I could ask you — hey! Round-Bear? Hello?"

I looked this way and that; I looked up and down! Damn it! He had been standing right there — whoa! That sly old dog was poling his canoe into the Everglade's night. The lady had gone, too.

I sat awhile thinking, listening, and letting my heart thump and pump about within my chest. Frankly, I was scared spitless; I did not relish leaving the magic circle of Round-Bear's camp. I had to invent the courage to drive away. However, the further I traveled, the more relaxed I became. In fact, I was quick to convince myself that, because I had been drugged, everything that I had seen, heard, or thought was the result of that old conjurer whispering in my ear. Yeah, sure, there was the answer! It was all delusional and triggered by my expectations and his insinuations. He told me what to see and to think and I bought into it, I'll betcha, betcha, betcha.

"Hocus-pocus, domin-ocus, and *shazam*," I laughed aloud. "Old Round-Bear might pull that hoogity-boogity stuff on his Indian pals, but those dudes ain't never seen Broadway." Suddenly I was slammed by such a terrible shriek that I nearly skidded into the black waters of the Everglades before my VW's engine sputtered out. Please, God, Allah, Yahweh, Adonai, Ain Soph, Osiris, Buddha, Jehovah Elohim, Peter Cottontail, Donald Duck, or whoever, don't let my engine explode now — *like hell*! A busted engine is child's play when compared with... with what? I ticked off other possibilities. Could it have been a pissed-off Florida panther, had I ran over the tail of a monster raccoon, or was it some banshee that was taking up residence within my half-fried brain?

Okay, I had no choice. I must check that engine no matter how dark it was out there.

I found my flashlight and was about to jerk my door handle when a second scream nearly blasted me from my seat. I twisted my ignition key — it worked! Even my engine seemed glad to start, so we rammed the hell out of there, each hoping that no alligator would be dumb enough to block our way. One of us would be dead meat!

I looked back once through my rearview mirror. Say what you want and think what you will; I would swear the lane that led back to Round-Bear's camp shimmered for one stuttering heartbeat.

Photo by Robert Morgan

Robert Tiger

8. Three Tough Tigers

Miccosukee Reservation
Tamiami Trail, Florida, 1972

My Tiger stood poised in the prow of our canoe, each nerve taut, every muscle tensed to strike. I made another stealthy thrust with my paddle to knife us into a black water lagoon choked with arrowroot spikes and hyacinth pads. A fat water moccasin bellied out of sight to our right; to our left a bullfrog dove for the muddy bottom without a croak.

A turn of my paddle eased us about until the silhouette of my Tiger and her pronged spear became etched like a statue against the blaze of another tropical sunset. Whispers of feathered wings flicked my attention up to where a squadron of snowy egrets waved away toward some secret roost. Her quick chin-jut ordered us through a maze of grey cypress knees that hunched together like watery tombstones. Wary of bloodsucking insects, I gave wide berth to a stand of maleleuca trees that were being smothered by moon vines and a scattering of bromeliads and ghost orchids — her hiss froze my paddle in mid-stroke. *Swishhhh-splash!* Donna Tiger's spear plunged into the water to quiver until she flipped a huge garfish into our canoe. I held my breath as that yard-long monster flipped, flopped, and slithered back until it lay between my feet. My toes instinctively curled inside my thin canvas sneakers while I thumbed through my mental dictionary. *Garfish: Any of several large predaceous freshwater ganoid fishes with hard enameled rhomboid*

161

scales and rank, tough flesh. In plainer terms: this was one badass prehistoric flesh-eating mutha that had the reputation of tasting like smoked monkey peckers.

"Looks like my brothers got the fire down to cookin' coals just in time," Donna Tiger said. "We'd better go in before it's too dark to see the snakes," she added with an impish grin.

Two plump water birds skittered ahead of the canoe as if to guide us to shore. I saw the flash of their white bills and recalled the Florida Cracker's rhyme to distinguish coots from the common mud hen: *White snoot — it's a coot! White snoot — it's a coot!*

That fish lay staring at me, its long teeth snapping a scant inch from my left foot. I watched its gills flex and pulse as if begging for water that would never come. I felt pity for this creature. Moments earlier, it had been an integral part of nature's scheme; now it was drowning in air. I wanted to toss it back, but that would not do. Donna's spear had created a gaping wound that was seeping blood. If the alligators didn't nab it, the wounded fish would die an agonizing death from the myriad of diseases that thrived in these mucky waters.

I attempted to make my peace. I whispered my name to introduce myself. It stopped snapping when I said that it would bring honor to me when its body became part of my own. It wriggled closer until its snout came to rest against my canvas sneaker. Yes, yes, I agree that most likely, it was losing consciousness and my imagination was attaching an illogical and anthropomorphic rationale to a random act committed by a creature in its death throes. On the other hand, perhaps that fish was wiser than I was to the realities of life. Perhaps it was accepting its place in the cycles of life and death. Whatever it was, my toes relaxed, but another old bugaboo returned to haunt me. Why must there be terror and pain attached to this constant turning of the Wheel of Life? Could not a truly loving and benevolent Creator have found a more humane way to sustain us all? Why was a violent death of one creature necessary to sustain the life of another, be they plants or animals? I have seen wild African buffalo devoured by lions while still alive. What had those buffalo done to our Creator to deserve that horror? Why —?

"My dad does that," Donna said.

"Does what?"

"He says stuff just like you did, especially after he's been hunting or fishing. It's the traditional way. That's neat."

A cruising alligator swerved its knobby snout toward us in the gathering gloom. Perhaps it scented fish blood. Paying no mind, Donna hopped into the shallows and tugged the prow of the canoe onto the bank. She stuck one finger through that gar's gills, strode into the light of the nearby campfire, and tossed it directly onto its hottest coals. Slap-crack-whiz! Embers flew everywhere as her victim flip-flopped back to cooler ground. Her brother Robert cracked its head with a stick and kicked it back only to have it flop out again. Young Spencer solved that problem with a rock.

"*Cheehan-toomo*," Robert chirped at me with a lop-sided grin. "You hungry?"

"Are you sure you can eat that thing? I've heard fishermen call them a trash fish. They leave a mess of them all along the canal banks."

"Aw, don't listen to those citified worm-drowners, black or white," he grumbled. "Don't they know gar meat's better than bass or sunfish or mollies or even a big bullhead!"

"Gar's got no parasites like all the rest of 'em, especially those dumb bass," Donna added. "And no matter how you cook 'em, catfish always tastes muddy." She sneaked a wink at me while squatting beside her youngest brother. "Spencer had to come along tonight because he's too scaaaaared to stay alone."

"Am not!"

"That's because he's only tennnnnnnn."

"That's a big fat lie, Donna!" he yelled. "I'm almost thirteen and you're going to Hell if you keep lying, pastor said so."

"Then you're still only twellllve."

"My birthday is only 10 weeks and four days away and you'd better remember it!"

"What do you want for your birthday, Spencer?" I asked.

"He wants to kiss girrrrls," Donna said while making smacking sounds with her lips.

"You're disgusting," Spencer moaned. To me he said, "I want a .22 rifle with a scope, six boxes of hollow-points and... and Robert's hunting knife."

"That'll be the day," Robert grunted.

"You told me I could have it this year!"

"You'd only cut your whistle off."

"He'd have to find it first," Donna chortled.

"Okay for you guys! I'll just go on home right now and when Mom and Dad get back from town I'll tell them what you're doing out here and you'll get bad luck just like that old drunk who drove his car into the pond over there and drowned or maybe you'll shoot yourself like Victor did — hey!"

Donna curled a fist beneath his nose.

"You shut up about that 'bad luck' stuff! It's not funny! And just maybe he'll come back to see you some night..."

Spencer suddenly made himself useful by flipping our fishy victim over to expose its charred scales. Come about, I thought! No one had cleaned it! They were cooking it guts and all.

"Can't clean gar," said Robert-the-mind-reader.

"Aw, everybody knows you can't clean gar," Spencer giggled.

"I tried it once," Donna said. "Couldn't even get my knife into its belly. That's why the old-time Indians cooked 'em this way." She pulled a switchblade knife from her jean's pocket, snapped it open, and flipped it at me. It sank point-first into a chunk of firewood that lay inches from my ankle. "Want to try?"

"Hey, if a Tiger says it, I'll believe it," I said.

She eyed the folding Buck knife on my belt.

"Can I see it?"

I handed it over; she shaved a strip of arm fuzz. Satisfied, she handed it back.

"That wouldn't do it, either," Spencer assured me. "It would take that big honkin' knife that Robert's gonna give me to cut up gar."

"Hush up!" Robert growled. "Mister Morgan needs to hear how the Everglades comes alive about now."

As if on his cue, thousands of beetles and bugs began whirring around us while bullfrogs belched a bumpy tune. This untamed opus was punctuated with an occasional *kwawk* of a hunting night heron and the *ch-ch-chirring* of fussing raccoons. Somewhere behind us, a quick splash and the crunching of a turtle shell signaled that the alligator had snagged a snack.

I watched Robert's face as he stared into the flames. He was a pensive sort who sought the deeper meanings in everything around him. Spencer adjusted his arms and expression to mimic his older brother's posture and countenance; if Robert sniffed, so did Spencer.

Donna was different from her brothers. She never stopped scanning the shadows that lurked beyond the rim of our firelight. In times past, she would have been a woman-warrior to be reckoned with. She impressed me, but so did her kin. These young Tigers were each slender in build with perfectly proportioned features, cheekbones, and well-formed ears with long lobes. They were quick to smile and slow to frown. I wondered how many wars, famines, and epidemics had determined which among their ancestral genes would survive; after all, they were the sum total of uncounted generations.

This led to a graver question: did they realize that the future of their gene pool rested solely in their hands?[23] Would they allow the current craze for sameness to destroy forevermore their distinct lineage? Perhaps, because of the Utopian teachings by pasty-faced theoretical sociologists, they might be tempted to dilute their genetic heritage and help to doom their race to disappear forever within some vast melting pot. Why was it deemed wrong, arrogant, or antisocial to wish to belong to something specific in a way that honors all those who came before? Why was it wrong to — Robert's voice yanked me back fireside.

"Our friend — you know who — said he'd heard you on the radio talking about seeing one of those Giant People somewhere out west. I guess that's why he called you, huh?"

Donna and Spencer leaned closer. I knew what was really being asked, so I repeated my story start to finish. When I began describing those eerie feelings I had just before my encounter, Spencer let out a groan.

"Boy, oh, boy, are you in for some bad luck if you looked 'em in the eye! You should never look 'em in the eye!"

"Why? What's wrong with that? You ever see one?"

"Who, me? Nuh-uh, man! Don't want to, neither!"

"Mom hit one with her car just last winter," Donna said, poking the gar's carcass with a stick. "She backed into it. I was late for school—"

"Donna's late for everything," Spencer assured me.

"She had to drive me over to where we catch the bus. She'd backed out of our driveway real fast, you know, and we whammed into something big. It was like hitting a big soft tree."

"If we missed the bus, she'd have to drive all the way into Miami," Robert explained.

"Did you see anything?" I asked.

"It was still dark; besides, I was too scared to look around. Mom did,

---

[23] Only Robert had purely Indian children. Donna never marred and died childless from diabetes, a disease all too common among Native Americans.

though. Then she floored it out of there."

"Maybe it was a dog?"

Donna shook her head so hard her hair whipped her face.

"We don't play around with stuff like that!"

"Mom and Dad are traditional that way," Robert said. "They don't ever make stuff up, especially when it comes to those Wild Ones."

"Dad sure didn't like it when Mom showed him the blood and the hair, though," Spencer laughed.

"What? Blood *and* hair? Please, please tell me she kept them!"

"Are you kidding?" Spencer snorted. "They got hosed off real quick."

"What about hair? All I need is one strand to make a match to what I already have…"

"Dad took it out and hung it in a tree out behind the house," Robert said. "He stayed up all night singing sacred songs, too."

"Why did he do that?"

All three Tigers stared at me as if I were stupid.

"So its owner could get it back, that's why," Robert said. "I got a whiff of it, though. It smelled just like them Ewash-shak-chobees. It was them, all right."

"Supper's ready," Donna announced while knocking the garfish carcass clear of the embers. A tube of pearly-white meat was revealed when she peeled away the charred scales. She scooped out its solidified guts with her fingers and flipped them into the fire — no muss, no fuss.

Spencer snatched a big chunk and popped it into his mouth. "Tell you what," he said between chews and swallows, "if you guys keep saying their names, your gonna get bad luck just like Victor — ow, ow, ow!"

"Keep it up and he'll come back to pull your toe," Donna hissed with a big pinch.

"*Nuh-uh*! Besides, I'm sleeping with Robert's knife," the boy chirped while tucking his feet for safety.

It was my turn to try the gar, and was I surprised! Its flesh was tender, sweet, and decidedly unfishy. I said so, too, but then moved to bring the subject back dead center.

"If your Mom hit one with her car, what's the chance they might not come back for a while?"

"They're here now," Donna said in a whisper.

"They're always around this time of the year because some of our elders sort of meet with them in sacred ways," Robert added in hushed tones.

"How?"

"That's shaman-business," he said.

"So what was one doing in your driveway?"

"Maybe he was waiting to follow Donna when she walked to the bus in the dark. They'd do that to protect her, you know."

"From what?"

He shrugged again, saying, "We don't have much trouble with 'gators, but you never know, especially when it gets colder and they like to bulk up. Or an old panther looking for an easy meal, maybe."

"I can always tell when they're watching me," Donna added.

"But they've never really bothered you, right?"

"No, but sometimes I feel like somebody's looking in at me when I'm in the shower at night. I know it isn't Spencer because I plugged the keyhole and our bathroom window is way too high up for shorties like him."

"Yuk!" spat Spencer. "I wouldn't be looking at *you*!"

"Describe those feelings, Donna, please?"

"It's like when you know somebody's looking at you but you can't catch 'em at it; it's that sort of stuff. You really know it's there by the smell, y'know? It's sort of like sour oil, but it ain't near as bad as that one white guy in Miami says. They don't smell anything like a skunk and they ain't apes; he's a liar. It's not a stink, either; it's just different.

"One night their smell stayed around so long that Robert even went out to look around."

"*I* would have gone, too, if you'd woken me up," Spencer chirped.

Robert laughed so hard he sprayed chunks of fish.

"Yeah, right, Spencer! You won't even go pee outside if it's dark!"

"No, sir, no, sir! I'll pee anytime I want! I'll pee right on that old Chobee's toes if he stands still long enough!"

"Then go do it right now."

"Where?"

"Over there where it's dark. It's gotta be dark or it won't count!"

"I-I-I don't have to go yet."

"Hey, if you're not brave enough to go in the dark, then you're not big enough to get my knife!"

Brave little Spencer marched off to the nearest bush that bordered our fire's rim light. He had hardly turned his back before Donna whizzed that gar's skull past his head to hear him yelp.

"Some of our uncles talk about seeing 'em, you know?" she said. "Buffalo Tiger — he's the Chairman of our tribe — and his brother Jimmy, too; they've seen them lots of times. Dad said Jessie Bert saw 'em out at Smallpox Tommy's camp one time, too."

Robert added, "See, we use those ugly old BIA houses for wintertime, but we'd rather sleep out in our chickees... until they show up. Then nobody sleeps outside except the old people. They ain't scared of nothin'."

"Some of our elders put stuff out for them," Donna said.

"Like peace offerings?"

"Naw, that's all movie crap," Robert bristled. "We never fought them! See, this was their country after the Calusa People left and that was way before the whites drove us out of our homes up north. When we got here, they say the Sha-wan-nook-chobee helped us learn how to make it in the 'glades, so now we share with them as we would with any friends, you know? That's the Indian way.

"Know what else? If you try trading them white man's food, they'll never touch it. Even if you hang out a deer, they still won't mess with it unless it's offered in the right way. Dad says that it takes years and years to make them trust you."

"Then they never steal food from your gardens or go through your garbage?"

Robert laughed.

"They ain't garbage pickers and they ain't thieves either. We leave potato chips and pickles and things on our picnic table all the time and if anything is gone it's either 'coons or birds — or Spencer."

"They trade other stuff with our elders, though," Donna added.

"'Stuff,' as in…?

"I think it's certain herbs and roots and leaves; stuff like that. It's not that they can't get it themselves, but it's sort of their way of sharing, you know?"

"I know some so-called Bigfoot researchers put out hamburgers and sardines and junk like that, so that's good to know," I said while scooping up a glob of garfish roe.

Robert stayed my hand.

"Better not."

"Oh, hell, I love caviar…"

"Some say gar eggs are poison."

Spencer came strutting back to the fire.

"See that? I peed in the dark, didn't I?"

"Yeah, but you got your sneakers wet," Donna said.

"Did not! That's only dew! Wanna smell? Do ya, do ya?"

Robert took my roe and offered it to Spencer.

"Here, try some."

Spencer eyed it warily.

"Uh, that's okay. You can have mine."

"We already had all we want but we saved some for you," Donna said. "See, you guys? I told you he was still too little!"

Spencer grabbed Robert's hand and sucked the glob off his finger. We three watched but he didn't turn green or puke or even belch, so Robert resumed his story.

"Anyway, when they are here — and they'll be here any time now — they hang around that big old hummock that you were told about. It's maybe a mile just beyond that big old slough. It's supposed to be a sacred burial mound for some old-time shamans, too. Dad thinks that's why the Big People hang out there and feel safe."

"Man, oh, man, Robert! Dad's gonna kill you if you keep telling secrets — *yaugh*," Spencer choked when his brother wrapped his hands over his mouth.

"Then maybe you'd better get your ass home by yourself right now, ass-wipe! G'won! Get going!" he snapped while shoving Spencer toward that long and very dark lane. There were no lights in any direction, and the thick canopy of interlocked pine boughs denied any hope of moonlight or star shine. It was indeed a path of inky blackness.

Swoosh! *Baroooooom*! An alligator whomped water and bellowed somewhere between the Tiger's home and our dead-end-road campfire. Spencer leapt back to grip a log seat with both hands.

"Nuh-uh! No, no, no! I ain't going and you can't make me," he burbled.

"Oh, yeah? Well, if you even *think* about telling on us, you'll never get my knife, understand? Never-never!"

Robert towed me out of earshot.

"I'll take you out, but we have to wait awhile."

"Right! But, why would you do this?"

"I dreamed it. I think I am supposed to — don't ask me again, okay?"

We returned to the fire to speak of other things until we spied the headlights of their father's truck approaching down the lane. My three Tigers hustled home with promises that we would meet again soon.

None of us expected that it would be early on the morrow.

Robert telephoned to claim that he had seen a giant Sha-wan-nook-chobee less than 100 yards from his house. I cancelled every commitment I had and rushed back to the reservation.

Robert and Spencer were uncommonly silent until we arrived at the end of that same lane where we had shared Donna's garfish. Suddenly submissive, Spencer followed yards behind when Robert led me to the southernmost edge of the dead-end road. Beneath a plastic Wonder Bread bag anchored by stones was a single humanlike but mammoth track complete with the dominant hallux, that "big toe" that helps to separate hominids from apes. It was no bear, either; their largest toes are in the center. I hunched down to study the scuffmarks and smudges in the soil and the grass. They clearly led back from the roadside to vanish into the stillest of the watery Everglades. True, too, the dual directions of the bent and broken reeds of saw grass and rushes indicated twin passages, one in and one out. Standing tiptoe, I could see no hint that whatever had passed that way had curved eastward toward the Tiger homestead.

Still and all, single tracks set my teeth on edge. I had been shown such fakes too many times.

I sneaked a quick look at Robert but his brow was furrowed and his eyes were fastened on the horizon to the south. Now I looked more closely at the track itself. A bear certainly had not made it. I measured an 8-inch width at the ball of the foot; it was the widest I had ever found. If real, this track was made by a humanoid and not an anthropoid.

Still, this imprint appeared too damned clean and too damned perfect to stifle my suspicious mind... until I noticed there were tiny rocks fixed into its mud. These rocks were muddy, too — they also contained tinier pieces of humus.

Photo by Robert Morgan

Figure 8: Track near the Tiger's home.

Photo by Robert Morgan

Figure 9: Robert Tiger pointing to the track the Tigers found. The hummock rising behind Robert Tiger became that day's destination.

"What happened, Robert?"

Stepping parallel to the path and several yards further into the reeds, I found similar pebbles had been either flipped over or mashed deep into the soggy earth. These indicated several yards of live movement and immense weight — or some faker was a wise SOB! Another quick glance at Robert confirmed that his attention was totally riveted not on me but on a distant hummock.

"It started up last night right after Mom and Dad left again to go to the Council meeting. Donna was in her room and I was in the kitchen. I had just opened a bag of hotdog buns —"

"And that's when ol' Donna started yellin' that she'd heard something bumping up against the house and she'd smelled it too and I thought Robert was trying to scare us so I came running out of my room to scare him back but he was in the kitchen making hotdogs so we all ran back to listen in Donna's room and, sure enough, we heard it too and that's when we smelled it — boy, did it stink — it was worse than Robert's feet," Spencer said in one breath.

"Did you go outside?"

"I shined a flashlight around the front yard," Robert nodded. "I didn't see anything, but that smell was there and I could just feel that something was out back in those weeds."

"Did you shine your light back there?"

"Dad says we should pretend to ignore them."

"So you didn't go back there?

"No."

"So when did the feeling go away?"

"Right after I'd gone back inside."

"Did you tell your parents when they came back?"

"No."

"Hell, no!" chimed Spencer.

"Then, this morning, Mom told me to put her mail out in our box. That's when I saw him. He was even tipped forward like he was about to cross the road but he froze when he saw me looking."

"Where's Donna now?"

"She left with Mom and Dad to go somewhere in town. I think they're going to a movie tonight."

"Okay, so let's think about this: had either of you two gone outside before you saw it?" The brothers wagged their heads in unison. "Did Donna go out earlier?"

The brothers shrugged.

"Did you tell anyone else about what we'd talked about last night?"

"No."

"Spencer?"

"No way!"

"Where's your mailbox? I can't see it from here."

"It's behind that one big tree way down there. Look, see how you can see the road? I put the mail in the box and started back across when I felt something, you know? I can't say what it was, but it made me stop in the middle. Maybe I saw it out of the corner of my eye, I don't know. That's when I looked down here and I saw what I thought was just some big old black man fishing, you know, like they do."

"You get a lot of non-Indian people doing that?"

"More than you'd expect. They don't seem to know they are on our reservation, you know?"

"What then?"

"He kind of froze. I think if he hadn't done that, I would have thought he was just another guy, like I said. But, he froze like he knew he'd been caught doing something. He had one foot on the road as if he was just coming out of the water and he stood real still as if he'd done something wrong. Even his arms were out as if he was about to take another step, you know, but he didn't. He looked at me so hard that I *felt* it. Man, did I feel it — oh, wait! This guy didn't have any clothes on, either."

"Robert was scared shitless," Spencer nodded.

"You keep saying it was a guy. How do you know?"

"I don't. It just seemed like a guy."

"So what did he do then?" I asked.

"He just sort of backed up."

"Fast, slow?"

"It was almost slow motion, you know, like you see in the movies. What was really strange is he didn't turn around! First, he stood still like a statue; then he just kind of rocked back on the foot that was still in the grass while the foot that was on the road just pulled back real slow-like. And then he was just gone. It was like he evaporated."

"Then what?"

"Robert came and got me and we took off," Spencer nodded.

"If we didn't, Mom and Dad would have made us go into town with them and Donna. We waited until they made the turn out before we got to look around. When we found this track, we ran back home to call you."

"Yessir! We ran like hell, too," Spencer nodded.

"You stayed home until I arrived?"

"Yup."

I turned the plastic bread wrapper over in my hands. "Then you just happened to have this in your pocket?"

"Get one, Spencer," Robert said coldly.

Spencer scooted to the opposite side of the road and disappeared among the weeds. In a flash, he reappeared with a torn sack of empty cans, bottles, plastic cups... and a plastic bun bag.

I asked Robert to repeat what he had seen. He did not expand his story nor embellish it. What he described was a naked biped that stood quite tall, had no waistline, and the one knee he could see was slightly bent. This person had wide shoulders and long arms, no discernible neck or facial features, but was covered head to toe with brownish-black hair that had a reddish tinge.

I knelt down to sniff the track; I detected nothing out of the ordinary.

Spencer snorted a laugh.

"Boy, I wouldn't do that if that was Robert's feet!"

We squatted together for a time watching and waiting for an impossible second sighting. The distant hummock that commanded our attention seemed to stare back. As the day began fading toward evening, Spencer got fidgety and began to pace. He was out of earshot before I asked Robert, "How soon can we go out to that hummock you mentioned?"

"I gotta think it out first."

"How about now?"

Robert's shoulders jerked, he sighed; he fidgeted; and sighed again before he waved his brother into my van.

"We're going to take you home, Spencer. Lock the doors and don't open 'em until I give you the signal."

Spencer's eyes went owl-like.

"What are you guys going to do — nooooo! Nuh-uh! You can't — you'd better not…"

Robert unsnapped his knife from his belt and pushed it into Spencer's hands.

"Oh, man, oh, man, oh, man," the boy stammered. "But what if you guys don't get back before Dad calls? He always calls when we're up to something. He's got six senses!"

"Just tell him I'm out somewhere with Mr. Morgan and I'll call him back when we get in, okay? You don't know where we went, either! You know why? Because you don't know!"

"Yes, I do! You guys are —"

"Give back my knife."

"Okay, okay…"

We took a pouty-faced Spencer home and waited until he was inside. I saw him peek out of the window as we roared off into the gathering dusk.

At the first intersection, we swerved a hard left and bounced out onto the Tamiami Trail Highway. Within the mile, we turned left again onto the Loop Road and I hid the van behind an old mission church. I took a pair of military-style flashlights out of my van, switched their lenses from clear to dull red, and tossed one to Robert. We not only didn't want to lose our night vision, we didn't want anyone from the village to spot us. For reasons neither of us understood, Robert and I shook hands before we slogged out toward that distant hummock. As we made our way, Robert nervously yanked up the center stalks of the razor-edged saw grass, bit off the tender milk-white tips, and then tossed the wands aside. He handed one to me. The heart of the saw grass tasted bland, but wherever my saliva touched it, it turned a soft rose color.

"It's starch, they say," Robert explained. "We always hear about hunters getting lost and starving in the glades. How can you starve with all this around? White people sure can be dumb." A small water snake slithered from our path. "See? Lots of food!"

"I've eaten rattlesnakes," I said. "They're not bad. Chickeny, in fact."

"You catch 'em yourself?"

"Yes, but I'll never-ever do that again," I said as I recalled my Gashpeta nights.

"Then why'd you do it?"

"I'd been bitten once when I was a kid in Idaho; I'd developed a real fear of snakes. I wanted to get rid of that feeling so I went to Bob Jenni, the curator of reptiles at the Oklahoma City Zoo. We went to the B-Bar-B Buffalo Ranch in Wyoming where they had a problem with rattlesnakes killing their buffalo. I helped Bob collect prairie rattlers there, but that's before I learned about the Snake People. Now I wish them well and thank them for allowing me to pass through their world."

Robert shot a surprised look back at me.

"I never heard a white guy talk like that! Don't tell Mom or Dad I said this, but they think you must have been an Indian in a past life."

"I think they might be right," I chuckled.

"Don't laugh!"

"I'm not laughing at you, Robert! I am laughing *with* you! I am glad to hear your family has kept the old beliefs alive, that's for sure."

"Yeah, but Dad doesn't want us to talk about it because we'd piss off the preachers and they can give us a lot of trouble through the BIA, you know? They'd go back to calling us heathens and savages again."

"Don't worry; your secret is safe with me."

Robert's pace slowed the nearer we came to the hummock. It was a great deal larger than I had thought. Hummocks are strange and wonderfully mysterious places. Marjorie Stoneman Douglas best described them in her definitive work, *The River of Grass*, that remains to this day as the best of all introductions to the true Everglades. The number of ignorant people who still refer to the Everglades as "that big swamp" always surprises me. Swamps are stagnant waters; the Everglades are far from being stagnant. Although measured in scant inches per day, the Everglades maintain a steady flow of fresh water from its source at Lake Okeechobee in central Florida southward over 100 miles until it finally empties into the Gulf of Mexico through a huge estuary. All across this immense river are islands of higher ground called hummocks or heads. While some hummocks are created by tree seeds that get caught around normal rock protrusions, most are the products of some long-ago alligator that wanted a personal pool to help trap fish during the dry seasons. The rims of mud that were piled up by that alligator's tail soon snagged seeds of the cabbage or sabal palms, the buttonwoods, willows, and the gumbo-limbo trees that dotted a vast prairie of saw grass. Naturally, when those captive seeds sprouted, their roots served to catch even more seeds and, in a few dozen years, a new hummock emerged.

My Tiger pal and I paused to survey our target through the gathering veil of darkness. Nearby were a few purple gallinules, some coots, and one great blue heron, all searching for a safe roost for the night. In the topmost fronds of the hummock's tallest cabbage palm, two anhingas stood guard with their black wings stretched out to drip dry before they too tucked in. To our right an American bittern was sneaking along, its striped feathers blending with the withered stalks around it. The moment I bent my head in its direction, it froze with its head pointed skyward; not a feather moved. It reminded me of something Norman Bates would have had hanging around his office at the Bates Motel in *Psycho* — Robert startled me by making soft hooting sounds. He whispered that the Nook-chobees used birdcalls and insect noises to keep track of one another, and, if one was still hanging around, his hoots might get us accepted as friendlies.

I said nothing, of course, but noted this added reference to the use of birdcalls to communicate. Did every Indian in America have this information embedded into their genetic memories at birth? Had my mother's white blood been enough to cancel my membership, or what? "Why must I learn these dad-blasted things the hard way?" I grumbled to myself.

My mind flitted back to the first time I had encountered this phenomenon. I was leading my second expedition to the base of Mount St. Helens in southern Washington. In a camp not far above Ape Cave, Alan Facemire, a professional cinematographer, and Bob Carr, now the resident archaeologist for the Archaeological and Historical Conservancy of Broward County, Florida, had recorded a strange series of owl-like hoots and barks which began each evening after sunset and continued until well past midnight. The cadence and position of each series made it appear that two or more owls were hunting the canyon rim below us, yet each time we moved to get a confirmation, there would be a single hoot louder than the others followed by dead silence. However, when we would appear to give up and return to our tent, those "owls" would hoot it up again. Back we would go only to begin the game again. Frustrating as...

When George Harrison arrived to chronicle our efforts as published in the 1971 October-November issue of *National Wildlife Magazine*, we played our tapes for him. As the magazine's managing editor and an avid outdoorsman and birder,[24] George had a broad range of experience under his belt, yet he also had been stumped. Later that night, he too heard the calls; they did nothing to solve the mystery. Later, I played those same tapes for Dr. James Butler, the Acting Director at the Corkscrew Swamp Sanctuary for the National Audubon Society. The closest he came to

---

[24] He is an editor for *Birds and Blooms*.

identifying those calls was *Bubo scandiacus*, the snowy owl. This presented two problems: Snowy owls are diurnal so they don't go hooting around at night to confuse lowly humans. Moreover, their hooting grounds are confined to their Arctic breeding grounds. Okay, fine! If no snowy owl in his right mind would be our tormentor, what (or who) was out there *imitating* a horny snowy owl... uh-oh! Could it be even remotely possible that this call had been handed down through untold generations yet first acquired in the primeval past and brought south via migrations — Robert Tiger snapped my attention back to the present by licking the palms of his hands, spreading his arms, and bowing his head. Damn! His pose was identical to Sonny's at Gashpeta!

Before I could ask if he was doing what I *thought* he was doing, he plunged straight into the hummock's dense underbrush and disappeared. I took a deep breath and burrowed in after him. Robert and I made plenty of noise (on purpose) as we thrashed through the fringes of willow and wax myrtle thickets — I froze when something scurried away beneath a thorny aralia. Swiping sweat from the tip of my nose, it took a few moments to pick up Robert's wake.

Feeling claustrophobic among the clutching leaves and vines, I was damned grateful to break into the wide clearing that crowned the hummock's highest ground. I felt better when I snapped on my flashlight to find him waiting there. Its soft red glow also revealed that we had entered a narrow glen set within a grove of buttonwood, gumbo-limbo, and a few white stopper trees. Surrounding us was a seemingly impenetrable wall of low palmetto bushes. I scanned my flashlight beam along the overhead where its canopy seemed stitched shut by a thick maze of drooping bromeliads. I was enchanted to find it was also splashed with dots of wild orchids that clung to all manner of branches and boughs. High in one lysoloma tree my beam found a tree snail that appeared as a single dash mark. Was this the rare *Linguus ornatus*? I slid my beam down to where several blue-mottled *L. barbouri* and one shiny bronze tree snail, *L. castaneozonatus,* were chugging their way up to join some secret snail party.

This magical wonderland dwelled unnoticed less than fifty miles west of downtown Miami; it was a world unchanged over hundreds of thousands or perhaps millions of years. It certainly appeared to be an excellent hideaway for...

"Look!" Robert hissed at me.

Close by were three rectangular piles of coral rocks neatly arranged side by side. I gulped to see old Mason jars arranged to the four cardinal points of the compass: north, east, west, and due south. I slipped past him for a closer look. Each sealing cap had rusted away yet those jars remained partially filled with a murky liquid.

My lips went dry as yesterday's toast. Were these akin to Dee-O-Det's sacred waters? Sweat stung my eyes to tears while I moved into their ring of power. I knelt to peer into the darkest crevices of these burial cairns where I spied bits of faded cloth and fragments of rotting wood.

"For God's sake, don't touch anything," Robert whispered.

"Okay, okay!"

"Maybe we'd better go..."

"We just got here! Let's see if we can find any old campfires or maybe some animal bones or hand-made shelters."

"What's that over there?" Robert croaked while pointing to deep impressions that had been hollowed into a thick carpet of soft humus. These depressions were set in a loose circle — *two of the five depressions had been recently sprinkled with layers of fresh leaves*!

Gently, cautiously, I laid myself down and stretched out in the nearest bed: it exceeded me by two feet or more. These weren't made by the smallish Everglades deer; they would not pluck leafs and fronds to lie on them; besides, deer curl up. I rolled over to sniff at the bed and to run my hands over the dried grasses. Their pungent stench conjured images of thick, dank, and oily hair. This hummock was no panther or bear's haven. Five bears sacking out together happened only in nursery rhymes; the real Ursus clan is notorious for roaming alone except when it's diddle-time.

My search for hair yielded nothing, so I stood up to peer in all directions. Whoever — whatever — used this outdoor bedroom had wonderful peek-a-boo views of all the open areas on three sides of the hummock; all three faced the approaches from the reservation or the roads.

"I don't see any bones or feathers or scraps of food lying around, do you?"

Robert shook his head.

I could easily ignore that. After all, the tropics have an abundance of efficient scavengers willing to claim anything that stops moving. Aside from these depressions, it appeared that nothing outside of the usual small animals had been out here for years...

"Listen!"

I froze at Robert's command. I heard nothing. It was dead silent. One glance at Robert's face and I knew that was his meaning.

"We'd better get back," Robert whispered while backing away.

I had little choice but to follow my guide. After all, I was there at his invitation; still, my inclination was to wait to see if the owners of those beds would come to claim them.

A natural scout, Robert chose to leave that burial hummock on a side at right angles to our point of entry. I assumed that his intent was to stay clear of the prying eyes of the reservation. Instead, we were being drawn along a path that was so wide that our sleeves barely brushed a single branch — then it hit us! It was far too wide and tall to have been made by those short, slender Florida deer or even the fattest of black bears. Robert jerked his chin forward to where our trail exited the hummock. The saw grass lay parted to cross an open prairie.

My Tiger buddy gasped, made an immediate right turn, and bolted straight into the thickest brush. Before I could follow suit, I felt more than heard a quivering low rumble that descended over us like an invisible blanket before rebounding up again. In that same instant an acrid smell of ozone permeated that hummock while a brilliant blue-white light flashed — no, it flickered — for less than a heartbeat to illuminate each tree, bush, stick, and blade of grass around us. I felt it more than saw it; more strangely, it was then that I recalled — if that is the correct term — that when I was in that trancelike state at Round-Bear's chickee, I had caught glimpses of Victor Osceola dodging bolts of that exact sort of light as he was scrambling about in that weird valley. It was then, too, that I had first smelled that ozone-ish odor — Robert's shout spurred me to action.

"Run, run!"

I dove in after him and together we tripped, sprawled, and scrambled off that sacred hummock. Without stopping, we slogged side by side due west through the saw grass prairie like twin human airboats. We paused to catch our breath only when we had crossed that open ground. Chests heaving, sides aching, we swiveled around to stare back at that hummock. The eerie light had vanished as if it had never existed, the earth was not quivering, and the bullfrogs were once again cranking up to full volume.

"Wait, wait, Robert," I gasped. "Let's go back! Come on, Tiger! Let's go back right now, and maybe wait a while longer until —"

"You're crazy, man!"

"Okay, okay — look, I'll sleep in my van tonight and at first light we can try again and —"

"I ain't going anywhere until I see a medicine maker who knows about those sky-lights," he yelled and bolted off again.

"Shit! Sky-lights? What frigging sky-lights?" I yelled while he kept tossing back unintelligible words in his native tongue. I yelled over and over again until he shouted back in English, "Ain't you never heard of lights that come from the sky? I ain't messing with 'em, man! That's bad luck!"

Those words, bad luck, bad luck, bad luck, kept running through my mind until we were safely locked inside my van, and rolling back to the rez.

"Let's get a cup of coffee or a coke or something. Maybe we could get Spencer and build another fire, what do you say? Maybe they'll come back..."

"We really messed up by going to one of their sleeping places! I gotta do the Black Drink or something to get myself straight. Maybe at the Green Corn Dance I can get some help."

"Okay, but let's go back one more time when it's daylight. It's those shadows that spooked us, that's all."

"I-I can't! You won't ever shoot them, will you? Swear to God?"

"You know I won't — and I won't go out there again without you, either."

"Promise?"

"Didn't I just say it?"

I had barely come to a halt beside his driveway before he bailed out, only to lean back to ask, "Betty and me are getting married in a month or two. Can you come?"

"Oh, no! Why didn't you tell me, buddy? I am so sorry! I'm already committed to leave and I have people meeting me on the West Coast."

"Oh..."

"Robert, I am so sorry! Damn, why didn't you tell me? She's such a great girl! Lucky you! Look, I promise we'll get together before I leave, okay? Maybe next week?"

"Yeah, sure. See ya."

I waited until lights were flicking on in every room in the house before I pulled away. I was hoping that those sky-lights didn't notice that

I was alone when I pulled out onto that long and deserted highway that led back to the bright lights of Miami.

9. Born Again Psychic

Miami, Florida, 1972

I was betwixt dog-tired and frenetic by the time I reached my haven of rest. I wanted nothing more than a hot-hot shower and a long flop down, perchance not to dream a single blessed thing. It was not to be. The lovely Reverend Joanne Barton[25] had left an urgent message on my answering machine asking that I rush over to act as a fill-in for a guest whom she feared would arrive too late to make that evening's radio broadcast. Ms. Barton hosted an internationally syndicated program that dealt with not just religious experiences — that would have left me out — but also the more esoteric subjects including ghosts, apparitions, and other purported mystical encounters. Interestingly, she had become fascinated with my adventures with the Forest Giants and we had had fun talking about them both on and off the air.

Indeed, Joanne Barton was unusual in other ways, too, and they were all to the good. She was an open-minded yet devout Christian, all the while being genteel, gracious, accepting, and tolerant of those who saw things differently. She was as elegantly beautiful as the actresses Ingrid Bergman and Deborah Kerr.

Joanne's telephoned message also mentioned that she wanted me to meet her mystery guest because he, too, was intrigued by the Forest

---

[25] Her name has been changed to protect her privacy. Some of her current flock may not appreciate her being associated with my work or my opinions.

Giants. Blahhhhh! I was in no blinking mood to answer 20 blinking questions posed by blinking newbies to that subject. My attitude toward the doubting public had been steadily slipping into that belligerent mode of "You wanna know what I bloody well know, Bubba? Get off your Bubba bum, get your feet soaking wet for a few years, plow through neck-high mountain snow banks, get your eyes swollen shut by itchy-bitchy mosquitoes and no-see-ems, and spend your life's savings to locate evidence that most citified folks refuse to accept because they haven't yet made the library list, and then maybe — just maybe — you'll qualify to share a few of my findings!"

Of course, for all my bluster and bitching, I knew that I would keep those opinions to myself if Joanne Barton's guest showed up.

I returned her call to accept her invitation and, after an infusion of spirits for my spirit — cold, cold vodka — and a quick scrub down, I hit the road to North Miami Beach. Within the hour, I was tap-tap-tapping at the chamber door to her fashionable suite.

Joanne's guest indeed was a no-show — or so it seemed — so she switched the topic of that evening's broadcast to a field of science that I had coined as crypto-anthropology.[26] The hour went fast and, when finished, my hostess served chamomile tea and a platter of ladyfingers.

"Have you ever had an out-of-body experience?" Joanne asked with the bluntness that is shared between friends. My mind flashed back to Round-Bear's chickee and the vision of Victor Osceola's soul darting around and about that weird valley, but decided that I was too tired to go into that.

"Um, er, let's say that I've had some rather enlightening visions."

"But have *you* ever been separated in the spirit?" she asked.

"Do you remember those old Dracula movies where he couldn't be

---

[26] I dislike the arrogant use of the term cryptozoology when applied to the Forest Giants. Zoology implies they belong among the "lesser" creatures on earth rather than as part of the almighty human beings.

seen in a mirror? One night I thought I was passing in front of one in my bedroom but instead of seeing my reflection I saw my body lying asleep on the bed behind me."

"And?"

"The moment I turned around to look I was sucked back into it so hard that it woke me up. Sure enough, I was in that bed and nowhere near the mirror. Some strange dream, huh?"

"And?"

"Well, another time I was apartment sitting in Key West for my attorney pal, Ted Ernst — he was off on some jaunt who the hell knows where — and I'd been sort of meditating that night — no, don't even think it. I had *not* been back to Sloppy Joe's[27] that night, I swear. Anyway, I felt as if I was floating way, way up-up-up out of that apartment building, above the beach, and even above Key West itself. Looking down I could see cars moving around the city, stoplights flicking on and off — the whole nine yards. I got so high up that I could also see a stream of car headlights up the Keys past Tavernier and Key Largo and all the way to Miami. I recall sort of drifting around to look south where I saw the glow of Havana."

"You were floating free?"

"Yes — well, no, not really. I seemed to be tethered to my real body by a long, long string of sorts — it was shiny. But the moment I thought about it and got a little scared, I was zipped back into my corporeal body like I'd been drawn by a rubber band," I said while stifling a yawn. "I'm sorry, kiddo, but it's been quite a day. I think it's time for me to hit the sack."

"No, no, no, Bobby, you can't! Someone is coming just to meet you and he should be here any minute. He wants to talk to you about Bigfoot and UFOs. Reverend Zarley had a huge congregation in Akron, Ohio, right along with Rex Humbard and Ernest Angley when they started out

---

[27] Sloppy Joe's was a favorite Key West hangout for Ernest Hemingway.

— surely, you've heard of them. Isn't Akron close to your hometown —
oh goody," Joanne giggled as the door buzzer buzzed on cue. "See? It's
meant to be!"

My heart turned to ice. How dare she take advantage of our
friendship like that! Had I not cared enough to forgo my private dwell-
time to help her out of her bind — or had it all been a sham to get me
there? To make matters worse, didn't she just say he was some sort of
"Reverend?" Every one of those dinks that I'd met seemed determined to
convert me to their particular take on religion. Pray for this, have faith in
that, but always keep the Sabbath — but only in their particular house of
worship, of course. *Ka-ching!,* more coin in their offering plates...
Besides, without exception they all had bad breath — I gulped when
Joanne ushered in a handsome, trim, and tanned, middle-aged gentleman
dressed in a crispy clean white shirt, linen slacks with razor-like pleats,
and polished Bally loafers. He was so neat and orderly that I wished I
had pressed my Levi jeans.

"Robert, I was sure you'd want to meet the Reverend Doctor Victor
Zarley!"

His hand shot out to give me a firm handshake.

"Please do me the honor of calling me Victor."

"I-um, hullo..."

"You seem a bit surprised. Why?"

"Victor is not exactly as common as Joe or Jim or John..."

"And?"

"And I just lost a friend by that name."

"Lost, as in...?"

"Suicide."

"I'll pray for him, I promise. However, perhaps we should view this
as an omen of sorts that blessed our meeting. You do believe in omens,
Robert?"

"Maybe."

"Well, my apologies for being so late, but so much information was streaming in that I couldn't cut them off. They are very interested in you, Robert."

"I knew they would be," Joanne chirped while bustling off to the kitchen to make fresh tea.

"Were you at a revival meeting, Reverend Zarley?" I asked to be polite.

"It's 'Victor' to my friends, and we will be that, I am sure. As for being tardy, no. I was meditating with my guides."

Oh, crap, crap, *crap*! Now he'll want to sucker me into that "messages from God" stuff to convince me that he's been sent to save my soul. I wondered how long his holly-jolly mood would last if I told him that I suspected the oft-quoted phrase *Unless ye be born again, ye cannot enter the Kingdom of Heaven* had been watered down from *Unless ye be born again and again and again and again…* It is illogical to my plebian mindset that we have but a single shot at redemption for all eternity — that's one hell of a long time. After all, we are each born under such widely differing circumstances and the poorest of the poor, the severely crippled and deformed, the autistic, and the slower-to-learn certainly have more to overcome than those who are born strong, handsome, or wealthy. How in the hell could this be the fair plan of their supposedly loving God?

I wondered, too, if Zarley's formal education had mentioned that the Fifth Ecumenical Council in 553 A.D. concluded that no technical grounds exists that bars the belief in reincarnation for Catholic Christians. Of course, the naysayers had been quick to argue the technical differences between accepting the pre-existence of a soul as opposed to admitting that it might be reincarnated into a succession of differing bodies until we dummies got it right. Their rationale assumed that should members of their flocks suspect that they each have multiple chances at redemption, they might take a time or two to do whatever they chose until it was the last round. Zarley leaned close as if reading my thoughts.

"Shall we begin our friendship by being totally open with one another? I want you to know that I am no longer the dogmatic and somewhat narrow-minded theologian that I was trained to be. I have personally experienced, witnessed, and participated in things that were expunged from the original Scriptures by my predecessors, including the interpretation of the Book of Ezekiel. His encounter was with a space capsule that was manned by those whom we erroneously call aliens — don't look so shocked. Joanne told me a little about your own experiences and that's when I knew we were destined to meet.

"Moreover, the Bigfoot — or, as you more correctly call them, the Giant Forest People — fascinate me in more ways than you could possibly guess."

Nino's earlier warnings returned to whisper in my mind's ear, *Dee-O-Det told me to warn you about those people who only look like regular people, but they aren't. They're the ones who are always trying to snatch your soul so you can't go home, don't ya see?*

Was this fellow a Pretender or one of their deceiving soul snatchers, or just another do-good-feel-good soothsayer?

Whatever he was, I set him straight from the get-go.

"Reverend Zarley — er, Victor — I have no interest or intention of debating religious issues," I said. "Anyone can believe whatever they wish — so long as they don't push it on me."

"Good enough and fairly said!" he laughed. "We are on the same page. I am not here to interrogate or convert you; I am here to share and, perhaps, to learn from you. It's my understanding that you've had some incidents involving unexplained sky-lights that you can't attribute to known aircraft. Joanne said that you've had years of experience around airplanes in the U.S. Navy aboard an aircraft carrier. She also said that you once had the system's certification responsibility to an entire computer complex for the Federal Aviation Administration in Washington, DC."

"Yes and no, sir. The incidents involving aircraft that our controllers could not identify happened at the Air Route Traffic Control Center when we were located at the Washington National Airport. It was after we'd moved our Center to Leesburg, Virginia that I shared the certification responsibility for its operating computer system."

"But you did witness UFOs on federal radar tracking screens in connection with commercial airliners, right?"

"I'll answer that if we agree that this conversation is off the record. I'm having enough trouble convincing folks the Forest Giants are real without more quagmires."

"And that cuts both ways, especially for one in my position," Zarley laughed again. "Most of my former flock and indeed all my closest family members condemn me because they refuse to grasp certain truths.

"Robert, take this as you will, but my, um, let me call them my 'guiding advisors' promised that I would find an ally here tonight. Now that we've met, I can see they were right. Please believe that you can trust me as a confidant and, perhaps, we might help each other."

Had I heard him correctly? Had the Reverend Doctor Victor Zarley used the term "guiding advisors"? Preachers I'd known usually talked about esoteric stuff like angels, saints, sinners, sliders, and devils, but never once had they mentioned just plain guides or advisors. I thought briefly about asking if he had heard of Keepers, Pretenders, and Deceivers, but thought the better of it. After all, I'd only known him for what, 10 minutes?

"Robert, would you mind telling me exactly when your interest in these mysteries really took root?" he asked.

"Which mystery, sir? I was born to ask the why of everything and, when it comes to religion, I usually piss off everyone in sight."

"Let's start with Divine Intervention."

"Well, to be frank about it, I can live with the term intervention; it's the word 'divine' that makes me do a backstroke. I've had a tough time with anything called 'sacred' or 'holy' because these labels were made up by intellectual frauds so they could pretend to have some special insight and label everyone else to be either ignorant or unenlightened. Bull-pucky!"

I waited until Zarley stopped chuckling before I continued.

"I read history, but not just its dates. I know there was a time when the Holy Roman Catholic Church made it a sin for anyone to know how to read or write unless they were priests or monks. Many kings were illiterate and their commands were written by their priests; how many men and women were literally burned alive if they so much as owned a book? What was the Vatican afraid of? Literacy, that's what! And why? They had to keep people ignorant or they couldn't rule them in that ignorance.[28]

"Here's another question that I've often asked but have yet to get a decent reply: Why doesn't this God, who supposedly made us all, just speak clearly and openly with his creations? What's with all this secrecy and mystery and mumbo-jumbo about burning bushes and things that go bump in the night? And why speak to the masses only through so-called prophets? Aren't we all created equal? So treat us that way! It would be so easy; just open the sky up once each generation so that all people on earth, literate or illiterate, can see their Creator. Why doesn't this Creator speak in pictures to everyone from the Jivaro Indians to the Pope so they all can understand the message? If those pictures commanded that all wars, crimes, cruelties, and abuses must stop or else the wrongdoers would be zapped on the spot, what would happen? Now *that's* what I'd call Divine Intervention!

"Secondly, why does this so-called loving God create badly crippled or starving children while others are fat and perfect? Oh, we all know

---

[28] The film *The Name of the Rose* gives an illuminating glimpse into those Dark Ages.

that clichéd answer: 'God works in mysterious ways.' Well, that's for sure — except I would use the words baffling, cruel, distant, and discriminatory!

"As to the Christian Bible, the Torah and its Mitzvoth d'oraita,[29] the Koran, the Book of Mormon, or any purportedly inspired scripture, just because these collections are old doesn't make them wiser. It seems to me that too many preachers and prophets want us to spend our lives walking backward. The ta-dah surprise is that we can easily grasp all they claim to know. They are not special; we just choose to be lazy thinkers. I found more truth in Cabbala, the Zohar commentary, the ten Sephiroth, and the Sefer Yetzirah than in the Christian Bible. I have no problem thinking for myself and on my own, but that is exactly what most organized religions fear the most.

"Victor, may I ask you a yes-or-no question? Would you trust the future of your soul on the word of anyone who would allow a parent to be murdered so they could gain power?" Zarley's cautious nod prompted a second question. "Do you use the King James version of the English Bible, sir?"

"It's been a standard for centuries but it is being revised…"

"But it forms the basis even for those revisions, right? Well, the Good King James was the son of Mary, Queen of Scots. Mary had been held prisoner by her cousin, Queen Elizabeth of England, for what, 15-16 years? Elizabeth promised James that he would become her chosen successor to the throne of England but only if he would not interfere when she had his mother's head chopped off. Do I have that right? Yes?

"Sorry, pal, but I wouldn't take that man's word for a damned thing, most especially a Bible he authorized that rails against bearing false witness and murder while preaching that we should honor our mothers

---

[29] The Jewish Oral Law that contains 613 commandments that guide Jewish life.

and fathers and not be covetous![30] Your Good King James was a bloody hypocrite who assisted by consent in the murder of his mother for personal gain. I wouldn't believe him if he told me the time of day!

"Now as to the Second Commandment about not making or worshiping graven images, I see Christians groveling about in front of 'graven' statues of Yeshua, Miriam, and all sort of saints; that's hypocritical to the core and I'll have none of it. If I need help from God, I'll go directly to the source."

"Do you consider yourself an atheist?"

I heard my sigh. It was a big one.

"Why do folks who rely solely on faith always point the finger of atheism if someone dares to question their concept of the Creator? Isn't it obvious that some guiding force much greater than we can grasp has engineered life in all things? Just because I don't blindly accept that this power has a long white beard and looks like Moses doesn't mean I don't accept the obvious! The proof is all around us, for Pete's sake.

"Look, if you and I break down the carbon atoms that we extract from a rock specimen in one experiment and then do the same with a human bone, could you tell the difference in those atoms if I mixed them up and asked you to choose? One atom of carbon is the same as all the others, no matter its source. Therefore, when some kid picks up a rock and heaves it through a window, he's messing with the same elements from the rock and the window that are also in his hand and his entire body. However, he's taught to assume that he is much more important because he has a disease the rock and that glass don't have. It's called ego.

"It's like people who catch fish and claim that they don't feel pain so they start filleting them while they are still flopping and trying to get back into their element. Just because human ears can't hear its scream

---

[30] Commandments 5, 6, 9 and 10, unless you are a Roman Catholic or Lutheran, in which case it's 4, 5, 8, and 10.

when it is being sliced apart doesn't mean it isn't happening to that fish.

"Now that's called arrogance!

"I like to ask kids if they would like to know how to change history. If they say yes, I take them to a stony embankment and ask them to pick a stone out from it. Then I tell them they just changed history because they've moved something that had been dormant for millions of years. Most of them don't get it.

"In short, there are times when I am embarrassed to be called a human being. Enough said?"

Assuming that little outburst would slam the door on any further discussion with this hardcore preacher man, I moved to take my leave.

"No, no, please stay with us, Robert," Victor Zarley cried. "This may surprise you, but I agree with much of what you say. Now, please, you must tell me — tell us — about any experiences you personally may have had with the conscious separation of the soul from the material body. And when did you get serious about all this? What called you?"

"Look, I didn't say what I said to insult anyone and I am not looking for an argument. Do what you wish, say what you wish; it's all the same to me. Just count me out."

"You haven't insulted anyone so far, right, Joanne?" Zarley added a twinkle in his eye when adding, "But you must keep trying!"

I took a long and deep breath. While I was physically exhausted from that day's excitement, there was something in that man's eyes that made me feel that I was where I should be in that moment.

"Okay, okay. Aside from some stuff that happened when I was a kid — my grandfather's spirit definitely returned to our home shortly after he had died to tell my grandmother that her incessant grieving was bothering him — my personal awakening began shortly after my daughter Erika was born. To have that baby smile at me gave me a rush that I had never before felt, at least not in this life. She taught me an important lesson in physiology: I did not know that my pinky finger was linked to my heart. When she tugged it with that itsy-bitsy hand, I became all hers. Moreover, if fortune will allow, I shall choose to be her papa in every life to come for as long as my soul exists.

"That was when I decided that I wanted to know the unvarnished truth about life and death and everything in between. I wanted to stop the baloney and all the dreaming; I made a promise to myself to follow what I learned no matter where it led.

"Within an hour of making that pledge, I felt drawn — almost propelled — to the library at High Wyndham, the Virginia country estate I had leased from Paul and Edie Strang. There I found Paul Brunton's work, *A Search in Secret Egypt*, fairly leapt into my hands. That and his other works would open many doors for me; they became my primers."

I went on to relate my understanding of Brunton's experiences the night he had bribed a guard to lock him alone within the Great Pyramid at Giza. I described how I had imagined the same smothering closeness of the lifeless air that he had breathed. My heart had pounded along with his when he described shining his pale torch light around the dark antechamber and the hollow Grand Gallery. I had stooped when he had stooped and we had slithered one after the other beneath the giant blocking stone before we had stepped into the thick blackness that has made the King's Chamber forbidding for over 4,500 years.

Then, despite knowing that my mortal body was safe and sound by my fireside in the Blue Ridge Mountains, I had caught the scent of that ancient dust that Brunton disturbed with his scuffling boots. Even though he and I were separated by decades of years and thousands of miles, somehow we seemed to pause together to gasp for air beneath the pressing weight of those thousands of tons of solid stone that rose up and up and up into a limitless sky. Then, after Brunton and I had sunk down beside the altar-like structure that had never held a body, only then did another adventure commence that would forever change his (and my) view of life — hush-hush-hush, I thought. Enough had been said about that chamber for now. While I trusted Joanne and felt nearly as comfortable with Zarley, it was premature for me to reveal the next event that had unfolded in the depths of the Great Pyramid. It was something that I glimpsed in a nanosecond that resolved the mystery of the ankh.

Instead of sharing this, I moved on.

"I was also intrigued by another chapter wherein Brunton told of wandering about the Egyptian necropolis at Dair el Bahari. For some inexplicable reason he chose to return to his tourist quarters using an old donkey path that crossed a steep hill. Nearing its summit, he encountered a stranger perched atop a boulder as if awaiting him. This man spoke in cultured English, yet his features were Middle Eastern and his costume was the roughest of robes of the Bani Rasheed Bedouin. Brunton found this man's conversation fascinating and his eyes were positively spellbinding. It was then that he experienced his first truly clairvoyant[31] vision."

Joanne plopped her teacup down with a clatter.

"In what way? Tell us!" she demanded while dabbing her napkin here, there, and everywhere.

"As I recall — and it's been a dozen or more years since I last read it — Brunton described a tiny light that came out of nowhere to twirl like a wheel about his head. Somehow, his level of awareness was so drastically altered that it lasted for the remainder of his life."

Zarley leaned closer.

"What color was that wheel?" he asked. "Did it make any sound? Where had it come from?"

"I don't recall those details…"

"Did this person have a name?"

"I think Brunton said it was Ra-Man-Hotep or Rak-Man-Hotep — no, that's not right. Maybe it was Ra-Mak-Hotep. Look, Victor, I

---

[31] Clair (clear) voyant (to see) is the professed acquisition of knowledge or perception of objects or events through paranormal means instead of the five senses.

shouldn't be paraphrasing Brunton's work, so I'd suggest you get a copy."

"Don't you dare stop now or I won't sleep tonight!" Joanne whispered.

"At least tell us what you remember," Zarley said.

"Well, Brunton had agreed to meet him again the following day at the Temple of Luxor and that's where he was told that he was a member of an Order of Adepts."

Zarley's eyebrows lifted nearly to his hairline.

"Exactly how did he define an Adept — *exactly*?"

"He said they have the ability to consciously separate their eternal souls from their corporeal bodies. When these are separated, the soul can go just about anywhere while their physical body is at rest."

"And?"

"The soul — the really-real person — can return whenever it wishes."

"And you think that's possible?"

"Why not, if you believe that souls exist and survive the death of our physical bodies. If we have souls, as folks like you keep preaching — no offense meant — and if it survives the death of its earthly body, then why can't it zip out from time to time on its own?

"As a Native American mentor of mine put it, a body is like a living 'car' that the soul — the real us — drives around on earth. When that car runs out of gas or blows its engine, so to speak, we get another one."

"So you think an ordinary person can learn to perform the feat of consciously separating their soul from their body and also can return to it unharmed," Zarley asked.

"All they have to do is to follow a few simple rules — with lots of practice," I said while trying to hide my astonishment. This Zarley character was the first "ordained man of the cloth" whom I had met that was asking intelligent questions without trying to preach back at me.

"If it's that easy, why don't more people do it?" Joanne asked.

"I think lots of people do, but they don't talk about it. It wasn't that long ago that we'd all be burned at the stake as witches and heretics or stoned to death if we claimed such a thing. Know why? Because that particular truth would set the common person free and all those organized religions would lose their power to get into peoples' pockets. Those sanctimonious bastards will never give up those free meals without one hell of a fight."

I had not anticipated swimming in such deep waters; I prefer to keep such opinions to myself. But, they had asked, hadn't they?

"And to your mind, what might be a solution to this dilemma, my opinionated friend?" Victor asked with a smile and a wink.

"By taking responsibility for yourself," I heard the jaunty side of me snort back at him. "But it's so much easier to believe someone else died for your sins and paid with his blood — and therein lies the tender trap."

"And you don't accept that?"

"Not when that person refused to talk with gentiles! Look, even the oft-quoted Ten Commandments are blatantly misquoted."

"Are they?"

" 'Thou shall not kill' is dead-wrong — pun intended. The Hebrew word used, R'tzach, means 'murder.' Murder is a far cry from killing; they are distinguished by motive and intent. And Yeshua — why do you call him Jesus? — stated that he came for the 'lost sheep of Israel' and warned the Jews to not go the way of the gentiles. I'm not sure that Yeshua spoke much to anyone who wasn't Jewish... ah, but when I bring up this detail, I am told with sanctimonious fervor that the gentiles have become 'spiritual Israelites.' Yeah, right...

"In my opinion, Yeshua took what he had learned from the Essenes at Qumran and put it into action. He said nothing that had not been taught by those folks who had figured it out nearly 200 years before he was born."

Victor's chuckles and wagging head encouraged me, so I added, "Look, I am an egalitarian sort. Sure, it might take one person longer than another to learn how to consciously separate his soul from his earthly body, but what is possible for one is possible for all — *if they have a soul to start with.* I am not so sure that every person walking around has one."

"Would you consider yourself atheist?"

"I am more Buddhist in my thinking; our ultimate fates lie in our hands and not with an intermediary."

"Then you are anti-Christian?"

It always came to this, it seemed. If anyone dared to look through a different prism, they must be 'against' this or 'for' that.

"Let me put it this way, Reverend. If I were in the eighth year of grammar school and was challenged by someone who had chosen to remain stuck in grade five year after year — or life after life in this instance — why would I be 'against' them because my lessons had exceeded their own?"

"So faith-based religions are behind you because you know so much more?"

"Don't insult me, sir. You asked!"

"I'm just curious about your response."

"I am saying that you, Joanne, me, and everyone else have the right to choose their own path and to walk or run along that path at their chosen speed. One is no better or worse than the other is. Everyone has an equal right to think — to *think* — on their own. They also have the right to live any way they choose so long as they do not harm or interfere with others whose education, experiences, situations, or goals are different."

"Please go on…"

"I don't want to insult you or your beliefs and I don't intend to influence a single person…"

"No, no, Robert. Please."

"As I see it, the first hurdle is to set aside all the limitations these various religions created for us. We all talk about souls — but the moment we try to include them as a tangible and recognizable part of our life, everyone backs down.

"Look at me. Here I sit — or so you think. But, is this really me? I assure you, I am a hell of a lot prettier than this old body-car!" When he and Joanne stopped laughing, I added, "Look, if any person is malformed, retarded, limbless, or unattractive, does this also reflect their soul accurately or demean its relative value? Not in my book. I think every person's true soul is perfect and beautiful; it's these body-cars that our karmas have earned that can be misleading; that's not a true reflection of their worth. How they appear is a reward, a punishment, or a test that is deliberately selected not by some bearded judge in the sky, but by their eternal being that is demanding they earn their ticket Home..."

"Earlier, you hinted that you think there are people on this earth who are soulless. Do you believe that?"

"I do indeed."

"And I am sensing that you have had an experience that led you to that conclusion," Victor said with a small smile.

"What you are sensing is that I am a seeker of the unvarnished truth, whatever that might be. Whether it's good, bad, or indifferent is irrelevant to the facts. What is, is, so why not accept it? Moreover, I see the logic that souls deliberately select physical attributes, locations, circumstances, or even certain afflictions as elective teaching tools within the succession of their lives.

"The problem is that we are taught from the cradle that we are not in charge of our ultimate destiny and that our only hope is to win the approval of some great, mysterious, and unseen power by pleasing and praising it through persons who run around pretending to have special inside information. We are warned that we must have blind faith through them to be 'saved from the fires of Hell.' We are told that we cannot do anything about our future on our own and that our good works aren't enough.

"Most of us just stop trying, and that's when the evil sets in. And, if I am correct, it means the earthly bodies of those misguided souls will die and decay, but their driver-souls will be right back on the same old tread wheel for uncountable lives to come.

"In short, sir, I think that our true destiny lies entirely in our own hands. Those that preach the opposite are either misguided do-gooders or soulless bastards in their own right."

"What's your opinion of using LSD to expand awareness?" Victor asked.

"Speaking only for my personal path, I am confident that I can learn all that I seek to know by allowing my soul to be its own explorer. I don't need illusions or delusions; drugs can fog the issues and can be misleading."

"And have you used them?"

I remembered Round-Bear and his teas...

"Not knowingly."

"And you know that archaeologists have confirmed that Egyptian priests used drugs in their religions."

"Yes, Reverend Zarley, but I would guess that was after the true Adepts were driven underground and Egypt was in decline. Any priest or preacher, then or now, that resorts to using drugs to make their point is an out-and-out phony. Even today — correct me if I am wrong, for you are better schooled than I am — many charismatic fakers, imitators, and outright evil priests and preachers feed off the fears of the innocent and the ignorant and work them into frenzies by any means possible.

"Then consider how the true meaning of the ankh and how the root meaning of the religion of Osiris is being misinterpreted —"

Victor scooted to the edge of his seat to ask, "Please tell me what you believe that meaning to be."

"It was something I glimpsed when I was imagining being with Brunton in one of those chambers. A plain stone dais held a wooden bench that was draped over with a cloth. A person was lying on it. Around him were six or eight persons; I could not tell if they were men or women. They were singing or perhaps chanting — I heard them only for a split-second.

"Everyone was dressed in white robes except the one squatting behind that person's head. I think — it was dim, you know — I think he wore dark blue or maybe it was a purple robe.

"Anyway, I glimpsed a wisp of something akin to a vapor emerging from the top of that person's head — the one lying down. But, when I blinked, I was back in my chair in Virginia."

"And how does that connect to the ankh?"

"The way that person was positioned on the dais could be represented by the lower part of the ankh and the loop at its top could symbolize the emergence of the soul from the head. I believe that the ankh is nothing more than a reminder that the soul can be separated from the body at will."

"Then what were you witnessing?"

"How can I say for sure? Perhaps this was the transformation of a neophyte into a true Adept and he was being taught how to consciously separate his soul — the real him — from his corporeal body.

"From what I've read, even the eminent curator of Egyptian Antiquities for the Royal British Museum, E. A. Wallis Budge, missed that mark when he tried to explain the Osirian religion —"

"Budge's works are also in your library? Good for you," Zarley laughed.

"I also have his interpretation of the hieroglyphic transcript of the papyrus of Ani; the so-called *Book of the Dead*. I very much appreciate his book *Osiris, the Egyptian Religion of Resurrection,* as well as his

Amulets and Talismans."

"How then did Budge miss the mark with Osiris?"

"I am greatly simplifying this, so bear with me. What if the original legend of Osiris and Isis was meant to be symbolic to the lives of every human being who ever lived? Isis and Osiris were brother and sister but ruled as one, thus demonstrating that we humans have male and female traits in equal measure but express one or the other according to our chosen mission. It's no accident of nature; we are in control of that. We are what we have chosen to be.

"However, Osiris was caught by an enemy — perhaps one who only *pretends* to be human — and he was cut up and his pieces scattered. His sister-wife Isis — his other half — had to find them one at a time to become whole again. Is this not a fair representation of our lives? We choose to return again and again until we 'find' our missing parts and become whole again.

"Perhaps this also is paraphrased into the most fundamental concept of Yin and Yang. It seems logical that when souls are freed of human bodies and in the spirit form, they have no need to be expressed as either male or female but are androgynous. They only assume either the male or the female body-cars for the purposes of procreation on earth while each soul — the drivers of those cars — maintains equality among all others. After all, why would a soul in its spirit form need a sexual mechanism whose purpose is confined to earthly procreation? Is it not logical that we enter such corporeal states solely to provide vehicles for succeeding souls?"

"Wait, wait," Joanne protested. "What about those ghosts who are recognized as someone's mother or father or whatever?"

"Perhaps those are freed souls who resume a guise that is familiar to the viewer?"

"Well, all right," she muttered. "But what about those male or female ghosts who are seen by total strangers?"

"We are getting far afield from Egypt…"

"Just give me your opinion, please, and then I'll hush," Joanne said and batted her eyes as only a genteel lady can do.

"Perhaps such hauntings are caused by souls who died in such a shocked, angry, or confused state that they refused the guides who came to assist in their transition. Consider the circumstances of legitimate hauntings: usually these are disturbed souls who believe they must continue to pursue some task on earth."

"So how can we help them? Isn't that our duty?" kind Joanne asked.

"I've had a small measure of success that you might try. Kenny Miller, the actor and entertainer, once asked that I take over his housesitting chores at the Palm Beach Gardens home owned by his close friend, Burt Reynolds. Kenny mentioned before he left on his cruise that I should not use the smallest bedroom, but the remainder of the house was fine. However, I noted that it had a telephone extension that was convenient to where I chose to sleep. I saw no harm in using it.

"As is customary when one is staying in unfamiliar surroundings, one double-checks the locks on doors and windows. However, I was awakened at 2:00 AM by a cold breeze blowing through the sliding doors in the dining room, which I found standing wide open. I grabbed my .38 revolver and made the rounds. All was secure, including the exterior doors on the screened patio.

"The following morning those damned doors were open again!

"I teased my date Liz Leslie about Burt's house being haunted. Before we left to shop for items for dinner, I teasingly placed a matchbook on its edge in the forbidden room. I made a production out of challenging the 'ghost' to knock it over if he was real. When we returned and were ferrying bags of groceries into the kitchen, I made a mad dash to that room with the intent of knocking that matchbook over as a joke. Too late. It was lying in the center of the floor. Thinking Liz had pulled a fast one, I set it back up before rushing outside. However, when we returned together, that damned matchbook was back on the floor. Liz went home early.

"The following morning those damned patio doors were open again. Enough was enough. I set the table for two; I made toast and scrambled eggs and poured two cups of coffee and invited my ghost to join me! I then had a one-sided discussion with an empty chair. I explained what I was doing there and that I meant no harm or disrespect. I promised that I would not go into that 'taboo' room again out of respect.

"Maybe I overdid the eggs; maybe the coffee was too strong. Whatever the reason, my ghost let his food go cold. Nevertheless, those patio doors remained locked and I never had another feeling of foreboding.

"When Kenny arrived a week later, I met him in the carport with a few choice words. He laughed and asked if I had met the ghost! He explained that his clothes were routinely dumped out of the bedroom dresser and that a guest writer for *Variety* did not stay an entire night in that house. His guest swore that the ghost had left him a threatening note!"

"So why do you think that ghost stopped bothering you?" Joanne asked.

"I spoke civilly; I acknowledged his presence for what it was; and I showed concern and a bit of camaraderie. After all, these traumatized souls have refused to rest in between incarnations; they cling to what was instead of preparing for what will come next. Why would I add to their misery by acting cruelly? They can't hurt you; they can only cause you to hurt yourself. Treat them as you would anyone in that condition, but always with the respect they deserve. After all, they are the ones who are suffering."

"You keep saying 'he.' Did you see him?" she asked.

"No, that's just the impression I had, that's all."

"I've heard enough for tonight! Robert, I must introduce you to my friends very, very soon," Victor proclaimed while pumping my hand until my arm ached. "We must go somewhere very private and isolated in the Everglades — as far out as possible, all right? My friend is off the coast of South America just now but he might be free to meet you within a few days. Yes, yes, this is right and proper!"

"Um, uh, er, sure, Victor, as long as we do it soon. I am scheduled to return to my study area."

"No, no, no! You must take the time; this is more important than you can imagine! My friend is also busy with all this trouble in Argentina. He predicts they'll either have another revolution or they'll have to elect a new president soon — perhaps you might invite some of your Indian friends to join us. And don't worry, he is a lot like you; he's also very dedicated to his mission."

"And what mission is that?"

"He commands a space ship," he said while hustling to the door.

"Oh, right, sure," I grinned, expecting a laugh and a wink that never came. A glance at Joanne bought a small smile and a quick nod.

Victor paused with his hand on the doorknob.

"I communicate with him regularly and he's made me more the optimist and less the dogmatist; he's become an especially good friend. Perhaps he might take you for a ride." He blew a kiss at Joanne, adding, "You were right; Robert is perfect. Goodnight, all."

My drive home went swiftly, perhaps because there was very little traffic at that late hour, or maybe it only seemed that way because my mind was aching. It got worse when I heard Victor's voice on my message machine.

"We're on for tomorrow night. Let me know where we can meet around ten o'clock. Hope you can bring your Indian friends."

10. Shark Valley Rendezvous

Everglades National Park, 1972

Nino did nothing to ease my dilemma. First, he grilled me about Zarley's physical appearance, posture, his eyes, and his reactions to our conversation; then he advised that I not only accept his invitation, but that I should take along the two eldest Tiger cubs. That said, he also warned that we three must avoid looking into the eyes of any "weird-looking dinks" unless they were tall, slender, and somewhat human. If anything but an obvious "star person" showed up, we were to leave immediately. He reminded me too that no one, alien or human, could have any real power over us without our permission.

"Aw, here we go again!" I sputtered back. "I'm trying to keep my contacts with the Yampricos within the realm of accepted science, for Pete's sake! First, you send me to hang out where some mythical cannibal has everyone spooked and I'm sleeping with water jugs and talking snakes while some creep spotlights my camp! Then, when I do find her supposed cave, nobody will let me prove she was ever real because they're afraid I'd wake her up! After a thousand years? That's nuts!

"Then, after all those smoke and mirrors, some poor kid blows his brains out because he talked to me about legends, some old duffer in the middle of nowhere slips me a Mickey Finn and I get nightmares, I get chased off a burial mound by nothing I could see, and now you say I should go with some born-again Bible-thumper to meet the captain of a UFO? In the Everglades? Late at night?

"One of us should see a psychiatrist... and I think it's me! I want to deal in facts, damn it!"

Nino heaved one of his drawn-out sighs.

"Fine. Good. Take the easy path like everyone else..."

"Don't start! Just tell me where I can get some stone-cold facts! From here on out I want hard evidence that can be verified in a laboratory."

"*Waugh!* Maybe them glass-polishers ain't up to the task yet, ever think about that? Back when I was born, them so-called doctors didn't know enough to wash their hands in between operations — and nobody ever heard of them virus critters! Every dad-blasted generation thinks they know all there is, so they want to shut the books!"

"Yes, but —"

"What if this Zarley feller is tellin' the truth? And if he is, maybe you could learn a thing or two from them Star People! What's it gonna cost you to get out there to see?"

"Oh, sure, and next you'll have me talking to those little grey men with grasshopper eyes..."

"How many times do I gotta tell you them goblins are the bad guys and they ain't our 'Star People!?' Oh, and be sure to tell that Zarley feller he'd better watch his back because there's lots of 'Pretenders' around who might want to clean his clock before he lets their cats out of the bag."

"Yeah, right," I sighed. "What else?"

"Can't talk anymore! Minnie's goin' next door to call the men in the little white coats to come get me! Let me know..."

I argued with myself for hours before I telephoned the Tigers. Luckily, Robert answered. I explained the basics of the situation and invited him to bring Donna along to meet Reverend Zarley; however, I did not mention his first name. Robert promised to borrow his father's truck as if he and Donna were going to a late movie in Miami. The area we selected for this escapade was the northernmost entry to the Everglades National Park, the Shark Valley Loop Road. It was convenient for the Tigers as it was adjacent to their reservation; the ranger's mobile home was easy to bypass, as it was concealed amid a grove of pine trees and thick brush. After all, no one but alligators, rattlesnakes, panthers, bobcats, wild pigs, and huge tropical spiders dared stalk around that loop after dark.

Our rendezvous point would be Otis Shiver's Barbeque. A true old-timey Florida digs, it squatted like a relic of bygone days along the historic Tamiami Trail that links Miami to Tampa. Most "hamburger" tourists ignored his handcrafted cypress wood cook shack with its attached thatched Indian-style chickee dining area. That was a mistake. His "Cracker cookin'" was hard to beat: as he liked to say, "Stop by and put some *real* South in your mouth."

I had learned about Otis through Laymond Hardy, a local naturalist and biologist whom I had encountered following one of my lectures at the Miami Planetarium for the Florida Zoological Society. He had confided that he and Donald Blake, a professor who taught greenhouse management, had encountered a Bigfoot while returning from a field trip to collect biological specimens in the Florida Panhandle. Accompanying them had been a lab instructor from Florida State University and two students. The team had spent a full day mucking about in Mud Swamp, a dismal place banking the Apalachicola River. As dusk dissolved into night, the five men had crammed into an old sedan to maneuver the sandy lane that weaved through dense stands of scrub pines and saw palmettos to reach the nearest paved road. Unexpectedly, a naked, hair-covered, 7-foot, two-legged, black-skinned form leapt across the lane directly in front of them. There was no mistake: their headlights made it clear that this was a hominid and not a bear on its hind legs. The shaken driver stepped on the gas; no one spoke until they reached the nearest bar to gulp whiskey and beer. There they decided never to speak of this encounter in fear of professional ridicule.[32] Indeed, to this day the Apalachicola Swamp Man is counted as pure myth in these piney woods as is the la loupe-garou[33] of the bayou Cajuns of Louisiana.

I had found Hardy to be a fount of unusual information. Once when we were investigating a reported sighting near Davie, Florida, an elderly woman showed us small banana-shaped tracks that led from her mobile home to an abandoned citrus grove. She admitted that she had been feeding table scraps to this hairy baby. Everything had been fine until she tried to pick it up; it bit her ankle. The tracks convinced us that her "baby Bigfoot" was a young orangutan that may have escaped from the nearby menagerie of Frank Weed, an exotic animal importer.

On the return trip to Miami, Hardy confided that some years previous Otis Shiver had recruited him to help rob a grave at Fort Moultrie, South Carolina. Shiver wanted to recover the bones of that famous Creek Indian warrior, Asi-yahola, for his Indian friends. History books report that after "Osceola" had been tricked into captivity under a flag of truce with General T. S. Jesup, he and his sub-chief Bobcat were imprisoned under deplorable conditions. Some say Bobcat managed to escape, but Osceola died soon after his capture. It is generally held that the attending physician at the fort had removed his head before his body had been interred in a shallow grave in the fort cemetery along with "full military honors," a claim meant to pacify his tribe. Immersed in preserving fluids, the puckered head of this brave leader became a ghoulish oddity among our largely Christian nation while being a great insult to the Seminole and Creek Indian Nations. It was their belief that the spirit of warriors whose bodies remained on enemy soil could never

---

[32] Although Hardy was an enthusiastic and well-paid member of the 1974 American Yeti Expeditions, in his declining years he reverted to toeing the line of professional skepticism.

[33] The fabled man-werewolf that is most likely another band of Forest Giant People.

find true rest. Interestingly, after the Seminole Nation's entreaties to the U.S. government failed to gain the return of Osceola's remains, the jar containing his severed head was apparently consumed in a suspicious fire circa 1866. Exactly 100 years later, in 1966, it was reported that grave robbers had attempted, but failed, to remove Osceola's bones from that military cemetery.[34] Not to worry, Laymond Hardy had whispered with a conspiratorial smile, both Osceola's head and his bones were at rest in a secret Seminole burial place somewhere in his beloved Florida.

I arrived at Shiver's Barbeque to find Zarley already chatting with Donna and Robert Tiger. When he spotted me, he leapt to his feet to shake my hand.

"Robert, I am truly impressed with your young friends and I thank you for sharing them with me. They are perfect for this adventure. They've described your choice of areas; it sounds perfect. Shall we go?"

As we filed out of the door — Zarley would ride with me while the Tigers followed — Robert hissed in my ear, "You didn't say his name was Victor..."

"Oh? Didn't I? Sorry..."

"Rat-fink."

"See you there," I said.

"Maybe," he replied with the hint of a smile.

Having Zarley alone with me for at least a half hour or better gave me an opportunity to cut through the wrapping to get to the meat.

"Victor, please don't take offense, but do you truly believe you are in contact with some space ship commander and that we'll be meeting him tonight? Is this for real or are you measuring my gullibility index?"

He said nothing for a mile or so before he spoke.

"Up until a short time ago, my life had been fully dedicated to delivering the messages of the Holy Gospel; if it wasn't in the Bible or

---

[34] Authorities claim that the bones Shiver and Hardy were hawking as Osceola's were only animal bones. Was this face-saving or was it fact?

didn't follow its logic, I was trained not to believe it. I was totally immersed in the Lord's work. I had a beautiful wife and I was adored by my children. I had money, fame, and a generous flock. I had it all, or so I thought. However, following my true awakening, my family and my closest friends shunned me in a most hurtful way, and my once-loyal flock reviled me as someone who lost his soul to Satan. Almost every cent I had invested was taken from me, and I was cast out to become a beggar of favors. I own the clothes on my back, I make payments on a used car, and I live in a single furnished room."

Damn, damn, damn! I had no idea my question would cut so deeply. Wanting to take the point off that moment, I said in overly grave tones, "Victor, in your travels, have you noticed that the majority of people around the world, no matter their race, language, religion, or faith, share one specific prayer in common."

"Oh? And what might that be?"

"Please God, Yahweh, Adonai, Usen, Wakan Tonka, Allah, Buddha, or Who-the-hell-ever; please let me get through this day without a single new thought!"

"Oh, oh, oh, you must let me steal that one," Zarley gasped in between laughs. When he had sputtered down, he offered what I'd been waiting to hear. "Would you like to hear the rest of my story?"

"Of course I would, but be forewarned that I can't go over 10 minutes without finding something to laugh at, even if it's myself."

"I was on a prayer retreat in Palm Springs, California, when I got a strong calling that I must find a specific and secluded area in the surrounding desert. I was led to the northwestern part of the Joshua Tree National Monument. I drove around until I was led to hike back to a hill that was a mile or so off the road. I had barely sat down before I heard a voice — don't look at me like that, Robert, please. You have to understand: I did not hear it as you are hearing me now; it was within my mind. Of course, I had been warned at the seminary that such communications came only from Satan and I'd been ordered to shut them out. However — and this was equally strange — I did not sense any evil whatsoever. It was somewhat like you saying, 'I saw what I saw.' In my case 'I heard what I heard.' "

"Did anything sound familiar?"

"Yes, especially the voice. It had spoken to me before. Once, late at night when I was very tired, I heard it so clearly that I reached over to turn up the volume, but my radio wasn't on."

"What did it say?"

"Which time?"

"Palm Springs."

" 'We're glad you finally came to meet us,' as if I had been expected. Naturally, I had to consider that someone was playing a joke on me. But, how could they? No one could have preceded me. Strangely, I was not afraid even when I was instructed to sit beneath a certain Joshua tree. Then this voice began to speak about life, death, birth and rebirth, mortality and immortality, and how each fit into a greater puzzle. I listened until I became chilled. When I opened my eyes, the sun was going down."

"Wait, wait; excuse me, Victor. What time did you say you left Palm Springs?"

"I had left before 9:00 AM and I'd reached that area sometime between 10:00 and 11:00."

"And how long had it taken you to walk in?"

"Maybe a half hour."

"But now it's getting dark?"

"It was so late that I had to run back to my car and drive like a madman to make the dinner date I had with my colleagues."

"You must have fallen asleep, m'man. The desert can do that to you."

"That loss of time was only a part of it. I was in the shower before I realized how badly I'd been sunburned."

"Well, sure, if you'd been there all day…"

"But I'd been burned all over. Front, back, and everywhere. Even the soles of my feet and the cheeks of my ass! It was as if I had been put on a spit!"

"Maybe you got naked out there? I've done that lots of times when I wanted to feel wild and free —"

"I'd arrived fully dressed and awakened fully dressed. Robert, the mind has the capacity to block out any number of things. Literal months passed before I began to remember even fragments."

Victor Zarley's words reawakened a mislaid memory of my own and, in a flash, I recalled writhing about on the floor of Round-Bear's chickee while fighting being sucked out of myself. Losing my grasp, I felt that I had shot straight *into* that old shaman's mind through a tiny window that winked open just above his eyes but had shuttered closed again after I had whooshed past. I imagined — it could not have been real — that I was spiraling around and down through a long, moist tunnel at a dizzying speed before I dropped into a domed space high above a stony valley. Freefalling now, I spied below me a shining path that slipped out through a dark cleft set between two distant mountains. Once that thin path entered the valley floor, it went straight as an arrow across a vast plain as if rushing to end its journey. Most curiously, a myriad of dark and duller side trails bled away from the brighter route, each twisting back on themselves in a great maze but always reentering the main path further back from its goal — was this the true path that Victor Osceola had failed to follow? I didn't know; I couldn't think; the ground was rising toward me at a terrifying speed. I barely had time to turn my head to see that shining thread led through the gates of a vast, neat, and serene city that spread far beyond the valley and out of sight. Suspended above that city was a huge light of many colors that pulsed and glowed with a steady cadence much like a great heart. For no reason I could ever explain, I sensed that this city was an excellent place to rest before going Home…

"Where is Home?" I heard myself mumble.

"You mean mine? Akron, Ohio."

"No, Victor, I-I-er, I was just remembering something that I didn't know I'd forgotten."

"I know how you feel," he said with a grunt. "Everything about that day came back to me over time, but only in bits and pieces like a mind-puzzle."

"How do you know this commander is real?"

"Oh, I've met him and he's taken me for rides. At first, it was difficult for us to rendezvous in northern Ohio, but we managed a time or two over by Portage Lakes. I was surprised; the Captain and his crew are taller than we are; he has long hair and clear blue eyes."

Recalling Nino's warnings, I asked, "His hair wouldn't be blondish, would it?" I asked.

"Why in the world do you ask that?"

"Is he slender? Do they call themselves 'Star People'?"

Zarley's brows did some knitting.

"Then you've met them?"

"No, but I am curious. Who do they say they are?"

"Why, our Keepers, of course."

Those damned Keepers again!

"Hold on; we're here," I said as I snapped off my headlights before swerving off the main road toward the entrance to the Shark Valley Loop Road. Robert followed my lead and together we coasted beyond the view of the Everglades National Park ranger station to hide beneath the cloaking boughs of some giant Australian pine trees.

Softly clicking shut our car doors — metallic sounds travel quite a distance on moonless nights — Zarley, Robert, Donna, and I padded two-by-two around the locked gate to hustle down the lane that pierces the wildest heart of the Everglades. As darkness folded around us, I considered spitting into my palms and spreading my hands to cast some loving thoughts out to my snake brothers, but thought the better of it. I did not want to take the time to explain such pagan acts to Zarley; besides, I didn't know for sure it would work with frisky alligators.

We slowed from a dogtrot to a swift walk until we were miles below the ranger's hut and within sight of the Shark Valley Lookout Tower. There Zarley halted, his eyes fixed on the myriad of stars that speckled the southern horizon. Try as I might, I saw nothing unusual.

It could have been two minutes or maybe even ten before Zarley sank into a lotus position.

"He's on his way," he whispered to us.

Robert, Donna, and I backed away to form a tight cluster. I felt Donna's shiver despite the warmth of the night. Robert elbowed my ribs when a slow cadence of soft splashes — the sort made by an animal wading across that sopping saw grass prairie — drifted in from the direction of that sacred burial mound we had visited. Moreover, it lay less then three miles away as the crow flies.

"What if it's them?" Robert breathed.

"We didn't hurt anything! We didn't take anything!"

"They could get between us and the car."

"It's not them!"

"I think we should leave."

"Let me try something — stay still."

I spat into my palms and held my hands out like a Cochiti; I sent a mental loop of peace and apology out, out, out in the direction of those sounds — and they halted. One minute, two minutes, three minutes, four; frogs, great and small, commenced their croaks, peeps, burps, and belches and then a thousand insects joined their chorus, too.

Another half-hour dragged by. The air traffic to the southeast of our position was limited to the customary military aircraft in and out of Homestead Air Force Base while commercial flights streamed in and out of Miami International Airport to the northeast — Zarley's leap to his feet sent us scrambling. We watched him nod and move his lips without making a sound. Then, with a loud sigh, he spun about to announce, "They're leaving Venezuela now and should be here in a few minutes! Believe me; this night will change your lives forever."

"You, uh, did you say they'd be here in just a few minutes?" Donna asked.

"Indeed!"

"Isn't Venezuela a long way away?"

"We can't stay that late, Mister Zarley," Robert said. "We promised we'd come straight home after the movie."

"But they're almost here."

"Victor, hadn't you said they'd had problems in Argentina last evening?" I asked. "What are they doing in Venezuela now?"

"I never know where they will be next; after all, they patrol all Central and South America, too."

"And here?"

"Especially here."

"Patrol as in a military sense, huh?"

"Not exactly."

"Law enforcement?"

"Not exactly, no."

"For NATO, then? United Nations?"

"None of those," Victor chuckled. "Their sole mission is to prevent us from destroying this planet in total. We can fight all we want between ourselves, but they won't let us go that far."

What if I told you that Usen is about to pull the plug on us humans if we don't start toeing the line? Nino whispered to me out from my memory bank.

"So these, um, these 'Star People' can go anywhere they wish?"

"Yes, yes; that's all part of their job as our Keepers. After all, back in the beginning their kind were responsible for creating our prototypes to house those souls that had become too disruptive within their parent societies all around the galaxy. The Yampricos, Bigfoot, Forest Giants, Yeti, Sasquatch, or whatever else you want to call them, they're the true natives to this earth; we humans certainly aren't. But they served as the original gene pool the Star People had used to help us adapt to being here; of course, it was quite a span of earth years before we — our souls — were introduced."

Nino's raspy voice again came a-whispering in my inner ear, *We'd lose everything we've worked for up to now; we'll be back naked in caves, and we'll darned well deserve it. If we get sent back to square one, maybe the Keepers will have to use those Yampricos to start us up all over again.*

"Victor, you said that humans can fight all we want between ourselves but our Keepers won't let it go too far? What's too far, a worldwide nuclear war?"

"You're getting a chance to ask them — wait, wait," he said and turned back as if to listen to someone unseen.

Robert, Donna, and I again closed ranks. Try as I might, I saw nothing out of place amid the canopy of stars that twinkled, blinked, or hung out there still as stones. Then, as my eyes swept back and forth, I detected a single white dot rising up and out of a distant quadrant.

"They're almost here," Zarley tossed back at us. "They've probably sent a shuttle for us..."

"Is that it? Is it?" Robert gasped.

"Show me, show me!" Donna wailed while looking everywhere except where it was.

Victor quick-stepped closer to the tower as if to escape our chatter. I didn't care; my attention had been snapped earthward where a second object came glinting out of the gloom at treetop level. Closing fast and before I could croak a warning or dive for cover, this flying thingy veered sharply up and over our heads to vanish over the hummocks to the northwest. It had made not a single sound, yet I felt — or did I imagine — the shock wave of its passing?

Cotton-mouthed and speechless, I turned to find my Tigers slack-jawed and glassy-eyed. My mind raced down a short list of possibilities: this certainly had not been some giant night bird moving between its favorite fishing ponds; no bird glides that far and that fast nor so suddenly gains altitude on folded wings. On the other hand, could we have accidentally encountered a test of some new military drone or missile? My military experience, albeit outdated by decades, told me this too was improbable because there had been no sound or smell of propulsion exhaust of any sort... unless it was propelled by some new gadget that harnessed magnetics — Robert pointed south again. That other glowing sky-light he had been watching had stopped its approach and was hanging still in midair.

"Yessir," we heard Zarley saying to someone unseen. "Please repeat. Yes, I understand. I'll tell them." Turning to us, he said in a voice most disappointed, "The Commander sends his apologies and asks that we come again."

"What happened?"

"He said he had to go back immediately. He'll let me know when we can try again."

"I don't know, Victor. I'll be leaving for the Northwest fairly soon."

"And I'm getting married," Robert said.

"And I can't come out unless my brother does," Donna added. "I think we'd better go home now."

No one had much to say as we trudged back to our vehicles. The ride back to the lights of Miami seemed interminable. Victor was silent until we pulled into the deserted parking lot at Shiver's.

"When do you leave for Washington State?" he asked.

"As soon as I can get my team together; it won't be long."

"I was warned that many forces would try to stop us from even meeting. It was Joanne's power that arranged it, you know."

"Oh?"

"I didn't want to say anything in front of the Tiger kids, but the Commander said it would be easier to meet in Washington. There are too many eyes here. I'd also be honored to have the chance to see the First People eye to eye. Maybe I could talk with them in mind-pictures. Would you mind if I tagged along?"

"Hey, who knows what we would accomplish together, eh? You know how to contact me to make our plans, right? Call anytime."

"What happened tonight had nothing to do with you or me."

"We can try again. Goodnight, Victor. Sleep well."

He appeared older when he trudged away to his car where he paused to stare into the sky. I looked, too, and wondered if that one bright star that hung just above the horizon was really pulsing. Was that what the Reverend Victor Zarley was saluting when he lifted his arm?

11. Sand in My Eyes

"So what happened to that preacher fella?" Nino asked through his customary cloud of cigar smoke.

"Dunno," I tossed back. In truth, my attention was fastened on that undersized snout that came inching out beneath the hem of his couch. I hitched my Levi jeans up a tad to better expose my naked ankles, so white, so soft, and so easy to bite. Indeed, two bulging eyeballs of watery evil followed that twitching snout. Yes, yes, I should have looked away to feign innocent vulnerability but my expectations were levitating at the sight of that little red tongue licking those thin hairy lips — damn it! That little monster's eyeballs locked with my gaze and, like an idiot, I smiled. I heard a guttural whine as both eyes and snout disappeared. Crap! How had Cleo known that the Vaseline I had slathered all around my ankles was caked with white-hot pepper?

"Are you two gonna hook up along the line?" I heard Nino asking.

"I certainly hope so…"

"Huh? When did you hear from him?"

"What? Who?"

"That Zarley gink! Ain't that who we're talkin' about?"

"Oh-oh-oh, right! No, I haven't heard a word."

He stared at me for a moment before grunting, "That's funny, I can't hear the music."

Minnie-the-monitor stuck her head out of their bedroom doorway to cock her head this way and that.

"Are you going crazy again, old man? There ain't nobody playing no radio."

"Then why is ol' Guynatay waltzin' me around?"

"You can't waltz on one leg! I ain't gonna stand for no more nuts stuff, and that's that," she snapped and went back to folding laundry or whatever she was doing.

Aside from wondering why Nino insisted on calling me "guy" something-or-other, I had to admit that he spoke the truth about me "waltzing him around."

Indeed, Zarley and I had met after our incident at Shark Valley to make plans about where we would go out West and whom we would see. More importantly, he said he would arrange a face-to-face meeting for us with his space chums in some out-of-the-way rendezvous around Washington State's Mount St. Helens. Apparently — and according to him — his starship pilot thought it an excellent choice. Was I dubious? Definitely — but not for reasons he might assume. It wasn't that I thought it impossible that extraterrestrial beings might exist; hell, run the numbers of probability that we are truly alone in this entire universe. The question was why would they give a hoot?

Zarley had disappeared for the interceding two weeks as if to put his affairs in order while I spent as much time as possible with my daughter, packed my gear into my VW van, and renewed my contacts around Cougar, Washington. All was set and a team of enthusiastic researchers had agreed to join us. Included were Dr. Jim Butler, biologist, archaeologist Robert Carr, anthropologist Peter Lipsio, newly graduated biologist Ed Dillon, vacationing Lt. Harry Marcus of the Dade County Sheriff's Department, Jim McClarin, and Eva Phillips.

I had reached the parking lot of the Dinner Key Marina in Coconut Grove the evening of our scheduled departure. Zarley was to arrive by taxi by 7:00 PM to follow my motor home to storage using my van. We would then proceed to his apartment to gather his gear. We expected to be on the Florida Turnpike before midnight... but our deadline came and passed with no sign of him. Naturally, I telephoned him repeatedly but had no answer. By 11:30 PM, I knew I was stuck and would have to wait until morning to make other arrangements. Disgusted, I was flicking off the lights to my Sightseer coach when I heard a car skid to a halt and feet came crunching toward my door at a dead run. A disheveled, wide-eyed creature clad in filthy, sweaty clothing lunged inside to pant like a hunted animal. Gone was the confident seeker of truth whom I had come to know and to like and vanished were the intelligent glances and the ready smiles of a virile man who had always been clad in crisp, clean, and neat clothing. Before me stood a trembling shell who babbled how sorry he was, how confused he had been, and how very much he wanted to make our trip. Most importantly, Zarley kept repeating, he wanted me to meet his starship friends and assured me how they were anxious to meet me, too. Still, he had found it nearly impossible to break away from some new and mysterious person who had come to dominate his life. He went on to describe how this "Lydia"[35] had appeared on his doorstep one evening two weeks previous and, before the next dawning, he had fallen under her spell — his words, not mine. Over those succeeding weeks, she had drummed into him such a terror for his soul that he could not eat or sleep, let alone escape. I cringed for him when he whined about how it had taken all his strength to "sneak away" this evening when she was lolling in her nightly bubble bath.

"It's okay, calm down, we can handle it," I said as soothingly as I could. "Let's leave your car here and we'll drop the keys into the mail to Joanne and maybe she can..."

"I *can't* go! I-I have no money left and I didn't have time to get my

---

[35] Lydia was a region on the west coast of Asia Minor. In the New Testament, this is the name of a woman converted to Christianity by Saint Paul.

clothes."

"Lookit, I'll cover all the food and whatever; I have plenty of extra clothes for the bush and I'll stake you to a pair of boots. I am sure Joanne will help secure your things. Fair enough?"

"Noooooo! Lydia… she'd follow," he wailed.

"So bloody what? This witch ain't my mommy and she sure as hell isn't yours. The last time anyone had any control over me was before I figured out how the pins worked on my own diapers. Listen to me; by sunup we'll be in Louisiana and she can kiss our rosy —"

"No, Robert, no! You don't know her powers! She's pure, pure evil and, and, and… she has no soul!"

Blam! My door was flung open for second time that evening and this arachnid-like creature in too-tight, too-bright polyester peddle-pushers scuttled inside — it halted like a freeze-frame in an old horror movie the instant our eyes locked. It had one stumpy foot on my step well and the other on my compartment floor. I was mystified by the violent images that flashed past my mind's eye as it stood sneering up at me. Simultaneously, I felt a flutter of shame that I would so much as think of squashing a female of our species.

But was it?

Whatever it was, it withdrew the offending foot.

Even in the dim light, I could see that this mini-monster lacked a discernable female form, its flaming orange hair had been crisped by cheap tint, and too many facelifts had stretched its skin as taut as a Santeria drumhead. Twin obsidian eyes glinted up at me over a hawkish nose that had been pared an inch too short, and its twitching fingers were tipped with red nails that curved downward like a feline's claw fresh from a kill. As repulsive, what imitated human lips were only twin smears of hot pink lipstick that further accentuated the yellow of her teeth, each being small, square, and oddly gapped — I felt an instant need for a spray can of insecticide.

"You will come with me now, Victor," spider woman commanded. "And I mean *nowwwwww!*"

"Oh, oh, oh, my dear, dear Lydia," he whined. "I-I only came to explain to Robert that…"

"Explain what? To him? Who is he? He's a nobody, a nothing; he's an idiot!"

"Hold it, Baby Jane!" I snarled back. "Who in the hell are you to…"

"Victor! Get in my car!"

"I-I brought my own…"

"Mine!"

Without an argument, without standing up for his human-hood, a slump-shouldered Victor Zarley slumped out while Lydia cast warning glares and sneers my way before she stalked after him. The sound of tires squealing away toward Bayshore Drive faded into an uneasy tropical silence.

"… and I still feel rotten that I left him there. Maybe I should have believed him about her being soulless. Maybe I should have knocked…"

Nino flicked his eyes to where we knew Minnie was listening. He wriggled his eyebrows and shook his head to warn me to say no more for now, at least on that subject.

"Remember that valley you saw in your dream? Too bad that Osceola boy didn't make his run straight and true," he said while unwrapping a fresh cigar. "You know, nobody can dodge a doggoned thing this life throws at us; it doesn't do no good to rub out a sick or a busted up body. That's like shootin' your car because it gets dents or runs out of gas. The next one you get might have a bum motor or a transmission on the fritz so you'd appreciate what you had. See, all that happens to us has its reasons even when it don't look like it's fair. I figured when I lost this stick and most of my best grabbin' hand that I'd better learn to live with what's left. That way maybe I'll get a better deal next time around.

"Like that preacher man, that Miccosukee boy had big names to live up to. 'Victor' means a winner and 'Osceola' means Black Drink Crier. One of those *aiyicks meforsee* — that's a sort of medicine maker — they cook up a drink that's so nasty only the bravest of the young bucks can take it on. It's blackish-green looking stuff; mean as all get-out. Some guys puke so hard they get to see special things, if you know what I mean. Some even gotta change their walk-around names to better fit 'em."

"Their what?"

"What were you called when you were a little kid?"

"Bobby."

"Then what?"

"I grew into Bob when I was about 12 or so. I didn't like it much, though. That's what people do to get apples."

"And when did you start using 'Robert'?"

"It took a while before that fit; people expect you to be a serious person. I like to laugh too much."

"And that's why folks should be careful what handle they hang on some poor kid. What's good for a baby doesn't cut the mustard when it's time to get serious, and them that's named Bubba or Zeke or has some cutesy-pootsy spelling only makes it harder when they want to leave the crib to head up a bank or maybe run for governor or some-such."

" 'Nino' says you're a boy-son. Can I ask what your other Apache names were?"

"Aw, we only use them among our clans. You gotta earn 'em, though. The big one comes in private visions. If you don't keep it secret it'll lose its power."

"How many times have you changed your walk-around name?"

"Oh, whenever an old one got me into trouble."

"Ask Nino about the one he took from a gravestone. That's a good story," Minnie called out.

He whispered, "We ought to call her Minnie Eagle-Ears! She'd hear a rat in the grass a mile off."

"What's this about a gravestone?"

"Back when my time at Pahgotzinkay was over, Sid Wilson[36] — he used to work for ol' John Slaughter — he taught me English to get me by. The problem was every time I hung around these parts, I had to pretend I was *Nakai-ye,* a Mexican, so I took up the name Ramon Rodriquez."

"Why that one?"

"He wasn't using it anymore. Well sir, I soon found out being Mexican wasn't a bed of roses either in the white man's world, so I took to letting people call me whatever suited 'em. That went along just fine until this Social Security thing kicked in. Hell, I didn't have a birth certificate to stick with them made-up names, y'see, but I happened by a cemetery one time where they was putting up a new gravestone. They told me their customer was from a town nearby and it looked like a good name to me, so I borrowed it."

"But you'd need a birth certificate…"

"Aw, I just slipped a notary I knew a quick five bucks and a pint of rotgut to make one up for me. He mailed it off and in no time I was in-like-Flynn."

"All set then, huh?"

"Well, sort of. See, that dead fella was a heap younger than me and I got drafted when I was old enough to be a granddaddy!" Nino shook his head as if it still baffled him. "Oh well, this Apache was born to fight so it didn't make no never-mind."

"I hear you two whispering? Ain't polite, you know," Minnie called out again.

"Say, when's ol' Brownsey comin' over?" Nino yelled back while

---

[36] Sid Wilson was a lifelong friend to Nino. He was written up in *Life* magazine as America's oldest cowboy just before his death at age 102.

winking at me. "He's late!"

"Now you know we're going there! Can't you remember anything? And don't rush me! I'm almost ready!"

"Works every time," Nino grinned. "Say, Guy, let's all go over to Council Rocks and I'll show you where my grandfather met up with General Howard.[37] We'll go in Brownsey's Jeep. You'll like him; he was the last elected Marshall of Tombstone and, by golly, he was as good as any Earp born."

"Great! I'll just pop out to change into my hiking boots and grab a jacket — ow! Damn!"

I glimpsed Cleo diving back beneath Nino's couch after tasting my ankle. She was whining — and I was smiling. I hoped her mouth would burn for a week.

◊ ◊ ◊

Millie and Everett Brownsey's adobe home was located on the southwest corner of 2nd Street and Safford in the historic part of old Tombstone.[38] Two blocks south was the site of the fabled OK Corral gunfight between the Clanton and McLaury gang and the Earps. Two blocks west put you on the front porch of Wyatt Earp's house when he was marshal; two east and you could push through the doors to the Crystal Palace Saloon where everyone who was anyone in Tombstone's history bellied up to a bar that stands to this day.

Everett greeted us in typical western style: a huge smile, a crushing handshake, a wary eye, and a cowboy's craving to test the mettle of any new acquaintance. His eyes twinkled when Nino introduced me as someone looking for the Yampricos.

"You came to the right sharpshooter, Roberto," Everett chortled

---

[37] President Grant had sent General Oliver Otis Howard to make peace with the Chiricahua Apaches by acknowledging their ancestral area as a reservation. The scout Tom Jeffords, a friend first to Chief Cochise and later to Nino, was its first agent.

[38] The Brownseys found bones and a skull when they tried to create a garden. It seemed their plot of ground had once been an unmarked graveyard for Chinese miners.

through his handlebar moustache. "Give me a day or two to sight in my new 7 mm magnum and I'll bag one of them big monkeys for you."

"Brownsey used to trick shoot for Winchester so he sees everything through a doggoned gun sight," Nino snorted.

A cheerful woman with an ever-ready smile, Millie Brownsey promised that evening's late supper would begin with a kettle of Mexican beans that she and Minnie would slow cook over a bed of throbbing-hot mesquite coals. That said, she tossed in a second handful of raw chili peppers from her garden for good measure plus chunks of fatback bacon. We men folks were ordered to have our tails back no more than an hour or two after sundown. We were also promised "mesquitized" ranch-grown chickens, Texas-size steaks, and a long line of Irish potatoes.

Everett gave a hoot, jammed a dusty cowboy hat down around his ears, cinched up his inlaid turquoise and silver belt buckle, holstered a hog-leg Colt .45, tossed a canteen of water into his battered Jeepster station wagon, and waved Nino and me on board. We rattled out of town due north past the old Boot Hill cemetery that is reputed to hold the bones of the Clanton and McLaury boys who were felled in 1881 by the blazing guns of Doc Holliday and the Earp brothers at the OK Corral fandango. A scant mile further up the Benson Highway, Brownsey made a turn onto Middlemarch Road that bore east toward the rising escarpment of the Dragoon Mountains. Indeed, we were entering the last ancestral homeland of the fierce Chiricahua Apache nation.

"Know where you are, Guynatay?" Nino asked.

There he goes with that guy stuff again. It wasn't worth bringing up, so I just shrugged and said, "I read a lot about this area and I have all the topo[39] maps, but I won't say I know it until I've walked it stem-to-stern."

"Oh boy, oh boy," he laughed and slapped his knee. "My uncle

---

[39] topographical

Gothlaka[40] played a darned good trick along this here road. He hid a whole string of his best warriors in the brush, don't you know. They waited until a supply wagon train came out of old Fort Bowie on their way to Tucson. When the last wagon in line passed by that first warrior, he hopped on board from its rear-end and snuck up behind the driver. He, um, put him to sleep, y'see, and then shoved him off so he could take his place at drivin'. So long as that wagon kept in line, no one lookin' back would get the jitters. Then another warrior hopped on board the next wagon up and he'd do the same thing, see? That's the way they worked their way up the line…"

Brownsey rolled his eyes.

"Put 'em to sleep, my foot! Your relatives were slitting their throats!"

"Aw, they only did what they had t'do," Nino guffawed. "Came natural, don't you see," Nino cooed with a wink. "Anyway, they kept pullin' that trick until there was only the lead wagon left. When that ol' boy heard something bump up behind him, he turned around to find my uncle staring him eyeball-to-eyeball. Whoee!"

"Face-to-face with Geronimo? What happened?"

"Well, sir, that fella took only one good slice in the neck before he jumped off and played dead in the dirt while Gothlaka and his gang drove off with their booty. When they got out of sight that ol' white boy jumped up and didn't stop runnin' until he hit Tucson. He went kind of nuts after that, y'know. Couldn't get him to leave town. He's probably still there."

"That's a true story, but I can't remember that boy's name just now," Brownsey nodded as he took a left turn onto a sandy lane just where the Middlemarch begins to twist up through a narrow pass that eventually drops it into the distant Sulfur Valley.

Bouncing over a ribbed cattle guard, we mushed up a narrow, sandy

---

[40] The Apache name for the infamous Geronimo. He had married a daughter of Cochise and thus became Nino's uncle.

trail that wound through washes and thick chaparral. As we entered what had been the final bastion of the historic old Apacheria, I found myself wondering how many ghosts were still standing vigil among all those tan boulders.

"This old heathen saved my life, did he tell you that?" Brownsey asked as we lurched through another sandy wash.

"Aw, now don't go into all that again," Nino groaned.

"You got regrets for keeping me breathing?" Brownsey snapped.

"Only when you go to tellin' that doggoned story!"

"Here's how it went down, Roberto. When I got elected Marshal of Tombstone, I was dumb enough to think I could stop some of those drug runners that had been using an old landing strip we've got down toward Bisbee. It's close enough to the border that they were brush hopping up those canyons at night, y'see. Well, I'd cracked a few heads along the way and picked off so many loads that I got to be a burr under their saddle. Then one night I got a phone call from some Mexican yahoo pretending to be an informer who wanted to spill the beans on his partners. He said he was afraid to come to my office but he'd meet me over at the Crystal Palace Saloon on Allen Street. He must have thought I was dumb as a box of rocks. I loaded up two .45s and was almost out the door when I got another call from old Nino here. He'd been having a few snorts at that Palace, too, and he'd overheard two Mexicans talkin' about what they were going to do to me."

"I got reminded of ol' Virgil Earp getting bushwhacked in about that same place by ol' Pete Spence and that durned Ike Clanton.[41] Then they killed Morgan (Earp) to boot! Gonna kill a man, be man enough to look 'im in the eye first."

"Well sir, I went over all primed up to plug a couple of them drug runners," Brownsey went on. "Hell, by the time I got there more of them

---

[41] This was not proven in a court of law, but all evidence pointed that way as they had the motive, the opportunity, and the temperament.

skunks had come out of the woodwork. Now I had five to deal with. I was out-gunned the minute I walked in, but those yellow-bellies didn't count on this old one-legged, hooched-up redskin sittin' at the table behind 'em."

"Aw, I wasn't much help," Nino said with a chuckle. "All I had was a pea-shooter stuck in my boot and a pig sticker in my pocket."

"But you were friends?" I asked.

"Not then. Never met Brownsey formal-like. Maybe a nod here and there."

"So, why —"

"Why? You won't never see this Apache pass up a chance to roll in the dirt with any greaser[42] he can get in his sights! I got reasons a-plenty. They murdered my wife and lots of my people," Nino said grimly.

"So you weren't even a deputy?"

"Was I?"

"Oh, sure, sure! Don't you remember? I deputized you over the phone that same night," Brownsey said with a cackle and a wink. "That was quite a scrap — two against five — until they figured out one of us had a leg missing. They kicked Nino's wooden stick out from under him and down he went! One got to stomping on his stump before I got that monkey's head cracked. Anyway, Nino's jumpin' in cost him another chunk off his short leg."

"You got shot?"

"I got the gangrene from all that stomping. And that can hurt real bad," Nino said.

"I had a hell of a time getting him to the hospital," Brownsey said. "He thought those doctors would pull the sheet on him as soon as they

---

[42] Nino did not apply that derogatory term to the average Mexican, only to banditos and killers. Among his many Mexican friends was Pancho Villa. Nino had a picture of him on his wall, a gift from Poncho's widow.

figured he was Injun."[43]

"I wasn't ready to turn my toes up just yet, y'see," Nino said.

"Before I'd heard he was sick — been a couple weeks — he'd been using that Apache tea he makes from chaparral leaves. Boy, that stuff'll cure you or kill you."

"It's awful, all right," Nino gagged.

"I can't say that tea slowed his gangrene down, but something sure held the line for this old turd-bird. Like they say, Apaches are tough customers. Anyway, when I finally got him dragged over to that horse-pistol in Sierra Vista, I stood guard while they sawed him a good ten inches shorter on one side. I wore my badge so they'd know I carried some weight."

"Let's get off it; all this gabbin' is makin' my stump hurt."

"So you and Nino have known each other a long time, huh?"

"About 10-12 years."

"You mean you were 90 when you got in that brawl?"

"Haven't had a good one since," the old man grumbled.

Those two characters may have taken it all in stride, but most folks I know give up life's adventures by the time they hit 60, whining that they are too old for this or for that. Nino set one hell of a different example[44] for me.

The Jeepster rolled to rest below a jumble of huge boulders and outcroppings. Brownsey elected to wander off to rummage around the nearby ruins of an old Butterfield stage stop where the outlaw Curly Bill Brocius is reputed to have carved his name. Crutches also prevented Nino from negotiating the steep trail leading up to the actual treaty site. I was left to discover it on my own, and that suited me just fine.

The place the Chiricahuas knew as Council Rocks nestles amid a

---

[43] It was a commonly held belief that white doctors would pull the sheet over the older Indians and let them die as opposed to trying to save them.

[44] I am 72 as I write this and I still haven't figured out what I'll do if I ever grow up. Using his scale, I have 35 more years to think about it.

Photo by Robert Morgan

Figure 10: Robert Morgan pointing to the pictographs representing the treaty with Cochise.

vast jumble of huge boulders on the northwestern edge of the Dragoon Mountains. There on a bulging overhang, as if to hide from the casual eye, resides a cascade of fading pictographs of that first treaty made between Cochise's band and Oliver Otis Howard, the one-armed "Christian" general President Grant had sent westward to pacify the fierce Chiricahuas.

History affirms that Howard had been empowered by President Grant to establish the boundaries and to promise by treaty that this portion of the Apache's ancestral lands would "forever" be their reservation.[45] I had read too that Howard's remarkable guide had been Tom Jeffords, the blood brother to Cochise and the man made legendary by the biography, film, and subsequent television series, *Broken Arrow.*

---

[45] That solemn promise would be forgotten the moment Cochise died. The Apache Wars resumed when John Clum replaced Tom Jeffords as their Indian agent and forcibly removed the Chiricahuas to the north amid the quarrelsome White Mountain Apache band.

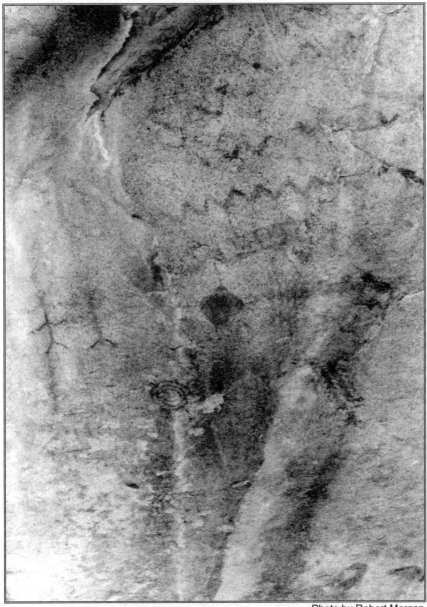

Photo by Robert Morgan

Figure 11: Pictographs representing the treaty with Cochise.

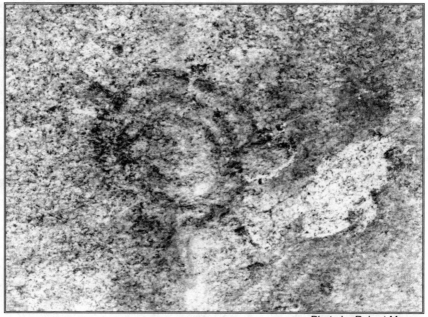

Photo by Robert Morgan

Figure 12: Cochise's signature.

Then something painted on the rock above me snapped me to attention. There was the fading but unmistakable sign of the famous Apache chief, Chies-Co-Chiese. His name translates into English as "hard (oak) wood." His symbol is composed of a series of blood-red concentric circles pierced by a wedge as if to split a log. Above it and to the right was also a clear depiction of an Apache Mountain Spirit, those whom superstitious Christians had erroneously dubbed as "Devil Dancers." I thrilled to realize that I was standing on the same sand where Cochise and his sons had stood, I could walk where Tom Jeffords had walked with General Howard, and perhaps I might sit where the shaman Dee-O-Det may have sat. Of course, it was all in my imagination, I am sure, yet the scent of hundreds of mesquite fires seemed to linger even though a century or more had passed. I vowed that one day I would return to make a series of close-up photographs and perhaps engage an

artist to create detailed sketches. After all, the relentless ravages of time
— or the stupidity of ignorant men — might one day deface this piece of
our great western history.

I sat first on this rock and then another and yet another before I
finally squatted onto the warm, warm sand itself. These were now my
rocks and my sand and I knew my estrangement from my soul's old
home in Apacheria had ended.

I waited patiently to soak up my first desert sunset of that trip. I was
not disappointed; indeed, the horizon steadily grew to a crescendo of
fiery orange flames before melting down and down into a vast wall of
shimmering gold and amber. Closer, across the valley, the Whetstone
Mountains drifted into cloaks of grays and blues that held scattered
blushes of lavender and royal purple. A single flash of lightning flickered
around the distant Rincon Mountains to the northwest to warn us that a
desert storm might soon blow our way. I wanted to stretch out not so
much to sleep but to ask my nagual, my unseen benefactor, to lead me
where I was certain we had wandered before — *waugh*! What was that?
Something was out there. Something was among the chaparral. It had not
made a noise, not exactly. It was neither a rustling breeze nor a dancing
dust devil; it wasn't a human voice nor was it the call of some wild thing.
It was as if something vast and huge was... sighing? Har! I had heard
that some natural sprits of desert lands play tricks on unsuspecting
minds, so I sat motionless while that dying sun gave its final kiss to the
gloaming.

I found Nino alone and staring as if mesmerized by a tiny fire.
Interestingly, the flickering lights were smoothing most of the wrinkles
that furrowed his face. Indeed, he appeared wise and noble and yet
capable of savagery.

"Did you see our treaty?" he asked as I settled down opposite him.

"Yes."

"Did you understand it?"

"I think so… instinctively, of course."

"Did you feel it up there?"

"Oh, I wouldn't dare touch it."

"That's not what I mean. Did you feel *it*?"

"Yes, sir. I think I did."

"Did you hear it, too?"

"… yes."

When Nino spoke again, his voice was weighted with melancholy overtones.

"I love this place more than any other on earth. There are times when I can smell the smoke from our old fires; sometimes I hear those kids playing when I was still sucking at my mother's nipple. That was such a grand time when we were all free and could ride for days in any direction and never leave our own land."

"In your book[46] you said you were taken into Mexico when you were what, two or three? How could you possibly remember all that?"

"Oh, I remember lots of things that aren't just from this life. I've been an Apache ever since I was first brought down to this earth, and that was a long, long time ago. Next time around I'll be an Apache all over again and I'll come and I'll sit where I'm sitting now and I'll give you the same answers if you'll come to ask me. There ain't a True Human Being on this earth who doesn't want to get back to the place of their first roots."

"You really believe that?"

"Why not? Look out there where all those restless souls are always running from pillar to post, moving here, moving there, always knowing that when they get one place that they'll soon be moving on to the next. They're really looking for a place among their own tribe, their own people; they just don't know it.

"Souls of True Human Beings rest easy only in certain places —

---

[46] *The First Hundred Years of Nino Cochise*, Abelard-Schuman, 1971.

that's the way it is for people like you and me and the Yampricos, too. The difference is they know who and what they are because no one can deceive 'em. See? They don't have them Deceivers after 'em all the time like we do."

In ways I cannot explain, I understood exactly what he meant. The problem had been, until then, that I didn't know that I knew.

"Did ol' Round-Bear give you anything special?" He stayed my hand when I reached for that little charm that I kept in my pocket. "That says he took you as a serious person. Did you ever read anything about Ghost Dancing and that Paiute prophet, Wovoka?"

"A little, but..."

"Do you know why Wovoka was trying to get the tribes to stop fighting among themselves?"

"As I recall, he wanted them to stand together against the whites, but not in warfare; he knew they had the bigger guns."

"That's part of it. Mostly, those Ghost Dancers were dancing to be forgiven for all their past foolishness. They wanted Usen or Wakan-Tonka to let the souls of all their ancestors who were still resting to come back quick to help them get back to the ways of the First Times before it became such a big honor to be a thief or a killer or to own slaves."

"You mean before the white man came?"

"Way, way before that — and don't go blaming everything on the whites. You gotta understand those Pretenders were already here making us fight one another even before ol' Columbus showed up. Hell's bells, it got so bad that no Indian woman dared to take a bath alone without worrying she'd get swiped by another tribe and made into a brood mare for the first buck that had enough skins to trade for her. Those weren't the happy times we like to pretend. Then, when we got our mitts on horses and guns, what did we do? We didn't go after the whites out of the gate; instead, we first used 'em to rub out the other tribes around us."

"It's only natural to attack an old enemy or to protect your food supply —"

"Horse pucky! Even when there was enough food for everyone, those goldurned bucks loved to go struttin' and dancin' to brag how tough they were and who was the biggest thief among 'em. They did that while their women made life miserable for all their slaves who did the real dirty work — American blacks think they were the first slaves in America. Hah! Pert near every tribe had 'em even before the English brought over what they called indentured servants, which is just a fancy name for a white slave. Just ask the Irish."

"But…"

"Facts are facts, and I don't care if you like 'em or not. We Indians had already done a good job at poisoning any peace in our lives a long time before them priests came to teach us their brand of baloney. Huh! It was nice of 'em to take a few hundred years to decide if we had souls, too!"

"But Nino, look what the whites did to Sitting Bull…"

"Bullets fired by Sioux killed him."

"Yes, but Chief Joseph…"

"He was tracked down by Crow and Cheyenne scouts for the white army — and didn't our own Apache scouts play bloodhound to chase down Gothlaka and old Nana and Victorio and Mangas Coloradas just for the white man's dollar, a jug of booze, and some pants with yellow stripes? You'd better talk to some tribal truth-tellers instead of their *story*-tellers before you go blaming things on the color of somebody's skin. Ol' Taglito had a red soul inside that white hide of his, to show you what I mean.

"See, before that Columbus fella ever dreamed about turning his snoot west, the Winnebagos were chasing the Dakotas out of Minnesota; Lakotas were killing off the Hidatsa, Mandans, Pawnees, and Crows, while those same Crows were crowding in on the Blackfeet. That's about the same time the Cheyenne had it in for the Shoshone and the ol'

Iroquois were burnin' alive all the Hurons they could catch!"

"But the People were only trying to live the perfect life —"

"Aw, Guy, that manure would make a rose bloom in the dead of winter! Listen to some of them words the real Ghost Dancers used when they sang, '*We, the True Human Beings of all nations, we of all tribes, we beg out Father Spirit to bring back all our ancestors and all our buffalo and make the earth roll back over the Others and drive them back to their stars. We want to return to the days of harmony as in the days of the beginning when we were all brothers and sisters and we shared everything and sang our thanks to the souls of the maize and the buffalo for sustaining our life.*' "

Nino sighed as if he had lived through it all, adding, "We woke up too late, and that's the truth of it. Usen got disgusted with all our squabbling so now we gotta earn another chance."

Closing that subject, he scooped up a large rock and dropped it onto the sand in between us. He asked that I describe it to him. Naturally, I played along with his game by describing every feature of that rock from my point of view. Then, thinking I was being smarter than the average bear, I crept around to his side to repeat the process while peering over his shoulder. He said nothing until I had strutted back to my side of the fire. My gloat didn't last long. He picked up the rock, flipped it bottom-side up, and slapped it down again. Not only had I forgotten its bottom, but all its angles had changed, too.

"What do you think about reincarnation?" he asked to let me off the hook.

"It makes sense, but I didn't know Indians believed in it."

"Once I got caught in the open by a gang of Mexican Rurales who wanted me dead. They'd chased me way south of the Cañon del Cobre. I was in big trouble because we didn't have maps in those days."

"I didn't know Indians could get lost," I chuckled.

"Yeah, just like white men never lie. Anyway, I popped out of this arroyo to look around. Dead ahead was a mountain that looked kind of familiar by its shape and all. Now, I knew darned well I'd never been there, but I was just as sure there was a fine camp of friendly folks just over that ridge. Plain as day, I knew they'd be camped where two rivers met; hell, I could pert-neer smell that good water. I took off lickety-split because my horse and me needed to wet our whistles.

"Well, sir, darned if I didn't scoot up this little canyon you could hardly see even if you knew it was there. Up I went just as if I knew what I was doing, and doggoned if I didn't find a slip-through crack at its far end just big enough for my pony and me. We lost them Rurales — or maybe they didn't want to follow this Apache into such a narrow place, eh? Good thing, though. When I busted out on the other side I almost got myself killed."

"More Rurales," I asked while my mind's eye conjured a vivid picture of two rivers meeting up amid a vast grove of huge cottonwood trees. For whatever reason, I also envisioned wattle-and-mud huts where naked children played and cooking fires were tended by their mamas. People were shuttling between pumpkin and squash patches and rows of ripening corn — but where were the himpers, those long breechcloths unique to the Apache? Where were their signature thigh-high kabun moccasins with the turned-up toes? I mentally rescanned this vision. There was not a single horse, a mule, a pig, a donkey or even a chicken to be seen. This was a primitive encampment, indeed.

Nino's chuckle drew me back to our present-day fireside.

"Wasn't no blamed water there! No trees, neither. Boy oh boy, was I in a pickle. I'd found the exact place I'd seen in my mind's eye except those two old riverbeds were long dry and it was as deserted as a graveyard.[47] It was all sand, so I had to sneak back around those Rurales

---

[47] Years after, Nino had occasion to lead a geologist employed by Colonel William C. Green, the Copper King, to that spot while exploring Northern Mexico for another place to mine copper. The geologist assured Nino that those riverbeds had been dry for over 1,000 years.

after dark."

"What does this have to do with reincarnation?"

"Do you remember that my first wife was Tarahumari?"

"Of course; Golden Bird was —"

"*Hsssst!*" he snapped. "Just say 'Bird'!"

How stupid of me! I knew that most traditional Indians avoid speaking aloud the names of the recently dead because they believe it interrupted their rest in between lives.

"But I've heard you referring aloud about Gothlaka, Dee-O-Det, Mangas, Nana, Chatto, Juh, and even your mother, father, and grandfather."

"Yeah, but they're probably back by now. It only takes about 70 years or so to do that jump-down, turn-around, y'know."

"Seventy years before… ?"

"Before they come back for another try."

"Oh, right. What about her? Maybe she's back, too."

"I'm sure she's waitin' so we can come back together, but I'll still have to take a little rest in between these lives, don't you see. They wear me out! Say, that'll be just right so you can join up with us again. How about it?"

"You mean me and you and, er, Bird? Yeah, great, but let's bring Riki, too. I'll be your kid and Riki can be mine again."

"Shake, partner. Now let me tell you something that's not in my book. Y'see, her father had brought what was left of his band up to Pahgotzinkay to ask for some protection. I guess that when my mother saw her, she'd decided then and there it was time to get me hitched up."

"Why didn't she want you to marry an Apache?"

"Aw, I was too mean and they were too, so it would've been one long tussle," he snorted and laughed. "Anyway, I got all spruced up and went over to my mother's cabin to meet this mystery girl. When she came in and sat down beside me, I felt as if I already knew her and she was that half of me that I didn't know was missing until she showed up and held my hand — what's the matter?"

"You said 'cabin.' I thought old-time Apaches lived in brush wickiups."

"I already told you when we first got to palaver! It's too doggoned cold up in them Sierras, so we built log cabins just like anybody would that had a lick of sense.

"Anyway, Bird was about 16 or so and was such a little thing. All Tarahumaris were little — except her father. He wasn't as big as me, but he was tall.

"Anyway, after we got hitched she told me I'd been her husband before."

"She meant in her dreams?"

"Way before that. She was hoping, too, that we could get our kids back, you know, the same ones we'd had when we lived down where those two rivers met. Then, we… what's eatin' at you now?"

"You mean that Gold, er, Bird remembered that place we were just talking about?"

"Darned tootin'! And she'd been there all right, but not in this life. She even drew a right smart map of it; hell, we'd had a whole blamed village with us back then. She knew all about those two rivers and she even drew a picture of that little mountain with its sneak-through canyon. I thought my heart would pop right out of my chest when she poked her finger down where she said we'd lived among them big old trees that used to be there.

"I hated to tell her it was all gone, but when I did, she said she wanted to go back just so's we could make our babies there just like we'd done before."

"Did you?"

"No, no… them Rurales, uh, they…"

How double-damned-dumb of me! He had graphically described that scene in his book about her being shot down while trying to reach his side during a firefight.

Nino's face grew old again.

"She's up in a little cave with my mother and my sister Nadine. I put Dee-O-Det with 'em, too," he said.

"I'll take you down to Pahgotzinkay if you want to go. We could take some flowers…"

He didn't answer so I excused myself to fetch something from the Jeepster that was never there. When I returned, I saw that tears had washed twin trails down his dusky cheeks. I offered him my handkerchief.

"They say Apaches don't cry, son," he said. "I guess I only get sand in my eyes."

"Time to hit the trail, boys," Brownsey bellowed as he rolled out of the brush. "We just got time enough for a few good belts before we tackle that big supper the women folks are fixin'!"

12. Meeting the Judge

Brownsey parked in front of the *Tombstone Epitaph* newspaper office, just around the corner from the Crystal Palace Saloon. Less than a century before, the Oriental[48] across 5th Street and the old Birdcage Theater[49] down the way on Allen, also had been favorite watering holes for characters right out of Clint Eastwood's film *The Good, the Bad, and the Ugly*.

Being Saturday night, the old Palace was crowded, smoky, and noisy. Stepping inside was akin to stepping back in time. Grainy photographs spotted around the walls from the 1880-90s proved that not much had changed since the times when Wyatt, Virgil, and Morgan Earp, Doc Holliday, Luke Short, Buckskin Frank Leslie, Billy the Kid Claiborne, Ike Clanton, Tom McLaury, Curly Bill Brocius, and Johnny Ringo had bellied up to this same bar of dark wood and polished brass.

Nino's favorite table — closest to the wall and left of the entrance — was being emptied by a clutch of tourists in baggy shorts and razzy T-shirts, so we snatched it. From there he and Brownsey could watch the doors and everyone in the joint. Some habits die hard.

We had barely settled onto our seats before a character calling himself Johnny Guitar sidled over to pay his respects. Spotting me as the

---

[48] Now it's a gift shop. Yuk!

[49] It's a museum! Oh, no! Where's Big Nose Kate and the rest of "the girls?" (sigh)

greenhorn, he welcomed me to where, he said, the world's ugliest women and dustiest cowboys came on weekends to wrestle around the dance floor to the racket made by the West's worst band. Deftly pocketing the tip left by the previous patrons, Johnny made for the far end of the bar before our waiter showed up to clear the table and take our order. He left muttering something about cheap-ass tourists.[50]

Our first round of cold brews had barely sloshed the grit off our tonsils before Nino's better eye went wide before narrowing. He was staring at an elderly man poised in the doorway like a specter from the past. This stick-thin fellow was ninety-five if he was a day, but he stood tall and as ramrod straight as a new post. His dress was black from the toes of his brushed cowboy boots to his trousers and vest and to his wide-brimmed hat. Only his dress shirt was white, and it was white-white. He looked neither left nor right as he did a slow saunter directly to the bar. He shoved the toe of his right boot up on the shiny brass rail and stared dead-ahead into the mirror.

I was thinking that this could easily be a bad guy in a 1935 Hoot Gibson movie when Nino breathed, "Ain't seen that killer out after dark in a coon's age. Looks like he's still cheatin' Old Harry, though."

Without a word spoken between them, the bartender placed a shot glass down in front of our specter and brimmed it with Old Crow whiskey. The thought zipped through my mind that this character might be playing the part of a gunfighter in some local drama. All he needed was a .45 Colt hog-leg six-shooter dangling from his waist and another bad guy at the far end of the bar waiting to slap leather…

"Ask the ol' judge to join us," Nino murmured.

"That's a judge?"

"In a way. See, if a fella was guilty of a crime and was wanted by the law and gave him any lip, he shot 'em on the spot."

"Huh? Why?"

---

[50] We three agreed to leave an extra tip for that poor guy. Sh! Don't tell.

Figure 13: William Thomas Warner with author and Hobie Earp (second cousin to Wyatt Earp), Tombstone, Arizona. 1979.

"Silent Bill — that's what most folks called him 'cause he's always been short on words but long on action. He was a sort of range detective, a regulator for hire on both sides of the border. He went after rustlers for the cattlemen associations and, when he ran out of them for target practice, he took up bounty huntin'."

"You mean that's an honest-to-God hired gunman?"

"Like as not he's never buried no dog who didn't bite — except that one time when he threw down on me in Cananea 'cause he thought I was somebody I wasn't."

"Where's that?"

"I already told you about that. Cananea is in Mexico."

"Wasn't 'throwing down' on you against the law?"

"Not in Mexico and never on an Apache anywhere they got caught off the rez," Nino snorted.

"Did he hunt down Apaches?"

"Never asked 'im."

"But now he's your friend?"

"William Thomas Warner doesn't make friends, but there's a few folks he'll nod to. Go ask him to join us for a toot."

I took a long, long swig of beer. From where I sat, I could look through the open door and into the street. I could see the exact spot where U.S. Marshall Virgil Earp's left arm had been shattered by some unknown bushwhackers on the night of December 28, 1881. That was just two months after Virgil, Wyatt, Morgan Earp, and Doc Holliday had shot it out with the Clantons and the McLaurys three blocks away in the vacant lot behind the OK Corral. When the smoke cleared — some 30 shots had been fired in 30 seconds — Tom and Frank McLaury and Billy Clanton lay dead. A few weeks later Morgan Earp was assassinated.

I did some fast math. All this Wild West shoot 'em up stuff had happened only 54 short years before I had been born, and well within my grandfather's lifetime. Yet here I sat hunched around a table with the last Apache alive that had been born free, an ex-marshal of Tombstone, and now I am supposed to invite an honest-to-God gunfighter to share our table?

Oh, what the hell, I thought; I'll play out my hand before all this thinking gives me a headache. I lapped up the dregs of my beer before performing my best imitation of a Western saunter up to the bar.

"We'd like to buy you a drink at our table, Mister Warner, sir," I said as I bellied up beside the man in black. Silent Bill tossed his whiskey down neat and quick without batting an eye, uttering a hello, a goodbye, or a kiss my rosy sit-upon.

A single rap of his glass brought the bartender scurrying back for another round of redeye.

"An old friend of yours would like you to join him," I said in a louder voice.

Photo by N. Erika Morgan

Figure 14: The oldest and best of the West gather for a brief reunion in Tombstone, AZ. Standing, left to right, Sid Wilson, at age 102 America's oldest living cowboy; Hobart Earp, 1956 fast-draw champion; Everett Brownsey, the last elected marshal of Tombstone. Seated, left to right, Nino Cochise, age 105, America's oldest Apache chief who had been born free; John R. Clarke, age 96, the last surviving original member of the Arizona Rangers; Silent Bill "Judge" Warner, age 92, America's last living range detective.

Must be stone deaf, I was thinking... until his skull swiveled on its spindly neck and I was being studied by two of the coldest blue eyes I have ever seen. I would have sworn his lips never moved under that grey mustache, but I heard him whisper, "Don't know you, son." With that, that gaunt geezer returned his gaze to the mirror.

Forget the saunter; I fairly slunk back to Nino's table to report. Before my butt could hit the chair, Nino snarled, "He pert'neer shot me down like a dirty dog in the street. You tell him I'll give 'im a new belly button if he turns down our invite!"

Quick-trotting back to the bar I said, "Excuse me, sir, I don't mean to

bother you again, but this friend of yours insists that you join us."
Ignored once more, I shot an exasperated glance at Nino. My weenie-
shrug made his upper lip curl, his best eye sparked fire, and I wondered if
he might have that gun in his boot again.

"Look, Mister Warner, Nino Cochise really would like it if..."

"Who?"

"Uhhhh, Nino Cochise. He said that I should invite you over to..."

William T. "Silent Bill" Warner drained that shot glass in a single
toss, patted some bills flat to the bar, and performed his signature saunter
over to our table... and danged if he didn't choose *my* chair to kick
around to fold onto.

I ponied up for another round of suds and whiskey all around before
ambling over to join them — yes, yes, I said "ambled." Let me explain:
to saunter in Tombstone is a surefire invitation for some tanked up
cowboy to roll you around in the dirt to make sure you have the right to
go around doing a Western saunter. Merely ambling, however, indicates
you might belong there — maybe.

On that note, allow me to share one more observation. Every red-
blooded male, no matter their origin or age, who is in Tombstone long
enough to hear their footsteps clumping along its raised wooden
sidewalks and who also hears those rinky-tinky plinkings of some out-of-
tune piano wafting above the buzz of a crowded saloon — and this
includes dudes fresh out of Brooklyn, London, Tokyo or wherever —
they all cease to walk, stride, or stroll. No sir; nuh-uh. They all
commence sauntering (!) along with a peculiar rolling gait as if they have
instant hemorrhoids and seeping saddle sores. Moreover, the words sure
become "shore," yes becomes "yup," and take a guess what no is. A
woman becomes a "ma'am," and a man becomes a "pardner" or an
"hombre" according to the situation.

Painfully conscious of the stares we were generating, I did my level
best to imitate Warner's chair-fold act — only then did I realize that I had

been outmaneuvered by these refugees from cowboy-and-Indian geriatric wards. Silent Bill's appropriation of my seat had placed me with *my* back to the door. Thus, I felt compelled to swing around from time to time to stare down potential bushwhackers as they sidled through the door. Thankfully, they were either slack-jawed tourists or more bleary-eyed good-time Charleys.

"You ever see one of them Yamprico fellers, Bill?" Nino asked.

That old goat jerked a thumb in my direction.

"You doin' the asking... or him?"

Nino vouched that I was his compadre, that he had formally adopted me as his son,[51] that I was sincere in trying to meet a Yamprico, and, by the bye, Hobie was looking forward to meeting me when he drifted in to hear about some of my adventures.

Too curious to wait, I asked who this Hobie character was.

"He's an Earp," Nino said.

"What sort of Earp?"

"There's only one kind of Earp! Hobie — don't ever call him Hobart — called yesterday. He's on his way down from Grass Valley. He's Wyatt's second or third cousin or something like that. He's just as fast, though."

"Hobie's fast," Silent Bill Warner agreed while loudly rapping his glass on the table for a refill.

"Fast as in...?"

"He's won some fast-draw competitions. Try him out when he gets here. I'll lend you my hog-leg if you want," Nino said.

"Only if I can use an M-16 at 300 yards. I'm dumb; I ain't stupid. So, how about those Yampricos?"

"Ever see one, Bill?" Nino asked again as the bartender appeared to

---

[51] He memorialized that honor in the inscription he placed in my copy of his autobiography. I was adopted in the Apache way. It's more lasting because it comes from the heart and it is an agreement not on paper but between two hearts. I take it quite seriously. He was more the father in spirit to me than my biological one.

refill Warner's glass to the brim, again without spilling a drop.

Warner stared into his fresh whiskey so long I thought he had forgotten the question. Then he shrugged and said, "Nope."

Thinking I might help jog a semi-atrophied memory, I offered, "Maybe you'd know them by the name Sasquatch, Bigfoot, the Abominable Snowman, Yeti, le loupe-garou, and —"

"Nope."

"I understand you first met Nino in Cananea? That's in Mexico, right?"

"Yup."

"And you almost shot him?"

"Pert-neer."

Nino said, "He thought I was that ol' Apachlakit — he still thinks all redskins look alike. But see, there was a big reward out for the Kid because he'd rubbed out some guards so ol' Bill here thought he'd cash in by passing off my carcass as his."

"He thought you were who?"

"He's talking about the Apache Kid," Warner said.

"What made you think Nino was him?" I asked.

"He fit the bill."

"*Waugh!*" Nino snapped. "If you'd faced it out instead of angling to bushwhack me, maybe when the dust settled it would've been me doin' the crowing!"

"Your book says you killed this Apache Kid — er — Apachlakit, when he tried to take over Pahgotzinkay," I interjected to keep the sparks down.

"Set a spell on that," said the suddenly not-so-silent William Thomas Warner. "I ain't sayin' Nino did and I can't say he didn't because I wasn't there, but there's been a heap of sightings of the Kid over the years since then, so I'm keepin' my books open."

"Yeah, and you'll be lookin' at them same dog-eared books until the cows come home 'cause I got the scars to prove it," Nino growled.

That comment would strike a chord in time. I would play his nurse-maid when Minnie became hospitalized. While helping him to bathe, I would spy a particularly long scar that seamed the inside of his right arm from armpit to elbow just as he had described in his book. I had also noted that his skin was brownish all over. Obviously, those detractors who would also claim that he was an imposter had not had that privilege.

"When you were out sneakin' around, did you ever see one of them flying saucer things?" Nino asked Warner while kicking my ankle under the table.

"Yup, I did, Nino."

My shock at such a quick response was followed by dread. How many hours would it take to drag out Warner's information if he kept speaking in monosyllables? What to do? I signaled the bartender to keep the refreshments flowing.

"I was ridin' herd on buff'ler on that reserve[52] they put up there in Montana country," Bill went on. "What I saw was real as rain. Weren't no aeroplanes back then,[53] but the contraptions I saw went to flittin' around faster than I could think. Then — whoosh! The whole gang went up the valley in an eye-blink."

"What did you do?" I asked.

"Collected my pay and went south faster than a scalded rabbit."

"Ever see any down this way?" Nino asked.

"Saw some along the San Pedro [River] down toward Colonel Greene's old place. Couldn't hear a whisper, but you sure could feel the weight when they passed over."

"When was that?" I asked.

"Don't recollect. Years back."

"Where'd they go?"

---

[52] National Bison Refuge was established in 1908 in Montana's Flathead Valley.
[53] The Wright Brothers took flight in 1903.

"They hung still for a spell near the old Clanton digs. Then two went straight up while their partner moseyed downriver toward Fairbank."

"Did it land there?"

"Didn't care to foller it."

"And...?"

"The last time was out past the old San Berna-doo.[54] Me and some Rangers was waitin' outside Skeleton Canyon for some smugglers to show. Came up short when them flyin' machines showed up to shine their sky-lights every which way. We hightailed it back to Nogales."

"Guy here saw one along the Rio Grande," Nino interjected. "About scared him blue."

Silent Bill Warner leaned close.

"Don't never let that light touch you, son."

"That's exactly what Nino says; I got the same advice from Round-Bear, too. He's a Seminole shaman."

"I don't hold much with heathen stuff," he snorted. "But some that run them machines ain't quite as human as some others, so watch your backside."

"Wait, wait! You think there's more than one kind?"

"I know so."

With that, he tossed off his last shot of whiskey, rose to his feet, touched Nino's shoulder, nodded to Brownsey, and gave my hand a firm shaking.

"Good luck on gettin' next to them Yampricos. I never saw one but I knowed good men what did, and them that said it weren't liars and I'll stand for 'em. And there was times when I felt things watchin' me that I couldn't see and heard stuff that didn't belong. My advice to you, young feller, is if you do get to see 'em, you'd best keep your mouth shut about it."

---

[54] The San Bernardino Ranch, AKA John Slaughter's Ranch, is a few miles east of present-day Nogales. See www.slaughterranch.com

"Why?"

"Upsettin' the apple carts of Bible-thumpers will send you to hell in a hand basket. You don't want to get between them and their offerin' plates. Much obliged for the redeye. G'night, boys."

Warner's sauntering exit tossed a blanket of melancholy over Nino. I wondered if he was thinking that he and Warner were among the remnants of a dying breed of men whose personas had been relegated to pretend movies filled with powdered-up actors who act tough but shoot blanks, paperback novels that lie a lot, and the fading pages of history books that could never do justice to their hearts and fire.

"I'll go to the john and then we'd better get our tails home for the grub," Brownsey said.

Nino sucked in a quick breath, and shook himself like a wet dog after Brownsey left the table.

"Gotta tell you somethin' quick, Guy. After I lost my mother, I went to work for ol' Colonel Greene at his copper mines at Cananea, yeah? Well, I got bored quick followin' him around t'Tucson and El Paso and places like that. He could see I was getting itchy for a long ride somewhere so he told me to guide some pimply-faced geologist from New Jersey out to find more copper. Greene didn't want that tenderfoot to lose his hair to some Yaqui-yori, don't you see?

"Well, this was an ugly gink who had maps and pencils and compasses sticking out of every pocket and always mumblin' about so many degrees this way, and so many minutes that way — nuts-stuff like that. After a week of him givin' a good horse a sore back with all them rock samples, I landed him down where those two rivers were supposed to meet but where I'd found no water."

"You mean where you and Gold — er — where you and Bird —"

"And that geologist didn't take an hour before he was tellin' me that he was dead certain there hadn't been water running through there for at least a couple hundred years or so, probably even a thousand."

"So that hadn't been the place you had imagined with her, after all?" Nino's jaw went slack as he stared at me.

"You can be dumber than a box of rocks! See, that's when all that other stuff started to make sense! This time around, I had time to think instead of worryin' about gettin' shot. While that ol' white boy went to chunking up rocks, I commenced to thinkin', but this time I let my 'other' mind do it. In no time, I was dead sure that I had lived right on that exact spot, and it wasn't no dream or wishful thinkin', neither. It was exactly what my Bird had described. That's why she wanted to go back there to make our babies all over again — that's the long and the short of it, son. Yessir, I even remembered all them houses of wattle-and-mud... what's wrong?"

"Er, um, what kind of trees were they? Exactly..." I gulped while recalling those images I had earlier that evening around our little fire. If he confirmed those trees were...

"Cottonwoods."

Oh, lordy-lord, lord-lord! How had I known that specific fact? Was it just a lucky guess? Moreover, what about that image I had had of me sitting across from him in that cave or cavern when we'd first met — his voice wrenched me back to the present.

"I'd even remembered then about havin' a whole family with a wife, kids, neighbors, and friends, the whole kit and caboodle! Now, you tell me how in the blue-blazes I could remember all that when I wasn't even married when I got there that first time!"

I was mystified. How could he be so cock-sure of these things? What had made him so open-minded to things that are beyond the ken of most everyone I had ever known? However, before I could ask more questions about those cottonwood trees, wattle huts, rivers flowing 1,000 years ago, I spotted Brownsey making his way back to us table by table, greeting this person, and gabbing with others. I had limited time to ask my final question in private. I explained that a new member of my

Science Advisory Board, E. E. Hedblom, MD, Captain, USN,[55] had proposed that I engage the services of one John Shelley of Portland, Maine, to "map-dowse" the presence of Yampricos even while I was tromping around the Cascade Mountains in the State of Washington. Naturally, I had assumed he was joking until Captain Hedblom had snapped that Mr. Shelley had been utilized by U.S. Naval Intelligence at the Brunswick Naval Air Station to map-dowse American flyers lost over the Gulf of Tonkin and the jungles of Vietnam. Amazingly, he had been 60-80% successful. The reason this was not publicized was obvious; one could only imagine the flak the Navy would get from the religious right for using such witchery. Nevertheless, as the good Captain said all too plainly, if John Shelley was good enough to save lives for the U.S. Navy, he sure as hell was good enough for me! To defuse the situation I had supplied Mr. Shelley with a duplicate map to the one I was using and agreed to confer with him each evening between 10:00 and midnight his time. I also had promised to check out any report he might share with me.

"What do you think, Nino? Did I do right?"

"Sure! Hell, I trusted that old coot Dee-O-Det and he never led me wrong. He saw all sorts of things in campfires and smoke and stuff like that. Maybe them things only provided the path for those whisperers to come help a feller out sometimes. Can't see 'em in the usual way, so they gotta do it somehow." He rapped his knuckles on the tabletop to help make his point. "Don't think you are ever alone. We got folks all around us watchin' out. You just gotta learn their language, see?"

"I-I don't know about all this…"

"Well, I think you do, Guynatay! Just stop analyzing everything like a white man! Let your red heart do some talkin'!"

"That's another thing. Why do you keep calling me 'guy' something

---

[55] I had been introduced to Captain Hedblom by anthropologist Peter Lipsio, a team member of our American Yeti Expeditions.

or other?"

"Huh! Thought I told you. I gave you a real name a while back. Forget that 'Bob' stuff. That's what kids do for apples. You are *Guy-nat'-ay!* Say it one way and it means *Not Afraid* because you go alone and without guns and such to meet up with them Yampricos. Say it another way and it sums up your dad-blasted temper!"[56]

"Time to tie on the feedbag, boys," Brownsey called out and waved us to follow him out. "Let's go quick or I'll be sleepin' in the shed again!"

Yes, indeedy! We devoured double-hot beans, steaks, chickens, potatoes, and everything else in sight until we were cross-eyed with contentment. Of course, in the presence of the ladies our conversation avoided any mention of Yampricos or sky-lights.

However, the time came for me to turn in. As is my wont, I like to be on the road just before sunrise. I had a long drive to the Mount St. Helens area of Washington where I was to rendezvous with a fresh team of serious researchers — mostly scientists — who had volunteered to help me solve the mystery of those giant people whom white folks like to call Bigfoot.

Brownsey was the last to wish me Godspeed with a hug and a grin.

"You be sure to call me if you need a sharpshooter to ride shotgun. I'll bag one of those big boogers for ya! Pow! Right between the eyes!"

"Goodnight, Brownsey..."

---

[56] I keep that meaning private for good reason.

13. Skookum Haunting

Cougar, Washington, 1973

"Morgan, wake up! There's been a sighting in Oregon! It's all over the radio — this is a hot one — less than 24 hours old! Hot, hot, hot," Peter Lipsio yelled while winging my boots in the general direction of my head.

Within the hour Peter, Harry Marcus, Bob Carr, Ed Dillon, and I were barreling away from the Mount St. Helens area for Oregon to rendezvous with Jim McClarin on site. Lipsio and Carr were respected anthropologists, and Marcus was a lieutenant with a Florida sheriff's department and an experienced crime scene analyst.

The only fly in our ointment was Dillon. He had good credentials as a recently graduated biologist, but he had an abrasive personality. He was one of those folks who made derisive comments about anything that was not his idea. We all know that type, but I put up with it. That turned out to be my mistake.

I was not surprised at the location of the reported encounter. The Dalles is a lovely town located at the mouth of the gorge where the Columbia River slices through the Cascade Mountain Range before making its final rush to the Pacific Ocean. Beyond its city lights and stretching eastward into Idaho are nearly two hundred miles of sparsely settled grasslands webbed by scrub oak coulees, huge wheat farms, lonely cattle ranches, and damned happy coyotes. However, it was west

264

of The Dalles that got the most Bigfoot action.[57] There, craggy canyons and hogback ridges wound down to the riverbanks from the foothills of Oregon's picture-perfect Mt. Hood. Across the Columbia River and north in Washington State hovered Mt. Adams, the rumbling and soon-to-erupt Mount St. Helens, and Mt. Rainier. This diamond-shaped segment of forests, mountains, and swift rivers had long been a hotbed of stories stretching back into the early nineteenth century when explorer David Thompson and the wandering artist Paul Kane recorded Indian beliefs about giant "skookums" that haunted the area. Indians that fished the Columbia or its tributaries made special fish racks set aside from their own as a sort of salute and tribute to those skookums. Moreover, while the native peoples swarmed to make the mountain huckleberry harvest each fall, they remembered to leave the red ones for their giant neighbors. These ancient practices remain to this day among the more traditional members of the Umatilla, Clatsop, Klickitat, Wasco, Wishram, and Yakima nations and the coastal tribes, too. Unlike most whites, they gladly share nature's bounty.

En route, Pete filled us in on that day's events. Persons of good reputation had made a report to the local police that a huge, hairy creature was seen wandering about the field across from the mobile home park where they lived. It had always walked erect, leaning down only to turn rocks over as if it was searching for rodents. Their report had made an instant uproar. Frightened mothers around the city and county locked their screen doors and windows, children hid under blankets, and macho men took to swabbing out the family shoulder-cannon.

The exact spot where these residents had sighted the "monster" had a recent history of high school students shooting at hairy giants said to lurk around the adjacent rock pit, and reliable deputy sheriffs had reported dark shapes leaping across roads come midnight.

---

[57] Obviously, sightings must be made by the human eye, and there are more eyes west of The Dalles than to the east.

Dusk had fallen by the time we arrived and already the site was crawling with armed macho men. Some, like Canadian researcher Rene Dahinden, had come from as far away as Canada in the hopes of slaughtering one of those monsters who dared to live without human permission. Disgusted by those with such obvious peanut-peckers, I slipped away to make my nightly call to John Shelley. He answered with the first ring and ordered me to leave The Dalles. According to his map-tapping dowsing rod, that Bigfoot was already 30-odd miles to the east, nearly across the Columbia River, and was about to enter a canyon that had a creek running through it. A quick check of the map indicated that Rock Creek Canyon was sparsely inhabited and provided a sheltered trek north to Satus Pass. Once across US Highway 97,[58] he would find sanctuary on the Yakima Indian Reservation and easy access to untold miles of wilderness in the vast Gifford Pinchot National Forest. Tactically, this was brilliant. He was long gone and the would-be mighty hunters would spend days and nights pointing their rifles at each other.

The problem for me was it was a good 35 miles away as the crow flies, and I'm no crow. I hurried back to gather my team to demand that we leave immediately. Only Jim McClarin elected to stay behind. I had no time to explain my mission due to his audience, but I regretted that he did not make this particular adventure.

Peter and I confessed our experiment once we were underway. We revealed that this secret advisor must be credited for all our recent successes that year. For instance, shortly after our arrival in Cougar, Shelley had described an area well known to me as a "possible" pass-through from Mount St. Helens south. However, he insisted there was a specific spot where he had observed a Forest Giant pausing and acting out of character. It was along the western bank of Swift Creek just south of where it emptied a marsh that formed the southern base to the

---

[58] The Forest Giants — Bigfoot — had been sighted several times crossing the road at that exact spot.

mountain. From there it flowed six to eight miles through a deepening canyon before spewing into Swift Creek Reservoir. I had spent so much time at that marsh that Jack Hoover and other local loggers teasingly called it "Morgan's Marsh." However, John's description of our target had been so precise that it led to the base of a specific pine tree. There, scant yards off a well-worn game trail we discovered a full 2½ gallons of rotting fecal matter. Our field examination indicated it could not possibly be elk or any other herbivore; it contained splintered bones and bits of hairs along with partially digested wiregrass;[59] and it appeared to have been made in one sitting. Naturally, we had rushed the entire mess over to Eastern Washington State University to place it under the microscopes of Drs. Grover Krantz and Tracy Blair. They confirmed the obvious; this huge mess had not come from any local bear,[60] lion, elk, moose, or deer. So what was it? Both had shrugged and said they would study the matter.

A full year would drag by before Grover would admit that our sample contained one or more enzymes that were in the gut of early Hominidae but had disappeared when Homo sapiens began using fire to break down complex foodstuffs. In short, what we had found probably had come from the gut of a hominid that predated modern man. Why had Grover refused to acknowledge this to science? That was his conundrum. To do so could prevent him from "harvesting" the physical specimens that science demands to prove the existence of our giant kin. Once proven, they could be protected by statute, but it would take not one but three bodies to provide the required comparisons to ensure each was not an anomaly in and of itself. In short, to admit his findings might prevent him from killing (murdering) the three specimens science demanded before it would recommend the survivors be protected from further harm.

Despite that success, Dillon issued a string of caustic remarks. After

---

[59] It was suggested that certain larger carnivores might use wiregrass to help cleanse their digestive tracts.
[60] Perhaps a Kodiak could make such a deposit, but not any grizzly in the lower 48.

all, dowsing had not been proven in the laboratories at his alma mater and therefore could not be taken seriously and we were damned fools off on a goose chase. I let him run down a bit before I offered to drop him off at a truck stop in Goldendale where he could either hitch a ride back to The Dalles or wait until we returned. He folded his arms and shut up.

It was nearing midnight when we reached the curve where State Route 192 crosses Rock Creek en route to Cleveland. The entire area was devoid of light or human habitation. I rammed the van into some dense bushes and we quickly padded our way up the shallow creek bed until we found a small clearing. Lipsio, Dillon, and Butler crossed the creek to the west while Harry and I stood pat. There, in the blackness of a moonless night, we fingered our cameras and waited.

An hour dragged passed. Then two. Pete stumbled over to whisper they thought they heard something approaching. Before I could respond, Harry Marcus hushed us. We held our breaths as something soft-footed came closer. There was no click of a hard hoof among the stones but a cadenced mashing of something massive. That something paused on the far side of some thick undergrowth not five yards away. I would have sworn it sucked in air through moist nostrils before it issued a single throaty grumble followed by a deafening silence.

"*Now*," I yelled while firing off my camera flash.[61] Quick-fingered Harry Marcus snapped on his flashlight to allow him and me to glimpse something over six feet tall, brawny, and reddish-black being swallowed amid a tangle of thick brush.

"Did you guys see *that*?" Harry croaked as the others splashed across the creek to wave their own lights this way and that.

Perhaps it had been a bear — do black bears grow that tall and run off on two legs — a grizzly would have charged, there were no moose around, and that sure as hell was no cow! Had John Shelley actually dowsed a Bigfoot? Had this been an actual encounter — or had our

---

[61] All I got were blurry bushes!

imaginations conjured it? After all, if Shelley had done this from 2,000 miles away, what could he do close up? We took a fast vote and each man (excepting Ed-the-Scoffer) offered to help with the ticket if he would fly out.

It was late, it had been a long day, and weariness took hold. We flipped out our sleeping bags and prepared to rest at least until dawn. Just before tucking in, I glanced up that canyon and caught a glimpse of a light in the sky slowly passing west to east. At that speed and altitude, it might have been a military helicopter on a training mission. I didn't dwell on it. I was too damned tired.

The following morning we returned to examine the target area. We found nothing of substance so we saddled up and left for our home base in Cougar where we knew Eva Phillips, a volunteer field researcher, would be waiting along with Jim Butler's wife Elaine.

I had a telephone call to make when we got back.

"Hello, Mister Shelley, how would you like to come out and give this a go on site? We'll all pitch in on your ticket —"

"I made reservations last night," he boomed back to me. "And don't worry about the money. A banker friend of mine from Montreal is donating all my expenses and sending you $500 to boot for some good walkie-talkies! Now listen: you people came close but you let him get around you along that western ridge. He's safe with the Yakimas now. However, there's something strange about dowsing these people. I get the feeling there's something more around them than I ask for. That's why I'm coming out. I'll see you next week."

It was tragic that Harry Marcus could not wait to meet John Shelley, but his vacation was over. I asked if he intended to share our adventures back at the Department.

"Are you nuts? I'm too close to retirement and I'd hate to go out on psycho leave."

Photo by Robert Morgan

John Shelly

14. Dowsers, Dsonoquas, and Keepers

I had no problem spotting the big Scotsman barging through the gate at the Portland Airport. His plaid Highlander cap gave him away. He stuck out one meaty hand and barked, "Nice to meet you. Let's get to work."

John instantly won everyone over with his honesty and good humor. Everyone except Dillon, that is, and when Ed sneered that he would like him to explain how dowsing worked as a science, Shelley admitted that he had no clue. Nevertheless, he would not deny its existence simply because it lacked a definition that science could or would accept. He also produced a file folder thick with letters of acknowledgement for his services from various state and local law enforcement agencies that he had helped locate lost campers, hikers, and children. Another letter came from a Christian relief worker acknowledging that John had successfully dowsed a well from his kitchen table in Maine that had brought water to a remote village in India. Ed's retort that modern technology could have done that too was shot down in the paragraphs that followed. Several attempts using traditional drilling methods had failed and John had been called only after the Indian government had given up. Shelley not only found the correct spot in a single hour, but he had accurately predicted the depth they must drill and, as astonishingly, the water flow of gallons per minute.

"I haven't the slightest idea how or even why it works. I only know that it does. Now then, let's cut through the meat and get to the bone. This is not magic and the rods I use have no special significance. I can use anything, a stick, a coat hanger, or a piece of plastic tubing. I bend them into two equal parts; and I hold one end in each hand and concentrate. I always ask for help and offer a sort of prayer to make sure that whatever I do is for the good of all living things. Then I ask the question and the rod answers."

"Is it magic?" Eva Phillips asked.

"Maybe it's a sort of psychic power and the rod just acts as a material indicator," Pete Lipsio offered.

"Maybe an extension of the Third Eye," said Bob Carr.[62]

"Or maybe a friendly ghost twitches it," McClarin chuckled.

"What's the toughest assignment you've had?" Eva asked with widened eyes and a shiver.

John's customary smile faded while he related a story about a child lost in Vermont. Following weeks of fruitless searching by the police, the desperate family had turned to him. John located the child's body in a small patch of woods a scant mile from home. The woods had been searched but not thoroughly enough. In result, the area police were now prone to use his services. Of course, they had to be careful not to cite him as a reference even though he may provide vital clues. After all, New England was known to have burned those they considered witches and outside science or religion.

Referring back to the water well, Dillon asked if John had charged by the gallon.

"Dowsing is a gift from God, my young friend," John said evenly. "I have never charged anyone, including you folks. And if I'm any help at

---

[62] Carr also had a special gift that has helped to make him one of the top archeologists in Florida.

Photo by Eva Phillips

Figure 15: John Shelly demonstrating dowsing to the researchers.

all, why don't you take the credit?"

Claiming that everyone who really tried could dowse, he invited us outside for a demonstration. The first to get a consistent response was Eva Phillips. When I teased her about having magic hands, she blushed, made a face, and then kicked me. She had every right; in time, she would prove the most consistently reliable witness in the group.

Show and Tell over, Shelley and I took a driving tour of our research area. I was in the middle of the account about those Arctic owl hoots when he commanded that I pull over. He trotted to a vantage point overlooking the Swift Reservoir that also provided a clear view of the wilderness to the east. He bowed his head for a moment before grasping each end of his dowsing rod. He held it level but slowly rotated his entire body in a clockwise direction. He completed the first revolution with no apparent reaction, but on the second go-around the tip of his dowsing rod appeared to dip once, twice — I stepped forward to grasp it between his hands and its tip — but it dipped twice more no matter how hard I squeezed. John grinned.

"Hell of a feeling, ain't it?"

I released my grip.

"What's going on?" I asked.

"One of those Forest Giants of yours is on the move. It's a young male…"

"How far away?"

Shelley bowed his head again until the rod dipped three times.

"About three-four miles."

"Which direction is he going?"

"North. But he's in no hurry."

"Male or female?"

"A young male."

John began another turning sweep. Once again, the tip quivered and bobbed, but then held steady to point to Mount St. Helens.

"Okay, we've got a female up there with a young one. They're near some falling water. There's a big male a few miles away — he's the top dog, the alpha of the family. Got a map?"

Does a baker have flour? I spread mine out and it barely took a minute before his rod was pat-patting an area on the southern slope of Mount St. Helens called June Lake. This was an island of beauty that had been isolated by a huge lava flow and long sheets of barren rocks. Loggers had clear-cut the old growth forest directly to the west, but the higher ground above the lake remained densely brushed and forested. Through it came a steady stream of glacier melt that cascaded over its brim to fall a good 100-200 feet into the lake. It was not just beautiful; it was spectacular.

"Ah-hah! I've been tracking this group for a couple of weeks. Mama and her baby stick around that bastion of safety while her mate goes out for food. Nevertheless, this young male over here is quite the roamer; last week he crossed the Columbia River and went into Oregon. He's probably on his way back. Since he's still alone I can guess he didn't find a girlfriend."

"Exactly where did he cross it?"

"Between that dam[63] and that place called Beacon Rock."

John's information seemed plausible. I knew of several sightings of the Forest Giants along that road on the Washington side and along Oregon's Interstate 84 near Bridle Falls.

"Morgan, why don't we try a little test to see how they react when humans enter their area with bad intentions? This would be a great way to find out if they have psychic abilities."

John outlined his plan. He would monitor the giants via map dowsing while I took a small strike force to make a feigned assault on that area above June Lake where mama and the baby were supposed to be in residence. Of course, we would not carry it too far, but with John monitoring their movements we could learn if they had the ability to communicate such intelligence over distances. I voted to try it, but John had a stipulation. We must do it after that night's dance.

"Dance? What dance?"

"Didn't I tell you? We're guests of honor at a real Kwakiutl shindig — and they are dancing something special for us!"

◊ ◊ ◊

An eagle-bone whistle shrilled from somewhere in the night outside the Kwakiutl-style cedar longhouse. The crowd of tourists, parents, and young students gasped when the thick wooden door boomed open to flare the fire in the center of the great room. Chief Lelooska[64] returned

---

[63] The Bonneville Dam.

[64] The Lelooska Cultural Foundation is in Ariel, Washington. Lelooska was born Don Smith and was a master totem pole and mask maker. Born part Cherokee, the elders of Canada's Kwakiutl recognized him as a reincarnated chief and welcomed him back into

the whistle and shouted a welcome in the native language of the Wakashan people called the Kwakiutl of the Canadian coast of British Columbia.

Lelooska cut an august figure. He was not a tall man, but he was broad and powerful. His dark eyes were quick and intelligent and his face reflected kindness while his bearing conveyed the dignity that comes from knowing one's true mission in life. Close by his side leaned the carved cedar staff of a Kwakiutl chief; down its length were the images of an eagle, a beaver, a grinning bear, a frog, and the fierce Dsonoqua, the dreaded Cannibal Woman of the Sasquatch, a member of the Timber Giant People the whites call Bigfoot. Draped over Lelooska's shoulders was a magnificent red-and-black woolen cloak partitioned by hundreds of hand-cut abalone shell buttons stitched into geometric patterns unique to the tribes of the coastal waters of the Pacific Northwest. Emblazoned across his ceremonial shirt was a stylized bear sitting on his haunches with his tongue sticking out and his claws poised for action. Around Lelooska's neck was curled a thick collar of woven cedar bark threads, and his hair was tucked up under a carved and painted cedar wooden headdress depicting an eagle with a red beak and angry eyes. Lelooska's nose appeared to have been pierced through at the septum with an ivory ring that hung down like a hollow flap below his lower lip and glinted yellow when he threw his head back and boomed a second singsong call. He used his drum-thumper to begin a marked cadence on a long and hollow log drum. Within a few beats, his wailing song and drumbeat was picked up by the six Kwakiutl Indians seated beside him.

Thus began the special dance given by Lelooska to honor his friend John Shelley and, by association, myself as the director of the American Yeti Expeditions. I would learn later that Lelooska had petitioned the

---

their tribe. The dances are still being performed. For more information check the web site http://www.lelooska.org.

Kwakiutl people in Vancouver, BC who owned the Dsonoqua dance for special permission to perform it for us. John nudged me when Lelooska's lithe sister, Patty Fawn, backed into the dancing area. Patty was puffing white downy feathers into the face of the hulking and hairy monster who shuffled in after her. A collective shudder swept through the audience; someone muffled a scream. The great black form lurched along in Patty's path, snuffling wetly through its carved cedar mask as if testing the air for danger — or food in the form of disobedient children. The door swung closed behind them with a hollow boom and the room became smaller. A thin man with owlish glasses snatched his towheaded child to his chest; his movement broke the spell of the soothing feathers and the Dsonoqua whirled to stare at them. Its blood-red lips were pursed as if to whistle, its hooked nose was flared by sharply curved nostrils, and heavy black eyebrows beetled its brow over colorless little eyes rimmed round with deep green sockets. Disheveled clumps of coarse black hair ringed its crested skull before hanging limply down to brush thick shoulders with greasy strands, while shorter tufts covered its entire body. Curiously, although the giant wore no clothing of any kind, a crude little basket made with red willow shoots hung suspended from one arm. The basket was just the size to hide a small child. The basket was empty. The Dsonoqua, the fabled "Cannibal Woman" of the Timber Giants, fastened a baleful eye on the unfortunate child. "Ohhhh, no," someone hissed. "Sit still," someone warned.

Patty leapt between the Dsonoqua dancer and the audience and puffed more feathers into its face while Lelooska's voice swelled and the drumbeat quickened. The Dsonoqua turned away as if mesmerized by the fleeting images of floating feathers and followed Patty in a shuffling, shambling gait as she backed around the room.

"Ho, Wild Sister," Lelooska cried. "We greet you and welcome you to the warmth of our fire."

Then, speaking to the audience, Lelooska related one of several versions of the legend of the Dsonoqua. A Kwakiutl maiden — a mere child — had been driven from her tribe to live alone in the forest through the lies of a jealous sister who accused her of being a witch. Given that the native peoples traditionally live in closely knit family units where children are never left alone, it is understandable that the frightened child had gone mad with fear. As she lay dying from exposure and hunger, a family of Timber Giants took pity and saved her.[65] Nourished back to health by their generous offerings of red huckleberries, roots, and raw fish, the girl's fear turned to fury. How dare her human relatives be so cruel to her while these giants were gentle and kind! In time, she became an avenging hunter of all bad children and would steal them from their beds come midnight. She believed she was saving the good and obedient children from the wiles of those like her evil sister.

Years later, the tribe realized the truth behind the incessant lies of that sister. They banished her to a lonely island where she ran into the sea to disappear beneath angry waves. Then, wanting to make amends to the child they had wronged, the tribe gathered at the edge of the forest to drum and to sing in the hope of calling her home again. However, when she appeared they were terror-stricken. She had transformed into a true wild person and had taken a Timber Giant as her husband. A truce was struck: if she, the Dsonoqua, would stop haunting her old tribe and stealing children, bad or not, she would be allowed to return once each year to warm herself beside their fires and to visit her family. As a parting gift, and because the sweet red huckleberries were now her favorite fruit, the tribe also promised never again to pick them, and they would be forever reserved for her and the tribe of wild Timber Giants.

That was one version of the legend. However, it was the dance and the magic of Lelooska's carved transformation mask that struck the most vibrant chords for me. The dancer passed three times around the fire. At

---

[65] Such acts of helping lost or injured humans are not uncommon. I have had several reliable reports of hikers being assisted by Forest Giants in recent history.

the end of each pass, its face would be turned away, but when it turned back, it revealed a mask within a mask. The first one was, of course, the "monster" face with its lips pursed to whistle and to imitate the calls of natural birds. The next mask revealed a much more human face, albeit an angry one. These were understandable according to the legend. However, that third and final mask struck the deepest chord for me. Were the aboriginal Indians acknowledging something that was escaping modern man because of our ego and desire to make ourselves appear exclusive to our Maker? Was this transformation mask their way of acknowledging a true brotherhood with those we call the Timber Giants, the Dsonoqua, Bigfoot, Sasquatch, Windigo, the Sha-wan-nook-chobee, Ewash-shak-chobee, Ewah-shak-koochi? Were they stating that they should be seen as someone more beautiful inside than was demonstrated by their outward appearance? Did that third mask admit that they, like us, have a soul?

My, my, my, I thought. Those allegedly "savage" natives who the Jesuit missionaries claimed were in dire straits until they brought them their version of the "only true religion" had the capacity to accept that all inhabitants on this earth had that essence called a spirit. I wondered if I too was offending God Almighty by harboring the thought that just maybe He (or She?) did indeed create all things equal.

◊ ◊ ◊

As planned, the following morning I dispatched a scouting team to check for fresh tracks around McBride Lake[66] as part of an ongoing operation separate from John's experiments. In the interim, he and I pored over the maps. His wand confirmed the Forest Giant family had remained in residence at June Lake while that younger male was still futzing around several miles to the south. Suddenly, the alpha male bolted away to a high crag closer to the main Forest Service road that wound to the west. I noted the time as 7:20 AM. According to John's rod,

---

[66] We had found fresh tracks there in 1971 in the presence of George Harrison, the managing editor of *National Wildlife Magazine* (see Oct/Nov issue).

that big boy remained there until 8:10 before returning to where the female and the child were waiting. My scouting team returned while we were still speculating about his odd behavior. During their debriefing, they mentioned that after drawing a blank at McBride Lake, they had made an unscheduled detour for a photo opportunity. An interesting cloud formation had made a donut-shaped halo around the snowcap of Mount St. Helens and the team had taken a detour to jockey for a better angle. When asked to locate the road on our map, it became clear that they had paused directly below where the Bigfoot family was resting. The time was somewhere between 7:00 and 7:30 AM. Had the alpha male reacted to their presence?

Shelley grumbled that he would be more careful. "I was so tied up with that big boy's movement I forgot to look to see what had caused it. I should have dowsed your team, too. I just didn't think to ask about it. Remember, a dowsing rod only answers questions, it doesn't volunteer anything."

I asked Shelley to confirm that the alpha family had stayed put. Pat-pat went the tip of his rod. It indicated that the bigger male was wandering off to the west toward McBride Lake and beyond, as was his daily wont. As usual, the female and her child remained close to June Lake and its protective crag.

An experiment was needed, albeit impromptu, to confirm John's accuracy and to learn more about our target's level of awareness. I decided to try John's plan of staging a phony assault on the Forest Giant family's sanctuary while John recorded the Alpha's reactions and his acumen.

Phase 1: Jim McClarin, Peter Lipsio, Bob Carr, and I would psyche ourselves up as if we were going to march into that Bigfoot's lair to murder the mother and child. I would urge that assault team to think "blood and guts." I surprised everyone by declaring that Peter should carry a weapon into the field[67] to make it more real. We would also carry daypacks that included survival and first aid kits and a walkie-talkie.

Phase 2: While our assault team drove the dozen miles to the foot of the ravine that lay directly below their assumed lair, Shelley, Dillon, and Eva would remain behind at the cabin to dowse every movement of the family, the alpha male, that lone wanderer, and us. Of course, Dillon objected until I reminded him that because he had lingering doubts about John's ability, I felt he should personally transcribe every tap of that rod and note the times.

Phase 3: The moment we arrived on site, we would launch our feigned attack, marching double-time while loudly singing "death to Bigfoot" songs and thinking nasty things. However, at the foot of the steepest rise we would spin around and return to the van and to Cougar. I did not wish to get so close that they would abandon their sanctuary. If it went well, this ruse should provide invaluable insight to their intelligence, awareness, and evasive strategies.

Phase 4: I intended to return later in the day to use John's map of the Alpha male's daily forage area to look for his tracks, hair, feces, or anything else to establish his physical presence. We were in dire need of a simultaneous sighting by multiple qualified personnel. Of course, clear photographs, fresh feces, and hair would add to the importance of such an encounter. I wanted everything short of a body.

We launched at high noon. Indeed, we yelled, sang, and chanted bloodthirsty slogans all the way to the mouth of that ravine where we bailed out and charged into the brush. Taking the lead, I followed a convenient game trail with long-legged McClarin kicking at my heels, Carr followed a few feet back, and the ever-cautious Lipsio brought up

---

[67] I had banned carrying any weapon into the field but I could not enforce that rule in camp. I knew that Lipsio and Dillon had guns within reach come sundown. Not a bad idea in bear country. However, in times to come I changed that rule to a complete ban when I realized that weapons cause psychological changes that impede peaceful contacts with the Forest Giants.

the rear. We had not made a mile before the thinning air had reduced our slogans to gasping wheezes. We were nearing our objective when the game trail vanished into a stand of tangled timber and boulders — I don't know which came first — heeding Bob Carr's yelled warning or slamming into an invisible wall of dread. Either way, I stopped and we piled up like four Stooges. Bob warned that we must not enter that stand of trees and I took him seriously. First off, I was aware of his uncanny ability to locate obscure archaeological sites, bones, and ruins; Laymond Hardy had sworn that he had psychic powers.

Perhaps in the safe harbor of bright city lights, one could offer that our sudden fears were brought on by our chanting and stoked by anticipation — that explanation could be offered by armchair skeptics who have never executed on-site explorations in remote places. Nevertheless, what had stopped us was nothing physical or tangible.

Carr moved closer to whisper, "You felt it, didn't you!"

"It was like running into a wall!"

"This isn't good. We are not welcome here. This is not good at all. They know, they know…"

"Stop thinking blood," I said. "Let's go back to see what John's little dipper says."

I assumed the position of rear guard as we descended at a quick trot and the further we got from that stand of trees, the better I felt. However, we all were startled when Ed Dillon popped out of the brush with his shotgun held at the ready.

"Jesus Christ, Morgan! That old man's so damned scared he's about to have a heart attack! He sent me to get you guys the hell out of here! What happened? What's going on?"

I was amazed to find John and Eva waiting beside Ed's jeep. The Scotsman's face was flushed and he was sweating. Before I could say a word, he snatched the walkie-talkie from my belt, flipped the power switch, and listened to it buzz to life.

"You forgot to turn this on, Morgan! *Damn it!* We've been yelling at you! You guys could have been killed! You're supposed to be the leader; you're supposed to be in charge of everyone's safety! How stupid can you get? Let's get the hell out of here! We've got some serious work to do!"

The drive back was unique; we rode in silence.

Once we reached the cabin, I asked, "What happened, John?"

"You tell me what stopped you from going to your objective. It was fear, right? You felt fear! Right?"

"Damned right we did! It happened to us at the same time. It was like running into a wall that was so cold I had the sweats! We didn't see or hear a damned thing! Now you tell me what you saw! What did that little map-tapper tell you?"

"That alpha male was on the move almost before you were out of sight. First, he ran back to the crag and then, while the female and the kid took off for higher ground, he dropped down through a stand of trees." He drew me to his map and rapped that area with one finger. "Look where he was! He was already there before you set foot on the ground! Then when you screwballs went charging up, he slipped around behind you."

"We felt something —" Bob Carr nodded.

"Nothing can move that fast without making a lot of noise," Jim McClarin argued. "Why didn't we hear him?"

"We were chanting, remember," Pete said.

If the day's events were true as John described, the old boy's defensive tactics were impressive. He had removed his family to safety, reconnoitered the advancing enemy force, outflanked them, and cut them off from escape. Even more, as if he had been taught Sun Tzu's ancient book, *The Art of War*, he had avoided conflict when the enemy chose retreat. If true, this mark of generalship could explain why the Bigfoot evades man so easily. On the other hand, was this all in our imaginations?

Evening was approaching, dinners were eaten half-heartedly, and John was permitted to rest on his cot. I knew we had to take better care of him; we knew he had come to help against the advice of his heart doctor. Left alone with him while the others went outside, I mentally walked around my rock of troubles. The danger in accepting that day's events at face value was twofold: nothing except circumstantial evidence suggested that dowsing actually worked. On the other hand, human ego has a way of either denying the existence of ideas beyond our common ken or exalting them by assigning anthropomorphic and even superhuman characteristics to anything that exceeds our personal experience. It was not that long ago when the most learned men of the Holy Roman Catholic Church called their Inquisitors down around poor old Galileo's ears because he had dared to claim that the earth revolved around the sun and not vice versa. After all, our egos demanded that the entire universe and all the heavens must revolve around Rome and Jerusalem. More recently, mid-twentieth century religious scholars continued their debate if Native American Indians had souls, the Office of the Inquisition[68] remained ready to examine heretics, only bad women enjoyed sex, and organized science denied the existence of the Komodo dragon, the panda bear, and the poor little platypus. Those thoughts and more were interrupted by Ed Dillon's loud wisecracking about dowsing, Bigfoot, and ex-waitresses (Eva) aspiring to understand science. Before I reached the door to tell him to take his vinegar elsewhere, John sat up, laced up his shoes, laid a heavy hand on my shoulder, and said, "Let's take a walk."

We strolled down through Cougar where the old Wildwood Inn, a gas station, a country store, and a one-woman post office centered the village

---

[68] It changed its name in 1908 and again in 1988 to appear less ominous. It is now known as the Congregation for the Doctrine of the Faith. It claims to have ceased torturing infidels and burning heretics alive. See *The Name of the Rose* for a peek into its workings.

of perhaps 150 or so year-round residents. Down the way, the Lone Pine Trailer Park and Motel awaited weekends to have its spaces filled. Each spring and summer the flush of logging crews and anglers fed the fragile economy; each fall hunters from Portland and Seattle came to bang away at the deer and dwindling elk herds. Then, with the approach of each dreary winter, the people of Cougar would hunker down to await spring for yet another transfusion of green grass and greener money.

"Listen, John, I'm going up there tomorrow to see what — "

"Let's try an experiment tonight. Look, I've been tracking these birds every day since Bloss Hedblom clued me in to where you were working. I was watching the movements of that June Lake gang before you got here. Every night for the past month and exactly at 11:00 PM they've moved down to that marsh as if they're expecting something. They aren't there long enough to feed. I think it's a rendezvous point of some sort."

"For another family, maybe?"

"That's what I want to find out and no amount of dowsing has given me an answer. It's easy to dowse for water; it's there or it isn't, and people and animals are easy, too. However, these folks can disappear in a heartbeat. A year ago and before we met I got a reading on four of them down around Mt. Shasta in California. I tracked them for a couple of months for the fun of it until they began hanging out in a marshy area just like what you have here. One night I got some wild magnetic readings and then, pow!, they vanished! No matter what I did, I kept drawing a blank. Then, about a week later, they were back exactly where I'd lost them."

"Maybe they just went into a cave or a lava tube?"

"That's not the end of it: something happened just before we did that thing in Rock Creek. I had clicked on this group but they were down in Roseburg, Oregon. As you might guess, there are dozens of bands like this all along this coast, but these three adults and their child caught my attention because they were making a beeline to what I knew was your area. They came straight to June Lake and damned if I didn't get that reading of magnetics again — and they disappeared just like the others! I dowsed all over hell and high water until they reappeared days later. In fact, that's the main reason I agreed to come out. I want to know where in the hell they go when they pull their disappearing act. Tonight is perfect. It's the dark of the moon and that's when I lost those dinks on Mt. Shasta. I want to be up there tonight just in case something else happens. Is it a deal?"

By 11:00 PM, our entire team was lined up along the logging road that borders the southernmost edge of the marsh. June Lake lay directly north and midway up the mountain. As John predicted, the night sky was moonless, black, and clear from horizon to horizon.

His plan was simple. We would fan out behind him as he followed where his rod pointed to any area of the marsh if the Forest Giants showed up. I asked Pete to take the far left of our line while Ed covered the right. Each of them was armed, but Pete also carried a flare gun. I was positioned directly behind John with my camera. Eva, Carr, and McClarin were spread in between at intervals of five to six yards.

We waited nearly an hour before John signaled that the Giants had arrived. Our line grew tighter as we slogged down the steep slope in his wake. He paused 30 yards in.

"The mama and the kid are hightailing back to the lake. But ol' papa is curious. He's just beyond that tree line. He's moving, moving…"

"Tell me if he shoots us the bird, Chief!" Ed giggled.

"… he's moving to the left, to the left — he's sticking to where the trees are — he's coming closer — watch it, watch it," John snapped and spun around. "Uh-oh! That Beta is coming in fast! It's that young one from down south… he's on that hill to the south of us — he's coming in!"

"He'll cut me off from my Jeep," Ed croaked.

"Don't move and don't panic!"

"Is it called panicking if I crap my pants?" McClarin cracked.

In between the chuckles and titters that took off the edge, Shelley switched between targets and our heads swiveled back and forth like robots on a string.

"Okay, okay, he's calming down. It's okay now; we can relax," John sighed and we sighed with him. "Beta's stopped on that slope behind us and our Alpha boy is still behind that line of trees." He took slow steps forward, cooing, "Come on, son, and come out. No one here will hurt you. We just want to get a good look and maybe take your picture. Come on, we can't see you..."

"Ain't that convenient?" Ed snorted.

"And why don't you shut up?" Eva snapped.

"Who are you to tell me to shut up, you little —"

"Enough, Dillon," I said and I damned well meant it.

"He's coming — no! He's stopped again," John whispered. "Now he's moving again; he's moving to our right... to the right... he's circling between us and the trees — he's heading for our road! Uh-oh! Beta's moving, too. He's coming down the slope behind us!"

"Jesus Christ," someone moaned. "Our cars!"

"Flare! Flare, flare, flare, goddam it, Pete!" I also fired my camera flash as if that would do any good. *"Flare!!!!"*

Kee-rack! Shhhhhh-boom! The marsh flashed alive like an eerie scene in a B-horror movie.

"He crossed the road, but now he's moving back toward Huckleberry Mountain again. Damn, damn, damn, they're both leaving the marsh. We're done."

No one gave the order or even the suggestion, yet we turned in unison to return to our vehicles. All our hopes dissolved first into disappointment and then descended into resentment. Was it because another chance to view a live Bigfoot had slipped past us, or did we feel bamboozled by someone we had trusted? After all, none of us had caught so much as a glimpse of our quarry. Accusing eyes fired darts at our dowser's back and he was left to walk alone.

After climbing the slope to reach the road, the old man paused to look back toward Mount St. Helens and June Lake. He ignored two invitations to take his seat in my van. Perhaps he had not heard them. I walked back to his side and repeated myself.

John shook his head, saying, "I'm going back down there. I want to go alone. I'll try to coax him to come back."

"Let's go. We'll leave everyone here."

"I want to be alone," he said and stepped off the bank to disappear into a black hole of shadows.

Naturally, Dillon grumbled, bitched, and sneered, so I told him to go and take anyone else who wished to leave. No one joined him so he chose to stand with Pete and McClarin to my right while Eva and Bob Carr were on my left. Only Pete and Ed carried weapons.

For the first half hour, we stood together in sober silence. However, that sky was much too beautiful to stay uptight. Adding to its mystique was the total lack of a breeze; there were no rustlings of night creatures or even hooty-hoots from owls on the prowl. Outside of the occasionally whispered word, the world had gone dead silent. It was then that I spotted a round dot of bright white light approaching at high speed in the sky southeast of our position. Its flight path was to the northwest and, if it continued its present course, it would pass over Seattle. I had been around aircraft since my early teens and had spent years at sea on an aircraft carrier that launched and recovered aircraft at all hours and under every condition imaginable. Coupled with my career with the Federal Aviation Administration, it was natural that I would pay attention to passing aircraft. This one began to puzzle me. Its perceived high speed did not match that extreme altitude.

"Airplane?" Eva asked.

"Yeah, but I've never seen one that evenly lighted. And where's its port and starboard wing lights?"

Bob Carr's laugh was nervous and tight.

"Maybe it's a satellite?"

"It's too low for a satellite. Maybe it's one of those super-secret test flights out of Nevada."

"Or a meteorite," Eva suggested.

"It's not falling, it's flying."

I spoke too soon. When it was directly above Mount St. Helens, that object — I could not yet ID it as an aircraft because no wings, tail, or elongated fuselage was discernible — it made an instant 90° change in course from level flight to dive straight down. There was no banking, no arc, and no glide. One moment, it was in level flight and the next, it was falling like a stone. There had been no flash of an explosion and there was no smoke or con trail. As bizarre, the closer it came to the mountain the dimmer it became until — poof — it vanished. We held our breaths awaiting the crash, the thump, the bang, the boom, the burst of flames, or some damned thing. Nevertheless, there was nothing. Nothing.

No one said anything for at least 30 seconds or perhaps it was a full minute. I recall asking Pete and Jim if they'd seen anything just before a bloodcurdling *"YEEEOOOOW!"* shrieked out of the marsh below us followed by the muffled sounds of running feet and groaning gasps.

"Get him out!" I shouted. "Pete! Ed! Get in there! Turn on your lights — get lights down there!"

Both armed men stood as if rooted until Eva Phillips bailed off the side of the road only to take a belly-slapping fall. To her everlasting credit, as she was skidding down that slope she held up her flashlight to shine the way for John Shelley. It was left to her, Carr, McClarin, and me to help the old man up those last few slippery yards.

"Did you hear it?" John gasped. Did you hear? It screamed in my ear! I didn't hear it coming — he crossed this road; he was here behind you! I was sitting on a stump — then it screamed! My, God, it was right beside me! Didn't you hear it?"

"I heard something," I said while calculating the time it would take to get a heart attack victim over winding mountains roads to the nearest hospital some 40 miles distant. It was not a happy prospect.

I sat John in the open doorway of my van while Eva hovered like a blond angel. The old man hung his head and locked his hands together to wring and twist.

"My God, my God, he screamed right in my ear! Didn't you hear it?"

"All we heard was you," Ed said evenly.

John's head snapped up and he stared at the cluster of young men who were watching him in silence.

I went alone to find a stump that he had used as a seat. I noted bent grass where he had walked about. In all fairness, it was too dark to look for other spoor; my tromping about would add to the confusion. A definitive examination must be done in the light of day. I returned to the road where my team was waiting. I took a poll. Everyone except Eva felt certain that John had issued that scream.

"First thing in the morning, I want a team up here to check this road. Let's start with that and go from there."

"Why bother?" Ed asked. "He did the screaming, man. Let's stop wasting time. This is bullshit."

"If any Bigfoot crossed this dirt road to bypass us and to sneak up on him, then he had to leave tracks. There'll be no traffic between now and then so you should have no problem finding them. Let's not say anything negative until we give it a fair shake. Fair enough?"

Shelley said nothing all the way back to Cougar except to reassure me that he was not in any physical pain. I could not convince him to return to the marsh. Instead, he caught the earliest flight he could get to return to Maine.

Ed Dillon gave me the report when his team returned that same evening.

"We covered everything, Chief. We covered the road on both sides, we went down into that stand of trees he was talking about, and we even found the stump he said he sat on. There was nothing down there but him."

It was as if an evil pall had fallen. The heart and the bank account for that year's expedition were drained and empty. It was time to fold our tents. Jim McClarin returned to California, Eva went to Denver, Colorado, Pete flew to Mamaroneck, New York, Bob Carr bused his way to Florida, and Ed Dillon went somewhere else. Once again, I headed south.

It was a long time before I remembered that strange flying object that had disappeared onto the slopes of Mount St. Helens just before all hell had broken loose.

15. Riding the Bad Luck Trail

A string of what Nino would call "bad luck" plagued those closest to me in my search for the truth. As I look back from the perspective of 2008, it seems likely that each death came about as a normal part of the speed bumps life takes delight in tossing at us. I cannot judge because I am still too close to the flame. No matter. I took each one personally. Why? Because I loved them all.

The Tigers: Donna seemed glad to hear from me when she answered the telephone, but her mood darkened when I said I was anxious to get back into the 'glades with her and her brothers. After all, my travels had kept me away for over three years and the only news I had in between was that Robert had been made a daddy twice over.

"My brother can't go with you anymore," she said. "He had bad luck."

My gut twisted. When a Native American uses that term, they don't mean they lost a wallet.

"Well, let's get together anyway," I said. "Can he call me? I'll be in Miami with my daughter all winter and we can come out anytime —"

"He can't. Robert's dead."

I assume that I said that I would drive out immediately. I hope I did. What I do know is that it wasn't long before I was knocking at their front door. Unlike other visits, the Tiger's radio was silent, the television

292

screen was dark, and there was nothing baking in the oven or bubbling on the stove excepting that forever coffeepot.

Donna greeted me with a longer and tighter hug than usual and she wore a face that had forgotten how to smile. She led me by the hand to the kitchen table where her mother sat swinging her head from side to side, perhaps hoping to transform her mental anguish into something physical, something that she could deal with.

Louise Tiger's thin hands shook when she lit a cigarette. She pushed it into the ashtray where another still smoldered.

"I still can't believe it, Mister Morgan," Louise said. "I still think my Robert's gonna walk smack through that door there and say 'Hiya Mom! What's for dinner?' But I have to believe he's gone, don't I? I saw him to the grave."

"What happened?"

She opened her mouth but made no sound. Instead, the corners of her eyes crinkled wet and her teeth crushed her lower lip.

"Look, Louise, I'll stop out again soon…"

"No, no, you stay! I want you to! My kids were always bragging on you, that you were their friend and all. You hungry? I'll fix somethin'."

"No, I am fine," I said, but she stumbled up anyway to open and close cupboard doors and the refrigerator, too. She took nothing out because they were bare. Donna quietly slipped out of the door. I heard a car start up and crunch away. She had not said goodbye.

"My Robert wanted to go out there to that Washington place with you," she said. "He thought it'd be fun to see real mountains. Except for visiting my folks up in the Smokies,[69] he never did see a real mountain. He saved every one of those postcards you sent, too. Yes, he did! Him and Spencer put them up in their room where they could show them off, and when you was on that Tom Snyder Show and that TV special about

---

[69] Louise was Cherokee.

monster mysteries,[70] they rounded up everyone they could find to watch you. Boy, did we have a gang here that night. My kids were so proud…"

"I'm glad," I said, and wished that I had sent more cards and called more often.

Louise snatched up my hand to lead me out of the kitchen and down a narrow hall to a bedroom.

"This was all Spencer's after Robert got married. Look what he did," she said. "He put his brother's stuff back where it always was."

Spencer had also created a ceremonial arrangement. Among the personal items that had been dear to him and Robert were my postcards and a faded topographical map of Mount St. Helens all dotted with stickpins that showed my old camps and study areas. Below that hung his knife, the one that Spencer had coveted. Beside it all was taped a photograph of the three siblings. They were laughing and hugging each other. Louise went from item to item to recount its history and what part it had played in their lives. She took her time.

Donna was emptying the bag of groceries fetched from the snack store down the lane when we returned to the kitchen.

"Do you know why Robert couldn't go out there with you that last time you'd asked?" Louise asked while Donna stacked slices of bologna in between pieces of white bread and handed them out. "He thought maybe his first baby might come early so he got married quick and got a job. He was like that. He wanted his wife and baby to be proud of him and themselves.

"He used to laugh and tell me that married life was getting him so fat that he'd bounce if he fell off those roofs he was working on. Wish to God he'd have bounced some when that car — oh, God, I sure wish he'd come through that door. He'd be so glad t'see you."

Louise Tiger was coughing but she lit a third cigarette anyway. "It was that death house that killed him! You know the one he rented down

---

[70] "Monsters: Myth or Mystery" was part of The Smithsonian Series.

the way? That's a death house for sure. Bobby and me, we tried to tell him to stay out of there but he wouldn't listen. See, he wanted his kids to be close to us and that house was all that was to be had out here. He was such a homebody; we loved him for that, too."

"I remember Spencer saying something about a house where everybody who lived there had bad luck. He thought it should be burned down," I said.

"Spencer-boy was as right as rain! Everybody that ever lived there went sorry. The first guy went crazy and beat his wife almost t'death before Bobby and me dragged him off. They say he hung himself. The next one drove his truck plumb off the end of the road and into that pond down yonder. Bobby and me heard him go roarin' by one night and he never came back up; that dead end's in deep water, you know. I was there when they fished him out. Killed hisself for sure." She sat nodding as if she had made a decision. "Somebody'll burn it down, just you watch and see, and I know what I'm talking about! Somebody's going to burn it for sure." Her flush of anger melted into pride when she added, "But our Robert-boy was such a bullhead sometimes, yes he was. Want another sandwich?"

I shook my head so she piled potato chips on my plate instead.

"Bobby wouldn't want me saying this so if he comes home I'll just change the subject, okay? Something was bothering Robert for some time. It was something bad that was coming in his dreams. I wanted him to go in for marriage counseling up at the Tribal Center, but he swore it weren't him and his wife, even though they bickered a lot. I just thought that most young'uns go through that until they get squared off right. But that weren't it, I see that now.

"I'd like to ask you something. Could it be that them 'Nock-chobees' got mad because he took you out there? Oh, he told me what he did and I know you didn't push him into anything. Both him and Donna said so, and neither me or Bobby are mad at you. The kids told us how you respected everything so you got nothing to be ashamed of. But something went wrong somewhere and one old shaman around here thinks that Robert got cursed because of he gave away a secret place where them big people felt safe."

"Louise, I wouldn't see why the Chobees would be mad at any of us. We didn't take or even touch anything. From what I've learned, they might chuck rocks or scream and yell if you got too close into their space, but that never happened either. But, well, did he go back out after I had left?"

"He was too busy getting married," Donna offered. "Besides, he wouldn't go without you."

"Then how about them flying saucer things and that crazy preacher?" Louise asked. "Maybe they played a part?"

"I can't see how or why. What Reverend Zarley showed us that night had nothing to do with those Chobees, but in truth I still don't know what it was. All I saw was something that moved fast — whoosh!"

"It was too fast for me to see it, either," Donna agreed.

"Lots of us out here have seen them sky-lights, but we leave 'em be," Louise said. "As for the Chobees, we know they come around every year; always have since way back when. Them what keeps the old ways trade little things to sort of shake hands with 'em, you know? Buffalo Tiger knows all about it but he won't tell anybody white because he's the Tribal Chairman and the whites would make fun of him — you know how they are. Now, that Buffalo, he's nobody's fool. The Tigers are good people, all of them; you can trust what they say. See, we treat this kind of thing different that whites. Bobby won't even say their name and won't talk about them as if it's a bad omen or something. And none of the tribal elders will talk about them, either."

"I've noticed that among many of the tribes I have visited from here to the Pacific Northwest to the deserts. Once I thought it was out of fear," I said. "Now I know there's more to it. They're helping to guard them from the whites because they kill anything they can't control…"

Louise suffered a small smile and a nod.

"All them big people want is to be left alone. But ol' Victor Osceola, he talked to you about them and my Robert did, too. And now they're both gone."

I took a deep breath before I asked, "What exactly happened to Robert?"

"He got hit by a phantom car," Donna said.

"A what?"

"Nobody saw it after it hit him. The cops looked both ways and there ain't no way off that road except east and west. They even set up roadblocks and looked in all the canals. Never found what hit him."

"Where did it happen?"

Louise smashed out her cigarette, cleared her throat, and said, "Right here on the rez. Right out on that Tamiami Trail — and there's something more to it than that, Mister Morgan. See, Robert was doing things that day that just wasn't him. He'd keep going to the door and staring out like he was looking for something. All I asked him to do was to go on down to the store at the end of our road here to fetch a loaf of bread. I really didn't need it, damn it, damn it, damn it! I was just trying to make him stop all that walkin' around! If I had known… oh, God, God, God!

"Instead of taking his truck, he took his brand new bright red motorcycle — I hate those things! Anyway, he got the bread and stuff, and then he did something that just wasn't smart. He drove out onto that highway and drove down to the next entrance — they say he was flying! *Why?* If he'd come back home along the reservation road he'd have been all right. Instead, he went out and got himself killed."

"Did he lose control? Did he hit a skunk or an opossum or a deer or a dog?"

"He got hit by something big and they dragged my baby's hands and face off! My boy's face was gone and so was both of his hands! They didn't even *stop*!"

"D-Did the highway patrol catch —"

"Nobody got caught! You know that road! It's straight as an arrow and there ain't no place to get off. So why did they never find nothin'? Tell me, Mister Morgan! Tell me that!"

"Louise, I don't... I'm sure... I guess... I..." I sputtered until the room went silent. I sat still. I did not move. Whatever could I say?

Louise drew in a long and bubbly breath and then said too calmly, "I know you won't laugh or I wouldn't say this. Bobby sat with some elders of his clan and they smoked and sang it out. Some of 'em think it was because Robert was out there fooling around with those Nock-chobees. You know how full-bloods are about stuff like that."

"I do."

"Me, I think it was either that death house he lived in or maybe one of them flying things shined a light in his eyes so he couldn't see. Either way, my Robert sure had some bad luck, didn't he?"

The bad luck for the Tigers did not end with Robert's murder. Young and happy-go-lucky Spencer would take a long and hard fall off a construction site. He would spend the remainder of his short life in a wheelchair until he died way before his time.

Donna would suffer with severe diabetes. No one knows why she refused her medications and chose instead to die.

Truly, truly, I miss all my Miccosukee friends so very much. Enju! That's what Nino would say. It means, "The end," or "I have spoken enough about that."

Gashpeta: Years had passed before I managed to return to that lovely pueblo of the northernmost tribe of the Keresan (K'eres) people.[71] When approaching for a drop-in visit, I spotted a familiar old truck outside the bar in Peña Blanca and slid to a stop. Its fresh bumper sticker about being "Cochiti and Proud" gave it away. I had barely cleared the

---

[71] Sometimes called The Drinkers of the Dew.

door and my eyes had not adjusted to the dim light before an even bigger Ernie had wrapped me into a bear hug. Laughing and slapping each other's backs, we had a few beers — okay, maybe some tequila shooters on the side — and we spoke of many things and of mice and men before he leaned close to say, "You don't have to worry about cannibal bones anymore, man. If they were there, they're gone now."

"Someone opened that cave?" I sputtered.

"No way! The dam backed up the water and that was that."

"Oh, crap! I'd forgotten about that dam."

"Boy, it sure has been a long time since you was here. This you gotta see! Let's go!"

The Cochiti Dam, one of the largest earthen dams in North America, had been completed a year or so following my visit. It created a lake of 545,000 acre feet of water, rises 251 feet above the bed of the old Rio Grande, and stretches over five miles up the canyon. Gashpeta and all those carved and painted rocks are under water. As Ernie had said, if any bones had been in Gashpeta, they would have been destroyed.

When I asked about Sonny, he said that he had disappeared among the bars in Albuquerque. No one had seen him in over a year.

Sees-Far Woman also had vanished; Ernie would not say how or why. I learned too that jolly, jolly Ernie was fighting severe diabetes, but he did not intend to give up his beer. I remember he and I returning to the bar, but I'll be damned if I recall leaving it.

Victor Zarley: I rendezvoused with Joanne Barton in Los Angeles to do another segment of her radio show. We were to broadcast from the theater on the historic Queen Mary I luxury liner that is permanently berthed at Long Beach. En route to the stage, that rascal led me down through the ship's engine rooms as if on a detour. I did not know that 18-year-old bilgediver, John Pedder, had been accidentally crushed to death there in a starboard tunnel by the automatic closing of the ship's watertight doors. I provided her and her troop with a thrill when I remarked about how very cold it felt in between those compartments. Only then did they reveal that Pedder's ghost was reportedly in residence.[72]

Ghosts or no, I was eager to receive the update about Zarley. Ever the wise lady, Joanne waited until evening to give me an extraordinarily disturbing report. In time, he had escaped his captoress but in doing so had been left nearly destitute. En route to Los Angeles to find Joanne, he had tarried in Las Vegas where he took random construction jobs. When he called and she mentioned that I was expected in due course, he promised to come for a reunion. However, he had not shown up. Instead, she received word that he had left Las Vegas with two young hitchhikers who were willing to pitch in for gas money. According to Joanne's informant, these three had paused to camp overnight in the Mojave not far from where Victor had had his claimed encounter with the commander of a UFO. He had left the hitchhikers to tend their campfire while he went off to meditate alone. When the hitchhikers awakened the following morning they discovered that he had died while sitting beneath a Joshua tree. Apparently, his heart had exploded.

Had it? Or had his soul taken that long-anticipated ride with a Keeper?

John Shelley: I paid what I presumed would be a how're-ya-doin' social call to a former member of my American Yeti Expedition field research team. The man had been among my most trusted confidants for more than one expedition. Of course, we spent the first hour updating who was where and doing what — but then his face turned as grim as a ghost. He admitted that he had lied to me and that may have helped to

---

[72] The ship's senior engineer allowed that the watertight doors had been closed as a safety factor due to fog. Anyone passing between compartments must open the doors manually. However, they close again automatically when the opening lever is released. Pedder didn't open the door wide enough and mistimed the speed and power of its return. I learned too that there is a cooling unit close by that could be emitting chilling (ghostly) breezes. RIP.

trigger a tragedy.[73] That lie had been issued the day after John Shelley had claimed that a Forest Giant had come down from Huckleberry Mountain, had crossed the dirt logging road near where we were standing guard, and had crept into the marsh to scream in his ear. The liars were the young men whom I had trusted to check on Shelley's claim. To a man, they had stated that no giant tracks could be found crossing the road or anywhere near where John had been sitting. In fact, they had not checked that area as thoroughly as they had claimed. Instead of spending hours, they had spent scant minutes. Their excuse was they had been certain that Shelley had made up the entire scenario. They also had chosen to ignore all those successes that John's gift had afforded us previously. They had also forgotten the two-and-one-half gallons of feces his rod had led us to and that his advice had placed us in the path of a creature some of us had seen in Rock Creek Canyon. Instead of trying to find legitimate evidence to support his claim they had spent that entire day impressing young female tourists they met at Ape Cave.

Unaware of such deplorable behavior, I had accepted Shelley's demand that he leave the following morning.

If this hideous confession was Hiroshima, Nagasaki would explode a few months later. My attorney and close friend Ted Ernst and I had made a point of paying a visit to our Science Advisory Board member Captain E. E. Hedblom, USN-retired. Because he had recommended Shelley to us, we felt that he deserved to know the truth as we knew it. Ever the gentleman, Hedblom had heard me out from start to finish without interruption. Then, as a man accustomed to command, he granted me no quarter for mistakes because it had happened on my watch. Like it or not, the buck had to stop with me, and he let me know his great disappointment.

If I had thought that my confession would ease my guilt, I was dead

---

[73] I lost contact after the visit, but I regret losing our relationship. I believe him to be a good person who had a brief lapse in judgment.

wrong. According to Hedblom, John Shelley had returned home from our sortie a shattered man. He had told the facts to Hedblom once and would never discuss it again. Worse, much, much worse, that master dowser who for years had freely donated his gift to all who called upon it for good causes had lost both his desire and his power to dowse. John Shelley died of a heart attack scant months following that eerie and mysterious scream that had sent him running for his life into the arms of irresponsible persons under my command. My regrets are profound and unutterable. Mea culpa, mea culpa, mea maxima culpa.

16. Searching For Shambhala

Moscow, Russia, 1990
(On the borders of Shambhala[74])

I winced when a circling falcon snagged a lone pigeon just above the cold and gray river. Trailing warm blood and crushed feathers, the hungry falcon bore its twitching victim to a bare limb atop a nearby tree there in Moscow's Gorky Park. A perfectly natural event, you say. Yes, yes, I know pigeons are but another sacrificial link in our world's unending food chain; I also know the balance of nature is such that one thing must surely die to allow another to live. No matter! To this day, I feel guilty. I should have cried out a warning.

I leaned closer to the Tibetan lama seated on the park bench beside me. His breathing seemed too shallow to support life. Only the scent of sweet jasmine incense assured me he was real.

"Why do we die?" I asked.

There was a long silence — it seemed interminable — before my holy friend murmured, "Why do you ask such a question? We do not die. Nothing dies."

I swatted at a fly that pestered my left hand, but missed. It pestered me too that the lama had not deigned to open his eyes.

---

[74] A mystical and fabled kingdom hidden in the Himalayas where peace and happiness exist forever.

"Sure we do," I replied almost angrily. "My mother died, my brother died, my father died, both my grandmother and my grandfather died, and some of my best friends died, too. In fact, hundreds of millions or maybe even billions or trillions of people before them have all died!"

Once again, he did not answer when I thought he should, so I sulked and punished him with my silence.

The brooding Kremlin stared back at me across the roiling waters of the broad Moskva River. I mused what terrible truths might still be locked behind its blood-red walls. I wondered too if its marble and stone halls still echoed with those old shouts of glory and phantom cries of pain, fear, and horror. Perhaps even the secrets of life and death were hidden there…

"What foolish person told you that death is real?" lama T'ziang Rinpoche asked while peeping out at me from behind heavily lidded eyes.

I stabbed a finger at the distant domes of St. Basil the Blessed in Red Square. "They did," I said. When my lama snorted, I added quickly, "Well, not them exactly. I'm not Russian Orthodox or any other sort of 'dox,' but as far back as I can remember preachers have preached about our coming deaths and the devil and the fires of Hell and how only a few of the super goody-good will ever be resurrected to live in heaven with the Father and the Son and the Holy Ghost forever and ever." I nearly tossed in one good old hallelujah, but thought the better of it.

The sound of flapping wings drew my attention up to where a large Russian hooded crow was settling onto the limb directly above that feasting falcon.

"I guess the rest of us will either burn in Hell or hang around Purgatory, wherever that is. Fat chance most of us poor slobs have, eh?"

"They lied, you know."

"Who lied?"

This time it was the lama who stabbed a finger at those onion-shaped domes of St. Basil's.

"Like death itself, those liars are an illusion."

"Death is no illusion; death is real," I insisted. "How can you sit there and say it isn't when —"

"It's your entire fault, you know."

"*My fault?* Good grief!"

"It's your fault for listening only with your body-mind; beware, for it is fallible. You must learn to listen with your soul-mind for it alone is *in*fallible."

I slapped again at some stupid fly that insisted on skittering around me.

"Everyone I know believes in death, so I have lots of company!"

"They are also being lied to. The moment you stop believing those lies, your fear of death will vanish like a puff of smoke. When that happens, fears of every shade must vanish, too, and you will be on the path to enlightenment. Um, yessss, this has always been so," T'ziang said, ever so smoothly.

"Ah, my teacher, my lama, my friend; if death is but an illusion, why are cemeteries filled with dead bodies?"

"Does a driver cease to exist simply because he changes the vessel that he calls an automobile? Like a driverless automobile turning to rust at a salvage yard, are not those body-vessels at the cemeteries empty of their souls?"

"Well, er, yes, but at least you admit bodies die!"

"No. Just as metal transforms to rust, the body returns to its basic elements; there is no death to such elements but merely a change of form."

"Yes, but a driver can get another car; so where do we go for a new body?" I asked as I flailed at that damned Kamikaze fly.

"Why must we go anywhere?"

"Oh, right, sure," I said as if I knew what he meant. Wanting to make light of it, I said, "So then we can choose what make, model, and color we want, too?"

"We are what we need to be so that we learn whatever it is we are here to learn. We also choose where our body-car will be created."

"Sure. Right... how?"

"Do we not choose our mothers?"

"I don't know, do we? And our fathers, too, I suppose."

"Sometimes."

That stupid fly dared to land on my left hand as if catching its breath. Slowly, slowly, I raised my right hand. I would prove the fact of death through its squashed little body — but then Lama T'ziang offered his hand to the fly. It hopped onto his palm like a trained flea. I watched the holy man lift his hand to his face until he and that tiny fly regarded one another. He spoke as if to the fly, "You know there are those few good and generous *tulkus* [75] whose souls choose to remain on earth and within each Circle of Life to serve as beacons to the slower-learning souls like our good friend here."

"Have you ever met a *tulkus*?" I asked for both the fly and myself because I knew he also wanted to know.

"The Dalai Lama is one, but there are many more."

"If we get tired of waltzing around this Circle of Life, when may we leave it?"

"Whenever we wish," T'ziang replied as the fly flew away.

"What would happen if everyone on earth wished it this very minute?"

"Then it would be so," he said with a shrug. "It is always up to each of us."

"I thought it was up to God."

"If God is all and everything, are we not part of God?"

Something with ice-cold teeth took a sharp nibble at my heart. I did

---

[75] A lama who chooses to be reincarnated to help humanity.

not care much for the idea that the control of my ultimate fate might be in my own hands. Rather, I wanted someone huge and wise and mysteriously divine and omnipotent to make all such important decisions.

I changed the subject.

"Tell me this, please. Does every human being on earth have a soul?"

"Are you asking if every human form possesses that particular blend of essences which compose that which we wish to perceive as self?"

"Er — yes, sure, I think so."

"No."

"But all human beings must have souls and all souls are created equal... aren't they?"

T'ziang regarded me much as he had the fly.

"That depends what you mean by the term 'equal'? Souls may differ in points of origin and their reasons to exist on this sphere we call earth. After all, each essence in its initial form is identical in value until it is modified by freely chosen experiences and circumstances. Thus, the equality of each soul lies only in that it is an equal part to a greater whole; it is that greater whole which remains divine and immutable. You may call that greater whole God if you wish."

"Oh, gee, thanks," I mumbled, as if I had understood. Thankfully, he went on without waiting for my response.

"May I continue the analogy of an automobile being similar to a body while its driver is similar to a soul? Let us observe too that automobiles are designed for differing purposes. Is it not logical that each driver might choose a vehicle to help it attain its own life's goals?"

"Er..."

"Is it not true too that the automobile chooses a path of least resistance if its driver stops steering? Worse, where might that driver end up if he hands the wheel to someone else?"

Those same cold teeth bit deeper into my heart.

"Are you suggesting, sir, that not all bodies have souls just like some cars might run without a driver? That would be impossible! I should think it's obvious that each human body walking around on the face of this earth has a soul driving it, right?"

"If you mean that particular blend of essence that uniquely composes..."

"Yes, yes, *yes*," I blurted impatiently. "Aren't they all alike? I mean, like good and bad drivers, there might be good souls and maybe some better souls and even a few not-so-good souls or even a bad soul comes along now and then to keep things in balance. Still and all, all human beings have souls that are created equal, is that right or not?"

"If you put it that way..."

"Of course I'm putting it that way!"

"Then the answer is no."

"B-But everyone *must* have a soul like ours!"

"Why?"

"Because God or Allah or Yahweh or Usen or whatever you want to call it made all the souls and made them in His, Her, or Its own image, that's why," I cried out from that wee space that dwells between fear and fury.

T'ziang lifted his gaze to that hungry crow and the blood-splattered falcon that held fast the limp body of the doomed pigeon, and sighed, "Why would such an omnipotent being need a nose to breathe through, ears to hear with, or teeth with which to chew? And, if you insist that such a Maker exists in a humanlike image, would not a She appear better suited to give birth throughout the universe than a He?"

With no wind left in my sails, I folded my arms tightly across my chest and clamped my mouth shut in a great pout. We sat side by side in silence while that great river flowed on and on toward its destiny. In time, I managed to unclamp my jaws enough to hiss, "Did I understand you to say that there are some human beings on this earth who have no souls at all — *ouch!"*

T'ziang had snapped a finger hard against my temple and instantly, in blips and flashes, streams of faces in all shapes and colors flashed past my mind's eye in quick succession. Most were smiling, warm, and quite loving; these were lovely to behold. However, spotted among them were those few who only split their lips as if to imitate a smile. These fake faces also differed in form, sex, and color yet they shared a terrible emptiness of spirit that spread out behind their cunning eyes like some barren desert. I detected not a shred of true human emotion among these living shells — no, wait-wait! That is not wholly true. These fakes had ample shares of greed, envy, hatred and, above all, deceit.

Throughout my vision, I kept hearing T'ziang's voice speaking quite calmly, saying to me, "Now you see there exists among us many imitators who are not 'human' as you or I would perceive humanness; they are here to snatch away our souls. Beware of these Pretenders."

"But why do they want to do that?"

"Pretenders resent our emotions; they cannot feel true love or even tenderness as we do. Being the jealous sort, they work endlessly to replace our yearnings for true enlightenment with dark anger, lust, and the greedy need to possess things, things, and more things.

"To the weary and to the gullible among us who trust in promises, these atavists teach that there is but one life for each of us on this earth so we should take what pleasures and comforts we can. Alas, they speak only of themselves and not of the true human beings. Much as any rough diamond must endure blows to cut each new facet to reveal its inner purity, our eternal souls must return to this earth over and again until we are fit to return to become part of our Maker.

"Now that you have seen this truth, no Soul Snatcher can deceive you ever again."

Just as suddenly as it had appeared — perhaps, my gasp broke the spell — that vision had vanished. Nothing around me had changed in

Gorky Park except three additional hooded crows had joined the vigil above that lone falcon. Afraid now, the falcon abandoned his victim and the crows greedily descended upon its remains in a great squabble of caws, squawks, and pecks, each snatching up a part of the pigeon's body-parts before flapping away in separate directions. Their act took on a new and frightening symbolism that jarred the very core of my being when my lama breathed close to my ear.

"Beware, beware, beware of the Soul Snatchers. They preach that you must have blind faith in things that you cannot see, smell, taste, hear, or feel. Remember too, Soul Snatchers fear the question why, but, even more, the question why not!"

"How else might I recognize them?"

"Their lips can imitate smiles but their eyes cannot."

"How old are you?" I asked my lama.

"I am as old as you."

His answer puzzled me for he was wrinkled and I was not. Before I could ask why that was so, that fly returned to rest again upon my hand. This time I lifted the fly to my face. I observed that each of its eyes had hundreds of facets. I wondered if each was a window to a life long past.

"Then how old am I?" I asked.

"Oh, my son, my friend, my brother, aren't we both as old as life itself?" replied a voice that may have come from either the lama… or the fly.

I smiled at the fly and the fly smiled too before it soared away.

"Where did the fly go?" I asked my lama.

"Like you and I, he seeks Shambhala."

Photo by N. Erika Morgan

Figure 16: The body-car of Robert W. Morgan searching for Shambhala.

About the Author

Robert W. Morgan encountered his first Sasquatch in 1957 while hiking in Mason County, WA. The Sasquatch stood erect and expressed surprise and curiosity, but not anger. Being from an Ohio steel town, he had never heard of such a creature. He later learned that he had come face-to-face with a legend and vowed to repeat his encounter. It was those intelligent eyes that most intrigued him.

Upon discharge from the service, the Federal Aviation Administration offered him a position in Washington, DC, including duties as a computer systems certifying engineer. Ill-suited to the constraints of government service, Morgan resigned to launch his first expedition to Mt. Adams, WA, where he encountered huge barefoot, bipedal tracks in fresh snow.

In 1969 Morgan convinced Skamania County, WA, Commissioner Conrad Lundy to create the nation's first county ordinance to protect the Bigfoot from "wanton slaying." Morgan's company, Vanguard Research Corporation, conducted several more expeditions. The 1971 feature article George Harrison wrote for National Wildlife Magazine described fresh tracks located in Harrison's presence under circumstances that prevented fakery. Robert also recruited a Science Advisory Board of 17 men and women, most with doctorates in a variety of complementary sciences. In 1974, he co-founded The American Anthropological Research Foundation (AARF) with attorney W. Ted Ernst to do research in "cryptoanthropology" and in other fields. Soon, his major sources of information became Native American elders and shamans.

Morgan and his teams have appeared in the Smithsonian TV Series, Monsters: Myth or Mystery, and the documentary, The Search for Bigfoot. He and field researcher Eliza Moorman reported to Dr. Krantz the longest string of bipedal hominid tracks (161) ever authenticated in North America.

Always active, Morgan can be contacted through the web site www.trueseekers.org.